S0-CUI-466

Britain in Balance

Britain in Balance

W. A. P. Manser

LONGMAN
in association with the Institute of Economic Affairs

LONGMAN GROUP LIMITED
London

Associated companies, branches and representatives throughout the world

First published 1971

ISBN 0 582 50029 x

Printed in Great Britain by
The Camelot Press Ltd, London and Southampton

Contents

List of Figures

Acknowledgements

We are grateful to the following for permission to reproduce copyright material:

Her Majesty's Stationery Office for tables from *The U.K. Balance of Payments 1968 and 1969*; National Economic Development Office for an extract from the *Motor Manufacturing EDC's January 1970 Report*; Macmillan and Company for an extract from *International Trade* (1927) by Taussig, and Penguin Books Limited for an extract from *British Economic Policy since the War* (1958) by Andrew Shonfield.

Figure 1 is based on statistics from *The U.K. Balance of Payments 1969* and *Economic Trends*, March 1970, with the permission of the Controller of Her Majesty's Stationery Office, and on statistics from *Abstracts of Historical Statistics*, with the permission of B. R. Mitchell and Phyllis Deene and Cambridge University Press. Figure 2 is based on statistics from *The U.K. Balance of Payments 1969* and from *Economic Trends* with the permission of the Controller of Her Majesty's Stationery Office. Figure 3 is based on a graph published by the Commission des Communantes Européennes, *10th General Report*. Figure 4 is redrawn from a graph in *Economic Age*, October 1967, and Figure 5 was drawn from figures supplied by the Department of the Environment, Transport Industries Branch. We are grateful to all the above for their permission to use this material.

Foreword

This book is intended for the layman. It is meant to serve two aims. Firstly, to set out, in satisfactorily clear terms, what the balance of payments problem is; secondly, to advance a personal view to the effect that the balance of payments ought not to be a matter of serious national concern. The first will, it is hoped, please and help the layman; the second will, it is hoped, also interest, although it may not persuade, the professional economist.

Come inflation, deflation, boom and slump, our foreign accounts have ruled our national mind for a quarter-century. But was this right? Were our self-inflicted economic penances so good for us? Was that encircling fence to a commercial and personal freedom abroad—exchange control—so very salutary?

The book is essentially a narrative. It sees, and tries to show, the balance of payments as an evolving story. This may irk the professional economist, who may, as the chronicle proceeds, feel that obvious next stages are missed. His patience is entreated. By the end of the book he will, it is confidently believed, agree that everything has been brought in and analysed.

A narrative of this form would stumble if it had to negotiate footnotes, references, parentheses, lengthy statistical tables, etc. Where possible, the source of facts quoted has been brought naturally into the text. References not so dealt with are contained in a source list at the end of the volume. These are indicated by footnote numbers throughout the text. If they distract the general reader, he is urged to ignore them; he will lose nothing thereby. They are solely to simplify reference to the end. The full statistical substantiation of the points made has also been consolidated in a number of tables in the Appendix. Some of these may prove not too boring to the general reader; but they are for the special delectation of the professional. As a further aid to convenient reading there is in the Appendix a glossary of the initials and the full names of international organisations mentioned in the book.

I am grateful to the editors of the *National Westminster Bank Review*, *The Banker*, *The Bankers' Magazine*, the director of the Committee on

Invisible Exports, for permission to reprint material which has already appeared in their columns.

I wish to give especial thanks to Mr John Wood who with great patience and skill advised on and co-ordinated the whole project from first to last; and to Miss Barbara Jervis who gave up many leisure hours to checking and advising on the designs and the text.

I 'Whatever Happened to the Balance of Payments?'

The balance of payments is like one of the more boring television serials. Episode succeeds episode, but nothing ever really seems to change, and you wonder how, and indeed whether, it will all end.

We have just been through one of the more colourful episodes. From the deep, apocalyptic post-devaluation gloom we emerged into the radiant surplus of 1970. In the golden days of June of that year, Mr Jenkins was still telling us that we had the strongest balance of payments in the world; the largest surplus in our history. Later, as the winter shadows darkened, crisis again loomed: this time it was inflation. Our economy had gone awry again, it seemed; and with the coming of spring, our payments surplus would melt like lingering snow. But this was only one episode in the unfolding story of the whole postwar period.

By common consent, the core of the problem lies in our trading abilities. 'It is time exporters got off their backsides and worked for Britain.' Thus, pungently, Prime Minister Harold Wilson, calling for an end to Britain's balance of payments troubles shortly after coming to power in 1964. This remark no doubt earned him some lifelong enmities among export managers; and some men who had spent months, if not years, selling British socks or chewing-gum in the steamier parts of Africa and Asia may well have had a momentary loss of control.

But he did no more than state succinctly the key formula for British economic recovery as it has been worked out during the postwar era: we as a nation are in trouble because our balance of payments does not, in fact, balance. And it does not balance because we import more goods than we export.

The eminently reasonable Mr Callaghan, then Chancellor of the Exchequer, in the 1967 devaluation debate, said:

> I am not seeking to ascribe any responsibility to anybody for failing to try to export, I am merely pointing out the fact that it is industry which does the exporting, and industry which imports, and if the two do not balance, eventually we get into a disequilibrium.

No one, indeed, could say fairer than that. And Mr Callaghan had on many previous occasions pointed out that the country was in deficit in its merchandise trade, and had been for years—£43 million in 1966, £225 million in 1965, £517 million in 1964 and so on back, with few exceptions, to the end of the war.

This is a fact which industry cannot deny. The country's 'visible' trade, by which we mean the import and export of physical, or visible objects—from shoelaces, whisky and coldcream, to bridges, oil and diesel-electric locomotives—is in deficit, sometimes severe, sometimes mild, but constantly in deficit and not in surplus.

Mr Callaghan and Mr Wilson were not the first to notice it, of course. Every Chancellor and every Prime Minister since the war has had it in the very centre of his thoughts and preoccupations.

'We have run', hallooed the redoubtable Dr Dalton—then Chancellor of the Exchequer—in August 1947, 'into a great storm', and launched himself into a speech full of the sights and sounds of danger. 'Our trouble is this yawning gap between exports and imports. Therefore all our measures must be aimed at narrowing the gap at both ends.'

The alarum was rung, therefore, long ago. No one can say that Britain was slow in sighting danger. 'Export or die' was a slogan coined by the end of 1947.

However, the trade deficit has not only gone on, but it really has not altered over all the quarter of a century that successive governments have been working on it. There was a great deficit in 1951—as much as £689 million—and 17 years later, after much toil at the same task, countless squeezes, voluntary restraints, alarums, excursions and a devaluation, the country was running a deficit of £534 million.

We have wrung our hands over this insoluble mystery. Why does Britain so stubbornly revert, year in and year out, to her habitual deficit? The diagnosis and the prescription, after all, have been clear enough and the curative treatment has certainly been applied. If there is an excess of imports over exports, this is because demand has got out of hand. Wages and prices rise. Inflation takes hold and gallops away, taking our export prices out of reach of our overseas customers; and so we get a deficit. Everyone knows this. It's a simple, well-defined condition, and the cure is simple and well recognised—deflation. You cut down demand, restrain the economy, and set all the above forces in reverse.

But we do it again and again; we restrain the economy even to breaking point, and still it doesn't work. The deficit comes back again and again. What is there special about Britain which prevents her from responding healthily to the cure when applied? To this central question heads have been bent, graphs drawn. Hardly an economist of standing in the UK has not contributed something to the pool of research. Outside the country, experts from the IMF, the OECD, the BIS, the central banks of the Group of Ten, the Brookings Institution, and numberless individual correspondents have laboured in their turn. Is it that Britain's technology is tired and old-fashioned, so that our industries cannot exploit the export opportunities created by restraint at home? Or are our exports still patterned on the old imperial style, and not sent to thrusting new markets? Or are we still making old-fashioned goods and not the innovations that sophisticated markets yearn for? Or is the quality wrong? Do we insist on British styles, where foreign tastes should be indulged? Do we service our customers badly? Do we visit them in bowlers, not speaking their language, handing out brochures in English technicalese? Are our managerial attitudes wrong? Is there a breakdown of communications with workers? Do we have too many strikes?

Or are we just darned lazy? 'For generations this country has not earned an honest living' said Ray Gunter, with the authority, no less, of Minister of Labour, in 1966. 'Half-time Britain' said William Allen, an American-orientated management consultant, in 1964, and deeply impressed those about him. '. . . The difficulty remains how to get a country moving when the majority would prefer to remain still'. Marc Ullmann, Jean-Jacques Servan-Schreiber's lieutenant on *L'Express*, commenting in *The Times*, in 1968, drew many a fascinating contrast between British languor and French vigour. But the 'Old Thunderer' itself, in that notable editorial of 1966, 'Why the £ is Weak' elevated the point into its fullest theoretical stature:

The £ is weak
Because Britain is living beyond her means
Because extra business is put before extra effort by too many people in all classes
Because too many working hours are turned into gambling hours
Because money is regarded by too many people of all classes as something to be got or won rather than earned
Because while France, Germany and Italy have had their 'economic miracles' Britain has not yet shown the willingness or capacity to make the effort to achieve her own 'miracle'
Because in all too many cases Britain loves the old instead of the new; seeks reasons not to do things rather than to do them
Because too many managements have been supine or unimaginative
Because there is on both sides of industry still too much hankering after restriction and too little eagerness for competition.
The £ could be strong if the British had the ears to hear, the eyes to see, and the will to recover their native sense and energy.

The response to these admonitory strictures demonstrated how convincing an explanation for Britain's trials this seemed to many readers:

'You are to be congratulated . . . for exposing the apathy and complete indifference of the British people during the past 20 years to the deplorable state of the nation.'

Many did not hesitate to point the finger at the British national character:

One need only to travel to any country of N.W. Europe to see . . . that there is an attitude which breeds progress, optimism and stability which is so absent from the British scene.

Or even at the lack of Christian ethics:

There is no such thing as an economic crisis—but purely a spiritual one. If the country reversed the race down hill process . . . and reverted to God in its code of living, in its many facets, all these troubles would cease.

Or at the lack of patriotism:

'We have unfortunately come to a situation where a great section of the population . . . is only interested in what their country can do for them and give little thought to what they can do for their country.'

It was a natural sequel to this act of national confession that, after devaluation in 1967, a few girls in Surbiton decided to work an hour extra each day to help put the country to rights again. This touching and simple patriotic impulse sparked, amid a burgeoning of Union Jacks, into a nation-wide 'I'm backing Britain' campaign. But then, when it came to organised labour, the trade union chiefs bluntly, where not coarsely, reminded the country that in this world men's time and products are sold, not given away, and that applying any other dispensation would not make the economy more prosperous, still less earn us more income from abroad. Thus the whole argument turned full circle back to the economics from which it had started.

And so the search goes on. What is it that prevents Britain from regaining her old commercial élan? No one has any doubt of the fault to be cured and of the method to be used. In this Whitehall and Government concur; there is as nearly as possible a national consensus of opinion on the issue. However, an old adage points out that when a point is accepted unanimously, then is the time to question its truth.

In this nation-wide symphony of view there is one jarring note. The jarring note is the simple fact that the deficit on trade in goods is not new. We have had it through all our history. Through prosperity and privation, through peace and war, victory and defeat, century after century, this country has run a continuous visible deficit.

II The Permanent Gap

This book is intended for the layman. The term is used with humility, not patronage. It is meant to refer to all those people in the country, intelligently attending to their work in business, commerce, in the universities and on the shop floor, who do not happen to be specialised in economics. They are people who read the papers, listen to the politicians, and probably remain frankly mystified. What is the key to all these contradictions of evidence, and policies that seem so right, and yet never succeed? What is this national failure so divorced from the real life of work, moderate achievement, pay and profit that they know? To the layman, the economist owes a duty of being explicit and of saying something consistent. As Lord Beeching said:

> . . . There rests upon economists as a body a special responsibility for making as clear as they can, as much as they can . . . to as many as are capable of using it. I think they owe a special debt of atonement to society for having obscured much that we might otherwise have continued to see quite clearly.

The last statement on the previous page may seem, to the layman, little short of staggering. In the context of current thought it is indeed staggering. However, it is probably the key to the problem and to the various contradictions that have arisen, as this book will attempt to demonstrate.

At first impact, however, the statement raises more questions than it answers. If a deficit on trade is not unusual what, then, is all the fuss about? Why wasn't this recognised before? And how does the economy manage to survive with a constant visible deficit? Does this mean that all the measures of deflation are unnecessary? And what is really wrong with the balance of payments, if anything at all? If there is something wrong with the balance of payments, what is the cure?

These questions must be answered.

Firstly, however, the main point has to be substantiated. Britain's present visible deficit is a feature that has existed throughout her recorded economic history.

This country has kept annual trade statistics for two and three-quarter centuries, since 1697 in fact—longer than any other country in the world.

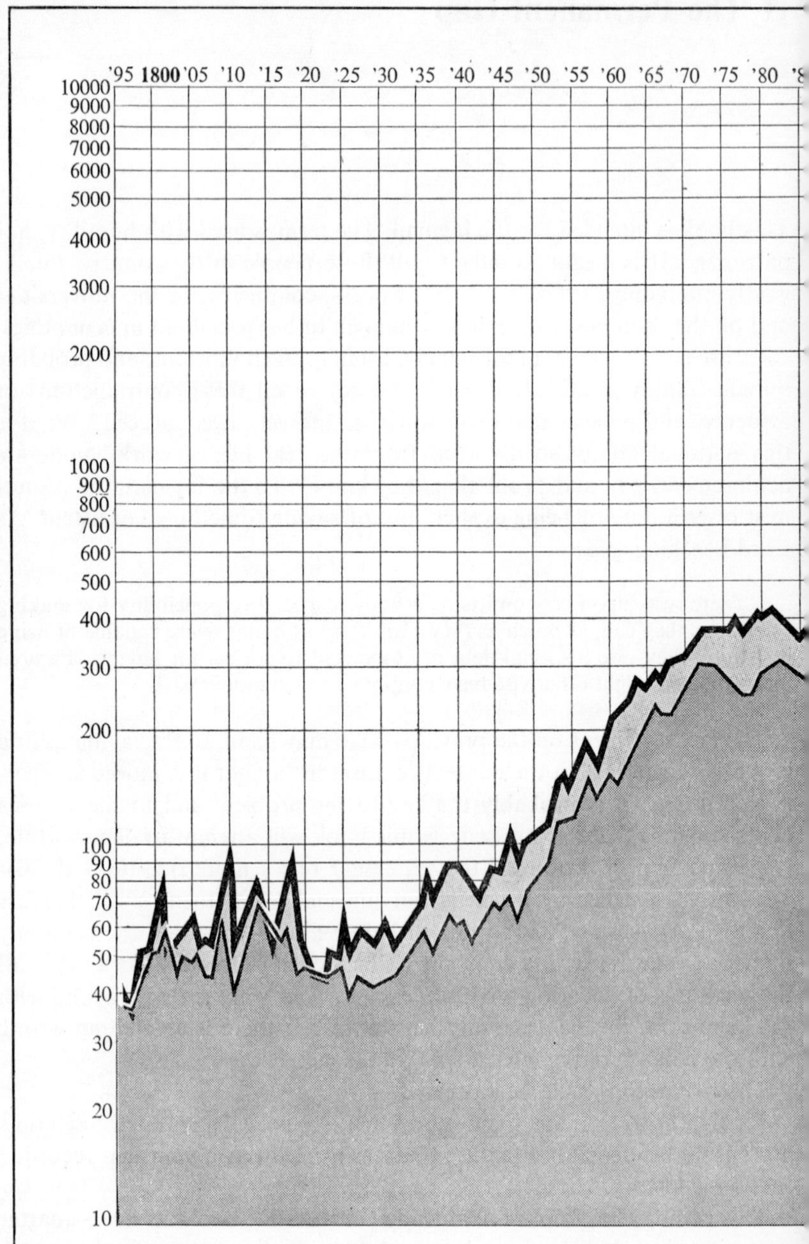

Figure 1. The Visible Gap, 1795–1969

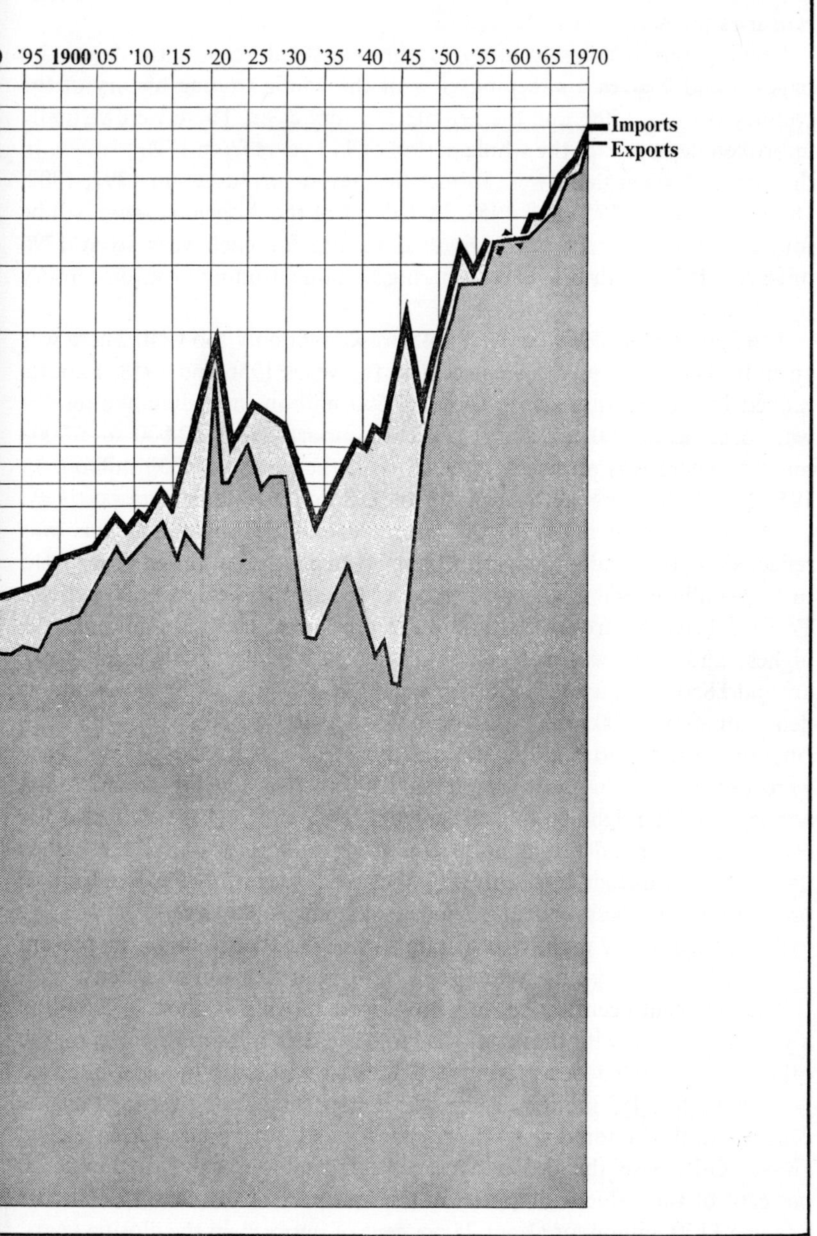
'95 1900 '05 '10 '15 '20 '25 '30 '35 '40 '45 '50 '55 '60 '65 1970
Imports
Exports

Prior to 1697 there is ample qualitative material going back several centuries farther.

Leaving out the first century of the statistical record, the figure on pages 6 and 7 gives a sweeping view of the whole trading history of the country back to 1796, and the net effect is very clear. There were virtually unbroken deficits over the whole period of 173 years from 1796 to 1969. In this span of years there were in fact just seven surpluses—in 1797, 1802, 1816, 1821, 1822, 1956 and 1958. In Table I of the Appendix there will be found a tabulation of the individual results for each year from 1796 onwards. It is worth briefly considering Britain's trading position century by century.

The figures from 1969 back to 1945 are known only too well. There was an unbroken series of deficits except in the years 1956 and 1958. Exports ranged in money value from some £1 500 million immediately after the war to some £6 000 million at present; imports from £2 000 to £7 000 million. There was an average deficit over the years of £300 million. In 1956 and 1958 there were surpluses of £53 and £29 million respectively.

The 1930s were a period of general economic blight and this was reflected in the trade aggregates. Annual export sales varied from £415 to £600 million, and imports ranged over the scale £675 to £1 000 million. Trade deficits ran from £260 million at the lowest to £430 million at the highest and there was a deficit in every year. In the 1920s exports ran around £850 million and imports over £1 000 million, giving a continuous deficit of some £300 million. From 1900 to 1910, the evening of the great Imperial era, exports ran at an annual rate of some £450 million. They were exceeded by imports averaging £580 million leaving an unbroken annual gap. It might be added here that the latter decade was also the evening of the great pre-inflation era. From this point on, as the figures unroll back through the centuries, they will seem small in relation to present day numbers—but this, to some extent, is illusory.

Such, then, is the picture of Britain's trade for the whole of the present century. In the sixty-nine years there have been sixty-seven deficits.

The nineteenth century began with exports moving at about £55 million a year and closed with these sales as large as £300 million. Imports, on the other hand, started out around £60 million and over the one hundred years grew to £450 million. There was a consistent deficit throughout the century. In the hundred years there were four surpluses only, as mentioned above. Otherwise the deficit averaged £15 million, equal to about 20 per cent of the value of imports, in the first part of the century and rose to some £150 million, or about 25 per cent of imports, in the closing years.

The century and three-quarters covered by the run of figures quoted above was, from the economic point of view, about the most vital in this country's history. It covered those years of Britain's emergence from the pre-industrial state and its transformation into a modern and highly developed economy. In the first half of the nineteenth century industrial production was, in Rostow's phrase at the 'take-off' stage and was growing at the rate of 38 per cent a decade, a performance unequalled before or since. Between 1800 and 1850 the population of England and Wales grew from 9·1 to 17·8 million, a rate of increase also unexcelled.[1]

By the middle of the century industrial production had moved into a steady and powerful gait. Since Britain had 'taken off' long before any other country she dominated world activity. In 1850, it is estimated, British manufacturing output equalled 40 per cent of the world's total; in 1870 it stood at 32 per cent and it was still 20 per cent in 1900. British manufactured exports accounted for 40 per cent of all world trade in manufactures in 1870 and for 30 per cent in 1900.[2]

Yet throughout she maintained a steady and large gap between exports and imports. The pattern of this deficit is worth noting. One good method of gauging the size of a deficit is to relate it to the total of imports. Thus if imports are £100 million and exports are £90 million, then the deficit, £10 million, is 10 per cent of imports; in other words, 10 per cent of the bill for imported merchandise is not being met out of proceeds from merchandise sales. Throughout the nineteenth century the deficit ran around 20–30 per cent of imports. The gap was about 30 per cent of imports in 1900–10, around 20–30 per cent in 1920–30, and between 40–45 per cent in 1930–39.[2]

Yet in the postwar period—the years in which the deficit for the first time became a standing national anxiety—the gap ran consistently below 10 per cent of imports, and often below 5 per cent. Not only are we concerned, therefore, with a deficit that has been normal since 1796, but with a deficit which is smaller than it was over the whole of these 173 years. (The contrast is strengthened by the fact that prior to the Second World War all imports were recorded 'c.i.f.', i.e., showing not just their price, but the cost of freight and insurance, etc., involved in getting them to Britain. As these are really invisible payments they have been hived off in postwar records and imports have been shown f.o.b. The gap, in earlier times, was, as a percentage of imports, naturally smaller than it would have been on a modern f.o.b. basis; i.e. without these extra charges—'free on board'.

However, it is important to look back beyond the nineteenth century.

There are two reasons for this. Firstly, the earlier years further illuminate the trading history of the country. Secondly, when we come to the eighteenth century we hit upon an aberration in the statistical record that is both remarkable in itself and highly significant for any interpretation of the country's economic history.

When the Parliament of 1694–95 decided that in order to have 'a faire and exact scheme of the ballance of trade', records should henceforth be kept, they appointed a functionary with the Latin-sounding title of Inspector-General of Imports and Exports. This man, William Culliford by name, was an archetype. His like can be found on any lunch-time stroll down Whitehall today. Long established in the Customs Service, he was incorruptible, highly conscientious, and not a little wary of the businessmen with whom he had to deal. He was also, as it happens, an anachronism. That type of impeccably sea-green Civil Servant did not become common until some time towards the end of the nineteenth century. The public and private standards of William Culliford's day were more those of a 20th century banana republic. He was perhaps not mistaken in refusing to trust his business contemporaries too far.

Culliford's problem was to be sure he got the right prices. His job was to give a value for the country's total imports and exports in each year. He set up massive ledgers in which consignments reaching and leaving the ports of England were individually entered; for instance:

To London from Africa: Gum arabeck: 45 cwt: at 34*s* to 44*s* per cwt: £87 15*s*. (i.e. at an average of 39*s*.).[3]

But was it 39*s* a hundredweight? It must be remembered that in an age where telephones, newspapers, commodity indices, advertising and supermarkets were not constantly publicising and standardising prices, it was very difficult to know what the cost of a particular product in any particular place would be. Culliford had the ancient Book of Rates in which standard values of merchandise were set out for customs duty purposes, but these were notorious for their inaccuracy.

Faced with these difficulties Culliford made a typical civil servant's decision, and a good one in the circumstances. He decided not to take the Book of Rates, nor yet the actual declarations of merchants, but to establish a new fixed price for every type of merchandise entering into the country's foreign trade, and this would remain constantly in force. These were known as the 'official values'.

Culliford, nevertheless, had to set his official values only after asking the people who knew—the merchants, shippers and others engaged in trade. Here was the rub. It must be borne in mind that in trade, customs duties long preceded statistics. For numberless centuries kings and governments in England had only enquired of merchants what their trade was in order to tax it. To this day our only knowledge of medieval imports and exports is drawn from the record of taxes. The year 1696–97 was, therefore, one of the first occasions in history on which English businessmen had been asked how much they exported or imported, out of pure interest in the answer, and the depth of their suspicion can be believed. It is highly likely that they understated their reply as regards imports to a man. As regards exports, it so happened that the Inspector-General's enquiries coincided with a broad change in policy under which exports were to be encouraged rather than be regarded, as hitherto, as a drain on the country's vitals. All taxes on exports were in course of being removed; indeed, for certain goods, 'bounties' or bonuses were being paid. Add to this the widespread inclination among merchants of the time, or of any time, to claim optimistic figures for sales and it is clear that anybody's statement of the value of his exports was likely to be above rather than below the mark. Culliford's enquiries were painstaking and he probably got as near the truth as he could. There is little doubt, however, that his values still magnified exports and understated imports.

The vital requisite of official values, however, was that they should be continuously reviewed. Culliford retired a few years later and was succeeded by Charles Davenant, who immediately embroiled himself in political affairs; the official values were largely neglected. Henry Martin, who succeeded him in 1713 and remained at the post for nine years, was conscientious; the official values were rechecked from time to time. After that a fate commonly allotted to eighteenth-century institutions overtook the post of Inspector-General; it became a sinecure. The actual work of recording was done by Assistant Inspectors-General, many of whom were competent, but the policy initiative was gone. After Henry Martin the official values were, for practical purposes, never again revised. They were left untouched for no less than 132 years, until 1854. In that time, as we now know, real prices changed out of recognition; and the records of Britain's foreign trade went hopelessly awry.

Over the whole span of the years from 1722 to 1855 the true prices of merchandise of course rose—they did so century in, century out. But whereas Britain's imports were mainly natural products—staple foods and raw materials—unchanging in themselves but becoming dearer through the inherent rise in money prices, her exports were manufactured goods, the costs of which were constantly modified by technological progress.

Britain's manufactured products in 1700, and those which entered into the export trade in subsequent years, arose from laborious and primitive methods. They were made with minimum ease and maximum cost. By 1854 industrial processes had been elaborated, streamlined and brought down to substantially lower costs per unit. Accordingly, export prices, although they continued to move upwards with the average level of prices, did not do so in the same way as import prices. In fact from about the 1790s to the 1850s industrial efficiency was going ahead so fast that export prices actually fell.

This we can see in a comparison of the true values and the official values in the early nineteenth century. The following was the position in 1800 (we will follow the terminology of historians and call true prices 'real' prices):

	Real (£*m*)	*Official* (£*m*)
Exports	52·4	43·2
Imports	62·3	30·6
Balance	−9·9	+12·6

Real prices had widely exceeded official values on both imports and exports. Import prices had gone ahead faster and, as a result, the apparent surplus registered in the trade statistics of £12·6 million concealed a real deficit of £9·9 million.

Next the position for 1853:

	Real (£*m*)	*Official* (£*m*)
Exports	115·7	242·0
Imports	148·5	123·1
Balance	−32·8	+118·9

Here, in the last year before the change of system, real import values were still ahead of the values shown in the official record. On the other hand export prices had fallen sharply. This accentuated the discrepancy between the balance shown by the official figures and that actually in existence. Instead of the handsome surplus of nearly £120 million which people believed in at the time, there was in fact a not insignificant deficit of £32·8 million.

The story is the same for all the years between 1800 and 1853, and of those before 1800. In brief, the official values showed a continuous surplus from 1697 to 1853, whereas, in fact, there was a continuous deficit.

It is in many ways extraordinary that a basic error in our trade figures should have persisted untouched for nearly a century and a half. There were extenuating circumstances, which will be noted later, but there is no real explanation. It is one of the puzzles of history still to be resolved. For present purposes the fact is that it happened. In the following words Albert Imlah summed up the position in his *Economic Elements in the Pax Britannica* of 1958:

> Year after year, through peace and war, dearth and plenty, high prices and low, the clerks meticulously multiplied their quantities by these unchanging rates. British 'official' trade values became progressively more useless as measures of current market values until the system was reformed in 1854.

The figures already shown on pages 6 and 7 for the years 1796 onwards are, of course, corrected for this error. For reasons which will be explained later, it was comparatively easy to work out, subsequently, the true values for the period back to 1796. For those readers who are interested, Table II in the Appendix shows the real values alongside the official values of trade in every year from 1796 to 1853.

Before 1796 we have no exact series of figures which we can substitute for those shown in the official record. As far as available statistics go, then, we still have for the years 1696 to 1795 only a run of trade surpluses which we know to be wrong.

Of this there can be no practical doubt. Even apart from the distortion of the official values there was a variety of factors peculiar to the eighteenth century which magnified exports and minimised imports. These are not worth recounting at length here, except for the remarkable instance of smuggling.

Smuggling today means a surreptitious extra bottle of whisky or leather wallet in a returning holiday-maker's bag; or at most it means a few professionals with a clandestine boatload. In the eighteenth century smuggling was a national industry. It occupied two million out of the thirteen million people living in England. 'Smugling and Roguing was the Reigning Commerce of . . . the English Coast, from the mouth of the Thames to Land's End' says Defoe, a contemporary observer. Involvement in smuggling was not considered a social misdeed. People in all walks of life from the highest to the lowest freely engaged in the traffic. A certain Reverend Woodforde is reported by G. M. Trevelyan,[4] as writing on March 29, 1777, 'Andrews the smuggler brought me this night about 11 o'clock a bagg of Hyson Tea 6 lb weight . . . I gave him some Geneva and paid him for the tea at 10*s* 6*d* per pound.' The reason for the trade lay, of course, in the universal and stringent rates of duty on imports. This stimulant to illicit entry, combined with the general laxity of public standards and the incompetence and corruption of the preventive service, led to contraband activity that amounted in itself to a major economic phenomenon.

The Younger Pitt[5] in 1784, shortly before he abolished duties, calculated that of the 13 million pounds of tea consumed in the United Kingdom at that time, only 5½ million had been brought in through the Customs and had paid duty. Many historians have calculated the volume of contraband; most agree that it could not have been less than 25 per cent of legitimate trade. Add on this percentage alone to the official figures for imports, and you have a startling deficit.

So much, then, for the whole run of recorded trade from 1697 to 1969. The conclusion is inescapable that over the whole 272 years the cost of imports decisively exceeded the return from exports.

Before 1696 there were no regular records of trade. Gregory King, the contemporary statistician, produced figures for 1688 which suggested imports of £7·1 million against exports of £4·3 million. A special survey ordered in 1669 threw up evidence suggesting that in the years 1663–69 exports were £4·1 million and imports £4·4 million. Before the Cromwellian wars exports probably equalled not more than 5–6 per cent of total national income. Foreign trade in those earlier times was not an activity of the nation as a whole. The major portion of the people, agricultural and rural as they were, fed, clothed and provided for themselves out of the land on which they lived. Imports were the perquisite of a few early manufacturers and of the rich who desired luxuries only obtainable abroad. 'Our stately fops admire themselves better in an Indian dressing gown than in one made at Spitalfields.' Even then, however, since exports consisted almost entirely of wool and woollen goods, it seems likely that the value of imports was higher.

Thus, going from the present day back to the beginning of our national life, back successively through the maturity, growth and infancy of our industrial economy and through the rural ages that preceded it, Britain appears to have been a net importing country.

III The Permanent Surplus

The notion, then, that Britain should be exporting a surplus is misplaced. Equally misplaced is the notion that she ever, in fact, did export a surplus.

This leads to the first question. How, through all these centuries, did Britain run a trade deficit and survive; and not only survive but grow from economic insignificance into mature prosperity? Clearly, though she had an unbroken deficit, she was not economically weak.

The answer is simple. Her 'visible' deficit was covered by her 'invisible' surplus. In other words, her shortfall in the exchange of physical commodities was made up by an excess of income on the sales of non-physical necessaries: banking, insurance, shipping and the like. Throughout her history Britain's 'invisible' earnings have generously exceeded her deficiency in 'visible' incomes. Table III in the Appendix shows the position for the whole span of years from 1826 to 1969. The combined surplus failed to appear only twice, once in the years 1846–50, and again in the period 1931–38. Apart from that, in every single year, including the whole of the postwar period from 1964 to the present day, the combination of the two has resulted in a surplus.

The term 'invisible' is an odd piece of jargon which requires fuller explanation. As far as we know, it originally came into use during debates on the balance of payments in the later decades of the nineteenth century. But it was first explicitly committed to writing during the 1930s, when the Board of Trade, for the first time, essayed some figures on the subject. These earnings, or sales, were called 'invisible' because to the Customs man, who traditionally has been charged with the task of counting imports and exports, they were indeed invisible. The practical British mind, aware after many unsuspecting centuries of a great benison in its overseas accounts, was first exercised by the problem of counting it.

In fact, this esoteric-sounding term represents two simple and perfectly everyday activities. Invisible earnings are the foreign currency earnings of the service trades and of overseas capital investment.

Services are a familiar enough idea nowadays in the home economy. It is well recognised that in business you do one of two equally essential things; you make goods or you ensure that they are distributed. Making goods is of course 'visible'. Ensuring their distribution is 'invisible'. It may mean providing a method of transporting them, i.e. it means being a shipper or railway or an airline. It may mean providing a way for buyer and seller to get together, i.e. you can be an agent, a merchant, a commodity broker, or a market operator. When in transit the goods must be secured against damage or loss, and if you do this you are an insurer. Similarly, the manufacturer or the buyer will need finance to tide them over the maturity period of their invoices, and if you provide this you are a banker. All these definitions are, of course, at their most restrictive. Insurance and banking, for example, are by no means confined to the physical movement of goods. Insuring all manner of persons and things against all manner of risks, and providing finance over a variety of periods, for building, expansion, mergers and other purposes are the function of our national insurance and banking industries. But beyond this, there is the service of accommodating and feeding persons on the move—the hotel and catering trades. There are the industries providing heat and light—gas, electricity, oil, etc. There is the communication industry—telephones, radio, films and so on. There is the teaching industry. Then there is the whole range of contractors, engineers, accountants, lawyers, surveyors and others vital to the economic process. These, briefly are the services; when they sell their speciality to foreigners they are 'invisible exporters'.

The notion that services are in some sense secondary to the main action, however widely it is held, is, of course, a false one. Only a very brave man would have made this suggestion to a British seaman in any century. Clearly, without financiers, merchants, railwaymen and engineers there would be no production, just as much as that without production there would be little need for any of the service activities. One is as vital as the other to the smooth advance of society.

Once this fact is absorbed, then, there will be no surprise over the statement that services account for fully half of the total activity of the country. Measured against the gross national product (GNP)—that is to say the total business account for the country in any one year—services accounted in 1967 for no less than 51 per cent of the total.[6] In countries farther afield they represented, for instance, as much as 60·1 per cent of GNP in the USA, 55·6 per cent in Canada and over 48·3 per cent in France. Similarly, services occupied 13 million out of the 26 million working population of the UK in 1968; that is, just 50 per cent.[7]

As economies mature, the service sector in fact tends to grow. This is understandable. After a while a country reaches the point where it has laid down the physical infrastructure of cities, harbours, railways, factories and so on. Its national output would tend more and more to come on to a repair and renewal basis. Similarly populations, however rich they become, do not significantly increase their intake of necessities; food is one of these. Industry and agriculture, then, tend not to grow as fast as the economy once a particular stage of development has been reached.

On the other hand, as industry becomes more complex and sophisticated, more training is needed; quicker information and therefore better communications are needed; executives need to meet and travel more often; bigger and more elaborate financing arrangements are wanted; a wider and more complicated marketing organisation is required. In their personal lives the same executives will travel more, eat out more, shop more, use more laundries, tailors, shoe repairers, barbers; they also read more, consult more solicitors, employ more accountants; and watch more television. The field of services constantly enlarges as business and social life becomes more varied and more intense.

The second half of invisibles—investment—is an equally day-to-day notion, despite the faintly mysterious penumbra in which overseas investment seems to have clothed itself. Investment is simultaneously the act of those having a business who wish to extend it by building new plant or offices, and those outside the business who have spare capital they want to turn to profit. Investment is the placing of capital in productive enterprise and it is the combined work of the two classes of people mentioned above. Much capital, probably about 60 per cent of all that invested, is found by the businessman himself from accumulated profits; the remainder he gets from outside, from investors, mainly via the Stock Exchange.

When this process occurs abroad you have overseas investment. The company concerned may use its own money to build factories or business premises in foreign countries; this is called 'direct' investment. When the investor, looking for somewhere to place his cash, sends his money abroad for the purchase of shares, this is 'portfolio' investment. The return on this investment abroad, whether in the form of dividends on shares, or of profits on the manufacturer's money directly invested in plant, etc., constitutes part of the invisible income for the country. And when it is remembered that the average return on capital invested overseas is 8½ per cent,[8] even after payment of foreign tax—i.e. on every £100 invested £8 10*s* 0*d* annually arises for the UK investor—it will be seen that this is a sizeable flow; this point will be illustrated more fully later.

Like services, investment is of course a huge part of our economic system. Production and economic progress could not proceed far without the use of capital, but the actual sums involved are enormous. Total investment by the UK, whether from the cash reserves of businesses themselves or from outside sources, amounted to £7 798 million in 1968.[9] Measuring this against the yardstick of GNP also, we have a proportion of about 22·5 per cent. This is not as large as the services sector, but this thought must be tempered by the remembrance that the total asset stock of the country, i.e., the accumulated fruit of all past years of investment, was £127 600 million in 1968, or about three-and-a-half times the GNP. Of course, what we have been speaking about so far is capital investment as a whole by the country, both within its borders and outside. For balance of payments purposes, we are concerned only with that slice which goes into foreign countries. The fraction is very much smaller; overall, about £2–300 million flow outwards each year for investment overseas, and the total asset stock overseas is about £11 000 million.

It is now time to put together these two large slices of our economic life and to look more closely at the size of their activities abroad. We must take into account both sides of the payments question. Clearly the country both sells and buys services abroad, and both sends and receives income on capital. This is the counterpart in invisibles to the import and export of goods in the visible sector. The following Table which shows invisible imports and exports for 1968 and 1969, also shows, for comparison, the same years' imports and exports of visibles at the top of the table:

	1968 (£*m*)	*1969* (£*m*)
Visibles		
Imports	6 807	7 153
Exports	6 273	7 056
Balance	−534	−97
Invisibles		
Imports	2 530	2 657
Exports	3 561	3 967
Balance	+1 031	+1 310
Balance of visibles and invisibles	+497	+1 213

We have already noted the major feature of the Table—the handsome way in which the favourable balance of invisible imports and exports covers the gap between visible purchases and sales.

It is also worth looking at the actual size of invisible receipts and debits. As will be seen, in 1969 invisible exports at £3 967 million were a full 60 per cent of visible exports, and if you add the two together, getting approximately £11 000 million for Britain's entire export performance for the year, then it will be seen that invisibles accounted for nearly 40 per cent of the total.

The large size of invisible earnings is of course not confined to the UK. The Committee on Invisible Exports in London has recently published a survey of the invisible earnings of the world. This shows that in 1967, the latest year for which comparable results can be shown, invisible exports at $67 400 million contrasted with visible exports at some $182 000 million. World invisible trade, therefore, contributed 27 per cent of total trade. No less than 31 major countries take part. A list of these countries, together with figures for their trade, is shown in Table IV in the Appendix.

A number of interesting facts can be deduced from this table. Firstly, Britain is now the largest invisible exporter after the United States. Germany, however, is a greater importer. Germany has much smaller invisible exports, and she therefore runs a deficit on her invisible account which in 1967 was very heavy—no less than DM 2 361 million, or about £250 million.

The United States, supernormal here as in everything else, dominates the head of the table, both in gross earnings and receipts and in the balance between them. However, if earnings per head are counted—presumably the best test of export performance—then the UK comes to the top.

Finally, a word on how the total of Britain's invisible earnings break down into the two main parts; services and investment income. The following are the figures for 1968 and 1969:

	1968 (£*m*)	*1969* (£*m*)
Services:		
Imports	2 028	2 186
Exports	2 502	2 695
Balance	+474	+509
Investment Income:		
Payments	502	471
Receipts	1 059	1 272
Balance	+557	+801
Total:	+1 031	+1 310

What is most important in the above breakdown is the major contribution to the net balance made by investment income. Of the total invisible surplus of £1 310 million no less than £801 million, 60 per cent of this, originated from investment income. The service activities, such as

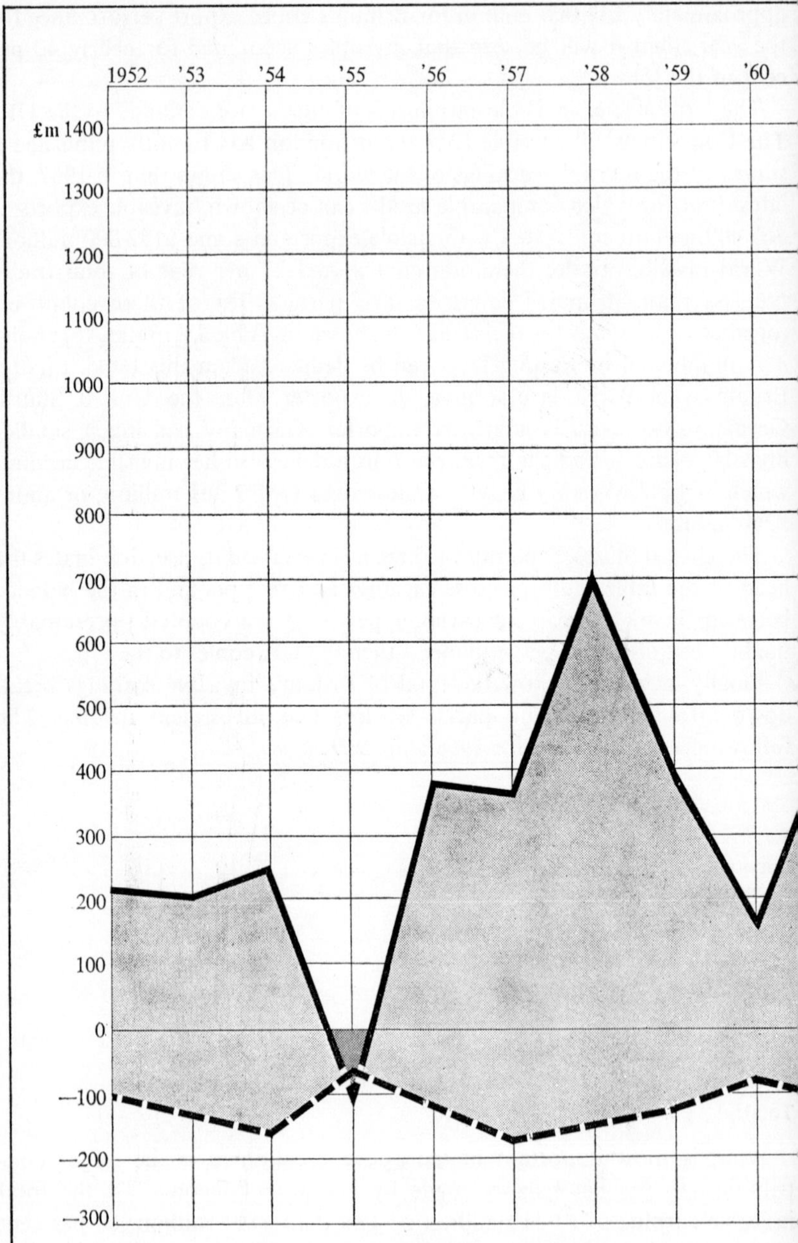

Figure 2. The Current and Long-term Capital Balance, 1952–1968

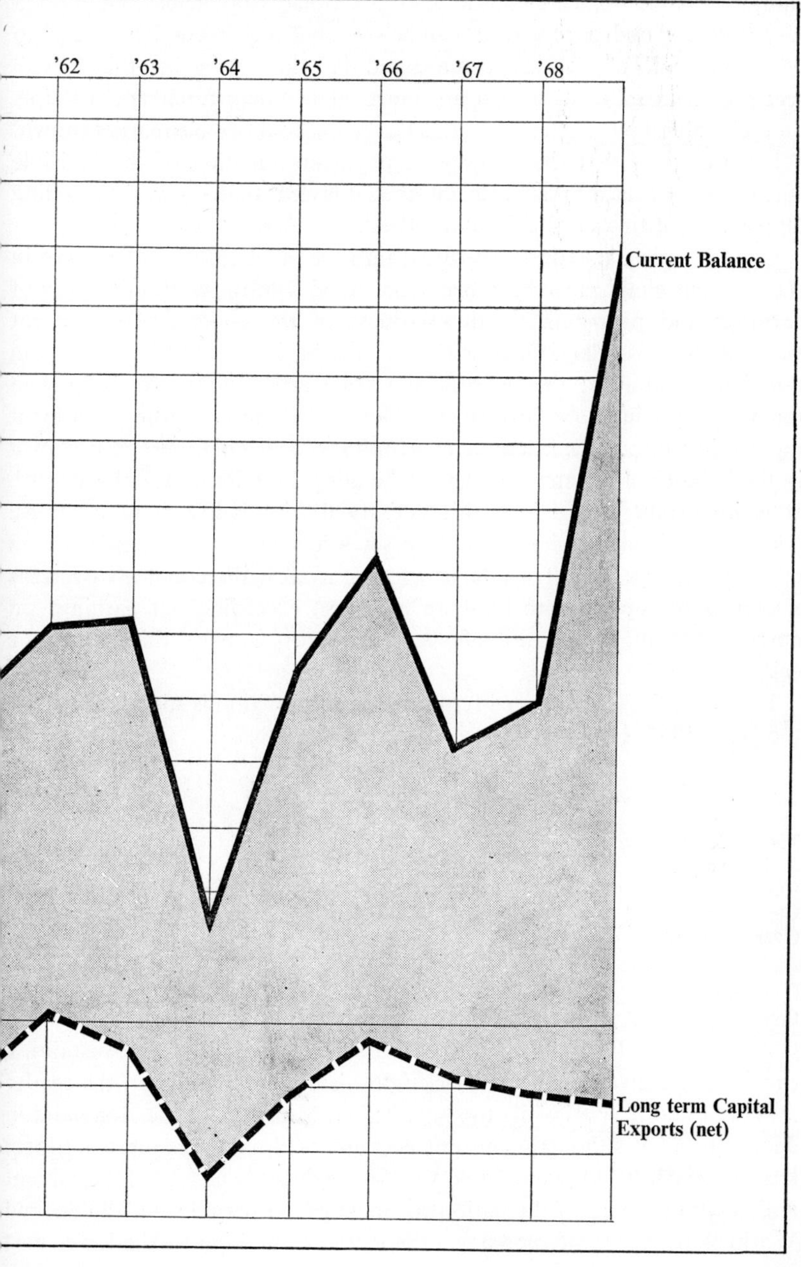
'62
'63
'64
'65
'66
'67
'68
Current Balance
Long term Capital Exports (net)

shipping, banking, merchanting and the other vital fields, maintain a higher flow of cash each way, as can be seen, but their accounts close off to relatively small balances between one and the other. As against this, British receipts on investment abroad are much higher than foreigners' receipts on their capital placed here, and this leaves the comfortable margin shown. When we recall that the balance of payments function of the invisible surplus is to offset the visible deficit, then it is clear that any item providing 60 per cent of this surplus is vital indeed.

One final piece remains to be fitted into the picture. In the above and in the previous chapter, we have been concerned with the continuing flow of earnings and payments on the business of the country—the 'current account', as it is called. Of course, as in any business, there is, apart from the daily cash flow, the process of setting aside money for long-term purposes, for, in short, investment. This is the source of the investment income just discussed. The placing of money, or capital, abroad is shown in the balance of payments under the heading 'long-term capital account'. It is important to see how this activity fits in with current earnings. As is self-evident, capital should be set aside only out of a surplus on current earnings, and it would be of little avail if the country's overseas resources of capital were built up at a cost exceeding our earnings on current account. Indeed, not a few commentators fear that this may be the case.

However, the figures speedily show that the position is sound. Thus, for the years 1967, 1968 and 1969:

	1967	*1968*	*1969*
	£m	*£m*	*£m*
Visible deficit	−454	−534	−97
Invisible surplus	+868	+1 031	+1 310
Current balance	+414	+497	+1 210
Capital outflow	−82	−110	+116
Overall balance	+332	+387	+1 326

The figure on pp. 20 and 21 shows a favourable current and long-term capital balance for the last decade.

And so on, back through the years. The record of self-sustaining earnings and investment goes back into history. At this point, the reader may well find it worthwhile to study Tables V and VI of the Appendix in detail. Table V shows the current account of the country on a uniform basis for the last 140 years. Table VI shows a detailed picture of the current and capital account of the nation for most of the period since the Second World War. At the present stage, the reader should ignore the lower part of the Tables, referring to Government. The influence of the latter is a part of the story that will be told later. As will be seen, and is stressed in the notes to the table, the continuing surplus on current account right through the nineteenth century firmly supported the capital investments that went on equally steadily; the quinquennial 1846–50 was the sole exception to this rule. In the twentieth century there has been only the blighted stretch through the thirties, when capital exports would have added a further minus to the current deficits. From 1952 onwards, full official statistics are available and Table VI shows these; except for only two years, the current and long-term capital accounts were fully viable.

What, then, if the trade and capital accounts of the nation are, and consistently have been, healthy, is the cause of the anxieties and difficulties that have surrounded sterling all through the postwar years?

IV The Real Problem

With the figures quoted at the end of the previous chapter, the account of the country's external transactions is not complete. One more figure needs to be added, a figure that has not so far been mentioned; however, it is of great importance. This is the figure foı official, or Government, expenditure overseas.

We have so far been concerned with everything that is bought and sold across the exchanges, with the buying and selling of goods and services and investment assets; with the work, in fact, of the nation as an industrial producer, investor, and commercial business operator. But money flows in and out of Britain for another reason. It flows out to pay for the activities of Government. These are not commercial, but serve political or military purposes. Funds leave the country to pay for embassies and delegations to international organisations, to meet UK subscriptions to world-wide bodies; and, much more important, to cover the cost of British naval and military establishments abroad and to provide military and civil aid, in the form of grants and loans, to other countries, mainly in the developing world. Total Government net overseas expenditure in 1968 and 1969 was £785 million and £942 million respectively. The following is the way this expenditure was made up in 1969:

Current expenditure	*£m*
Military costs (upkeep of bases overseas, etc.)	250
Purchase of military equipment (US aircraft and missiles)	61
Military grants (finance for other countries' defence forces)	9
Subscriptions and grants to military organisations (NATO, SEATO, CENTO, etc.)	7
Economic grants (cash grants and free goods and services to developing countries)	86
Administrative and diplomatic expenditure (embassies, etc.)	53
Subscriptions and contributions to international organisations (United Nations, OECD, etc.)	48
Interest and charges on official debts	329
Other	4
Total	847
Long-term capital	
Inter-Government loans (i.e. long-term loans made to developing countries), capital subscribed to international lending organisations, such as the International Development Association, the Asian Development Bank; less borrowing from US and German Governments to help defray costs of US aircraft, military bases in Germany, etc.	95
Total current and long-term outflow	942

These totals of annual expenditure by the Government must now go into the balance of payments account, making up the final external balance, as shown below. These figures set out therefore, for the first time in this book, the full external transactions of the United Kingdom.

	Private balance (£m)	*Official balance (£m)*	*Overall balance (£m)*
1958	+558	-410	+148
1959	+367	-479	-112
1960	+76	-533	-457
1961	+605	-541	+64
1962	+625	-611	+14
1963	+584	-619	-35
1964	-78	-666	-744
1965	+425	-677	-252
1966	+706	-754	-48
1967	+332	-793	-461
1968	+387	-785	-398
1969	+1 326	-942	+384

There, then, in the Table above, is the simple cause of Britain's balance of payments deficit. The nation, having made a surplus on its private dealings in goods and services and investment, then overspends this income for official purposes overseas. In every year there was a commercial surplus, save for one small exception, and in every year, without exception, there was an official deficit. In the single year, 1964, which did not run true to type, there was a minimal commercial deficit, and a heavy Government outflow—the combination of these producing the overall deficit for which that year was notorious. In eight out of the twelve years shown, the Government deficit was great enough to overcome the commercial net return and to put the country as a whole into debit. If the successive net balances on the commercial side, shown in the Table, are added up, and if the same is done for the Government side, then there emerges a figure of £5 800 million for the accumulated earnings of the private economy in the twelve years, and a figure of £7 810 million for the accumulated spending on the official side; leaving the country as a whole in final imbalance to the extent of £2 010 million.

This has been the pattern for the whole of the period since the war. Tables V and VI in the Appendix, again, will repay close attention. Table VI, especially, shows the unfailing official outflow in the postwar years. Not only was there a Government deficit in every single year, but it grew steadily as the period advanced. Over the same span of years there were consistent private surpluses, save only for the minor exceptions of 1955 and 1964. Whenever there was a deficit in the balance of payments as a whole, it was due, not to a commercial shortfall, but exclusively to a Government deficit; and even in the two exceptional years, the contribution of the private sector to the overall deficit was minimal.

The plain testimony of the figures, then, is unequivocal. Britain does not run a commercial deficit; she runs a political and military deficit. For the cause of her payments imbalance we need to look no farther than official activity. If there were no Government spending, there would be no deficit, and no balance of payments problem.

This is by no means the end of the story, as the succeeding chapters will attempt to show. There are many aspects to the matter; in particular many implications for economic policy. It does not follow that Government overseas activity should cease. However, the facts outlined above remain; and they are a vital key to the overall situation.

Why did deficit Government spending emerge as a problem only after the Second World War? As will be seen from Table V, the Government item did not appear in the balance of payments until the 1930s, and even then was both very small and self-cancelling. There was no significant one-way flow until 1946, and before 1946, of course, there was no balance of payments problem.

There were, naturally, official outgoings in the years before the war, going back over the centuries. But these were invariably balanced by receipts of similar nature from abroad. For instance, the Government of India is noted, in the sparse records available, as paying annual sums up to £200 million to the United Kingdom to help meet the latter's administrative costs in that country in the 1930s.[10] Moreover, the cost of maintaining armies and navies in foreign parts was not as high, in relation to national wealth, as later, and often the fuelling and refitting, particularly of naval vessels, could be done in colonial bases within the metropolitan financial frame. Finally, rightly or wrongly, the notion of economic aid to developing countries had not emerged before the war.

After the war Britain found herself in a world of nuclear submarines, guided missiles, supersonic bombers, and a range of technologically sophisticated systems and electronic devices. The cost of these soared well beyond the levels of anything that had been known before the war. Empires and colonies dissolved. A host of new, foreign countries emerged, no longer prepared to build their economic strength from their own resources and from foreign investment, but insistent on grants and aid from other governments. This was a cost unknown before the war; and Britain paid, and paid again. The straight line progression of official expenditure overseas, again, demonstrates the rate of expansion.

A standing official deficit, as was said earlier, is rare in the world. A glance at the following figures[11] will make this clear:

Balance of Government payments and receipts—1966

	($*m*)
USA	−6 385
UK	−1 288
France	−1
Germany	+339
Italy	−9
Belgium-Luxemburg	−46
Netherlands	−42
Sweden	−45
Canada (1965)	−5·5
Japan	+315
Australia	−131
New Zealand	−24·6

Of the twelve countries shown, only the first two have a balance, positive or negative, of any scale at all. The sums involved in other countries are tiny. This is because normal governmental cash flows balance. One state will pay out into the international official world about as much as it receives. This is in deference to the regulatory principle that determines commercial flows, as we have seen, and basically governs all international transactions. However, it does not apply to Britain, or to the United States. These two countries, alone in the world, run sizeable deficits on their official accounts. Both engage in economic aid to other countries, but it is not in this that they particularly distinguish themselves from the rest, all of whom join in this form of good work. It is the combination of these civil spendings with the great weight of military commitments that settles on them the standing burden of official deficits.

There are fifteen members of the NATO alliance, all of whom have assigned forces formally to the international command. How many have, in practice, shifted forces from their home bases? The following is an exact tally for 1968, and it has altered little since.[12] Apart from Britain and the USA, only three countries incurred the cost of stationing defence forces abroad. Belgium transferred to NATO's central front in West Germany a contingent of two mechanised divisions. The Netherlands stationed one armoured brigade in the area. Canada supplied an infantry brigade group and six air squadrons. Britain, on the other hand, supplied the British Army of the Rhine—three divisions of mixed armour, artillery and infantry, with ancillary communications and army aviation units; in addition there was a British tactical air force of 150 aircraft, tactical nuclear support units, and seaboard defence cover in the same theatre.

The total British complement amounted to 65 000 men. Against this, however, the American contribution was enormous; consisting of the United States Seventh Army of some 225 000 men, backed by tactical air forces, missile units, and a stockpile of nuclear warheads. It should perhaps be added that there were then two French divisions still in Germany, but they had been withdrawn from NATO, and their purpose was undetermined.

Outside Europe, there is the Far East and the whole unsettled arena of the Indian Ocean; with histories of conflict in Korea, Laos, Cambodia, Malaysia, Indonesia, South Arabia and Hong Kong; Africa and the Middle East, with recent troubles in Tanzania, Cyprus and Kenya, and the peripheral danger of the Arab-Israeli war. On the other side of the globe there is the whole of Latin America, dependent on outside arms for its continental defence, and the turbulent Caribbean. What are the forces deployed by the major military powers in these areas?

There were small French army and navy units stationed in North Africa, the French West Indies, and the Pacific. The Dutch had one battalion in Surinam and an amphibious group in the Antilles. Finland, Canada, Denmark and Sweden stationed 1 000 men each in Cyprus. In Vietnam, New Zealand had 540 men, Australia 8 000: South Korea, Thailand and the Philippines had sent 48 000, 2 500 and 2 100 men respectively.

The United States had 500 000 fighting men of all kinds engaged in the Vietnam war, together with massive logistic material costing over £1 000 million annually. She had 23 000 troops in Central America and the Caribbean. She maintained a transworld fleet in constant activity. She kept a strategic bomber force permanently airborne, and maintained air bases, missile and anti-missile stations, and early warning systems in all parts of the globe.

The United Kingdom had 60 000 men in Singapore and Hong Kong, 20 000 men in the Mediterranean, 7 000 men in the Persian Gulf and about 500 in the Caribbean, distributed between land bases, Air Force stations and H.M. ships, and backed up by a wealth of supporting material, organisation and personnel. British overseas military commitments accounted for approximately 50 per cent of the £2 300 million defence budget.

Thus the United States and the United Kingdom shouldered a foreign defence burden starkly out of proportion to that borne by their friends and allies.

The brunt that has fallen on the two countries has had exactly the same balance of payments consequences. The United States carries the enormous total burden of $7 500 million (£3 100 million) in net official spending overseas, civil as well as military. America, like Britain, maintains a consistent surplus on her commercial balance of payments. Indeed, no country not running a commercial surplus could contemplate the kind of overseas commitments these two countries undertake. But America, like Britain, runs into steady overall deficit because the Government involvement outruns the private sector's earnings. In this the United States' balance of payments[13] is cast in exactly the same mould as Britain's, and this fact is rarely perceived.

	Private balance (*$m*)	*Government balance* (*$m*)	*Total balance* (*$m*)
1960	+3 969	-5 154	-1 545
1961	+5 297	-5 975	-678
1962	+4 186	-5 978	-1 792
1963	+3 902	-6 091	-2 189
1964	+5 265	-5 445	-180
1965	+3 768	-5 676	-1 908
1966	+5 015	-7 572	-2 557
1967	+5 386	-8 767	-2 881
1968	+6 919	-8 217	-1 298
1969	+5 529	-8 461	-2 932

The picture is consistent. A private surplus in every year, a larger Government deficit, and a consequent overall deficit year by year. This pattern, as with the UK, extends back to the war, but not farther. There has been a surplus on American private account indefinitely back into the past. There have been major Government deficits, however, only since 1950, and an overall balance of payments deficit only since that time.

The force of the UK and American position is illustrated by the equivalent German and Japanese circumstances. The table on page 27 shows that these two countries, famed for their successful balance of payments management, were running a perceptible net gain on Government account. This is because these two countries enjoy the reverse of the process on which the UK and the USA have been engaged. Instead of sending their national defence forces overseas, they have been the host of those despatched by others, principally, of course, the Americans and the British. The German government thus received no less than DM5 347 million on this account in 1968 (about £560 million), and DM 4 898 in 1966 (about £437 million), while the Japanese takings in 1966 were $466 million (about £170 million).[14]

It is instructive to calculate what would have been the balance of payments out-turn for these two countries if, instead of these incoming payments, there had been outflows of the size borne by the UK, i.e. of some £250 million. This clearly would have involved for Germany an absolute turn-round in 1966 of £690 million—from a gain of £437 million to a loss of £250 million. The German balance of payments outcome, overall, for 1966 was a surplus of £92 million. If, then, she had borne the overseas military costs of the United Kingdom, she would have been in overall deficit to the tune of £598 million. The United Kingdom has only incurred a deficit of this size twice since the war, once in 1951 and once in 1964. She had in 1966 a deficit of £128 million. Germany should, therefore, in her enjoyment of balance of payments surpluses, be thankful for her exemption from the burden of foreign military costs. The Japanese position is similar. Instead of her actual payments surplus of £120 million, she would have run a deficit of £300 million. There are, of course, the much-publicised German 'offsets' of her military receipts—the purchases of British goods, and loans she has contracted to provide. There is very little firm information on how extensive or effective these offsets are. In any case their intended effect is only to bring the German account back to neutral. They do not add in the actual costs the UK incurs. Even taking the offsets into consideration, the Germans would still be in deficit, in the above example, by £160 million.

* * * * *

So much for the facts. The four chapters so far have shown the real form of the balance of payments. Now for the argument.

There is much to be gone through. There is a case for official expenditure itself, one that can be made out on economic, moral, political and military grounds; one that has weight and must be examined. There is the question whether we should not try to change the overall pattern of the balance of payments: should we change parts other than the official expenditure account? Behind all this are the pressing background questions. Why have these basic facts gone unrecognised for so long? Why do we insist on the need to correct a supposed commercial deficit? Why does Britain's trade fall into this see-saw of visible deficits and invisible surpluses anyway? Let us begin with the last.

V The Essence of Our Economy

Why has a country which in the nineteenth century bestrode the industrial world and which today is one of the five largest producers in the world, run a consistent merchandise deficit over the whole of its economic history?

For answer, consider the United States, a country running a historically great visible surplus. The United States occupies 3 600 000 square miles of territory ranging from the arctic to the sub-tropics; it is one of the world's biggest producers of grain, meat, oil, timber, coal and textiles. It is not only self-sufficient in food; it produces a great surplus which is devoted either to exports or stockpiling.[15]

The vast expanse of that country contains in abundance virtually every mineral and natural resource needed to sustain human life and nourish industry. The USA is rich in deposits of bauxite, copper, iron ore, lead, zinc, manganese; she is not only a producer but the leading producer of 24 of the 51 metals known to the world. She has fruit, vegetables, both temperate and tropical, fish, water power and natural gas in abundance.

Foreign trade, not surprisingly, is a small part of the United States' economy and her visible trade is in surplus.

The course of the British economy has been quite different. An island of 94 000 square miles, i.e. 36 times smaller than the USA, Britain has had four significant raw materials only in her economic history: wool, coal, iron ore and natural gas. The last of these dates from 1966 only. Wool was exhausted by the early nineteenth century. This paucity of natural resources, as we have seen, was of little consequence before the eighteenth century, that is to say before the industrial era. Britain's largely rural population provided its own needs in housing, clothing, food and in such rough contrivances as passed for machinery. But Britain, as a potential industrial enterprise, had nothing on the premises.

She could have continued indefinitely as a rural undeveloped country, as could indeed any country in her circumstances. But this was not the will of her inhabitants. Industrialisation therefore came to these islands: indeed it came earlier than anywhere else. The results of this industrialisation were good, and inevitable; a high standard of living, a wealth of machinery and personal convenience, and an advanced and emancipated society.

But this could not be achieved without a compensatory effect elsewhere, and this occurred in the country's import bill.

Firstly, and obviously, Britain became heavily dependent on the foreign-based raw materials needed for her new manufactures. She needed raw cotton and wool for her textile industries; she needed timber, leather, oil-seeds, nuts and kernels, natural rubber for constructional and mechanical work; she needed pulp and waste for paper and boardmaking; dyestuffs, natural resins; linen, hemp, jute and ramie for industrial as well as personal materials, asphalt, clay, sulphur and asbestos; quartz, nickel, chrome, tungsten, lead and a whole host of other metals and materials for her growing industrial society, which could only come from countries overseas. As time went on, and her factories and plants multiplied and diversified, the range of goods she required from abroad grew also, and, if anything, her dependence on foreign resources intensified. As her manufactures became more sophisticated, so materials which had been novelties before, became commonplace necessities; industry could hardly operate today without mica and molybdenum—which was far from the case in the early nineteenth century. Then, of her few home-based raw materials, coal and iron ore began to flag in relation to the advancing scale of the industries they were supporting. Coal increasingly gave way to the more flexible and efficient advantages of oil so that today half of all Britain's imports, by weight, are oil. This extraordinary statistic aptly reflects the falling contribution of Britain's indigenous resources. In addition, the great iron-ore deposits of Yorkshire, Glamorgan and elsewhere that fed the dark mills of the Victorian ironmasters have long since shrunk, and what remains is tiny compared with the rich ores of Africa, South America and Sweden. The modern British steel industry uses 33 million tons of iron ore a year, of which 17 million comes from overseas.[16] Finally, as every economist from Ricardo to Harrod has pointed out, it pays a country to concentrate on the products in which it has the most advanced techniques, and to leave other countries to make items needing a lesser degree of proficiency. Accordingly Britain, which has kept in the mainstream of technological progress, has relied increasingly on other countries to do the preliminary or intermediate manufacturing. Thus, she has had a steadily growing import of 'semi-processed materials' and 'semi-manufactured goods'.

Industrialisation in this country therefore means a massive and persistent inflow of materials from abroad. It had, however, a fundamental effect on imports in another way: there was a major demographic change. The English were transformed, in a few decades, from a rural to an urban people. The uprush of factories swept farm labourers off the land and into the towns. Britain needed more food from sources outside this country. Imports of foodstuffs, thenceforth, swelled the already growing tide of industrial raw materials.

A glance at Table I of the Appendix will show the drastic effects these two forces had on the size of British trade. Between the years 1796–1800 and 1825–30, imports went up from an annual average of just over £47 million to one of £60 million, an increase of 28 per cent. In the 30 years from 1850 to 1880, imports went up from about £100 million to £400 million—a 400 per cent increase. This was, it should be remembered, a real increase—not one inflated by rising prices. For comparison, real imports between the end of the Second World War and the present have barely doubled. Virtually the whole of this import bill consisted of food and industrial materials. In 1854, of an overall import bill of £152 million, £48 million or 31 per cent was for food, and the rest, save for some £2 million was for raw and semi-processed materials. The same, of course, is true for today. In 1968, for instance, 24 per cent of imports were in the form of food, and probably nearly 50 per cent in the form of raw and semi-processed materials and semi-manufactures.[17]

Industrialisation, then, brought an unparalleled upsurge in the imports of this country, and the inflow has been maintained ever since. Exports also, because of the new machine-made articles available, were to grow powerfully, as will be seen, but the logic of the situation was that the new sales would not outweigh the double factor operating on imports. Thus the visible trade gap—which already of course existed—was not altered by the Industrial Revolution. Moreover the margin between inflows and outflows, although proportionately not much different, was very much larger in real terms, because the actual size of imports and exports had grown tremendously. So the net upshot of the Industrial Revolution was to present the country with a much greater merchandise deficit.

At this point, the invisible surplus came into play with crucial effect. It should never be forgotten that the Industrial Revolution came at a stage when the economic development of this country had already reached a degree of maturity. In other words, Britain was an organised commercial and financial community long before it was an industrial one and this fact was of critical importance. It is worth pausing for a moment to recall the expansion of British mercantile enterprise that was already completed when industrial imports and exports began their upswing in the late eighteenth century.[18]

By the reign of the first Elizabeth, English ships and seamen had penetrated the far corners of the globe and they pursued voyages extensively in the ensuing decades and centuries. Cabot, Hawkins, Frobisher, Drake and Raleigh brought the English flag to, and founded English settlements along the coasts of Newfoundland, Labrador, Virginia and throughout the East. These men were not, as the romantic interpretation of history might suggest, at sea principally to promote British prestige, to view exotic new lands, or to explore little-known oceans and continents. They were there for trade, and monetary gain. The British, then as now, had their sights firmly fixed on the practical goals of this world: wealth, no less than glory, was their watchword. Cabot and Frobisher, in their search for the North-west Passage, Drake in his circumnavigation of the globe, were after a route to the East, to the spices, perfumes and rich merchandise to be obtained there and carried, for profit, to Europe. Hawkins' triangular voyages between Europe, Africa and America were a cross-freight exercise. No one who has read the literature of the time, from Shakespeare to Hakluyt, can be in any doubt of the continuing aim.

> What English ship did heretofore anchor in the mighty river of Plate? Pass and repass the impassable Strait of Magellan, range along the coast of Chile, Peru and all the backside of Nova Hispania, farther than any Christian ever passed . . . and last of all return richly laden with the commodities of China?

Note Hakluyt's concluding question.

Seaborne trade led to merchanting. The model for Shakespeare's *Merchant of Venice* could, with little difficulty, have been found in Wapping or Rotherhithe. By the end of the sixteenth century London and Bristol were full of men buying and selling the produce of the East and the Americas, sometimes by the shipload, sometimes in 'parcels' of goods, then to buyers both here and in other countries. Out of merchanting was born insurance, the guarantee of ships and their cargoes on the high seas. From the spread of merchanting and the immobilisation of money in cargoes consigned over long sea voyages arose the need for credit and then for banking. Last, but not least, came overseas investment. The English mariners, as they passed, founded settlements, not as the start of Empire, but as posts for more trade. Cabot and Frobisher created colonies in the north-east of what is now Canada; Hawkins, Gilbert and Smith sowed communities along the eastern seaboard of today's United States. More extensively, Queen Elizabeth's gold, reluctantly disbursed, founded the East India Company in 1601 and, with it, access to the then endless wealth of the Indian sub-continent. Hudson's Bay Company and others followed in their time. The modern United Africa Company can for instance trace its origins back to a company founded by the King brothers in 1695 to carry on trade with West Africa. Into all these posts and colonies passed English money, not just for the purchase of local foods and produce, but for warehouses, homes, harbours and roads. This was British overseas investment at work and it began before the Tudors' reign was out.

By the time the Industrial Revolution was well advanced—say by the end of the eighteenth century—all of these invisible trades and enterprises were in full swing. The British merchant fleet was the largest afloat. There were British investments in Canada, India, the West Indies and elsewhere, and these were bringing back income in increasing strength to this country. There was a flourishing market in the shares of this overseas capital, the South Sea Bubble of 1720 being no more than a spectacular instance of how these overseas ventures could occasionally go awry. By 1795 the Bank of England had been in existence for a century.[19] A sizeable money market had come into being and inland commercial bills had been legal for about a century. Banking was established: Barings had set up in London and Exeter in 1762, and Rothschilds were to be at work in London before five years of the next century had elapsed; the Committee of London Clearing Banks was only five years away. The men meeting regularly in a City coffee house in the seventeenth century transformed themselves into Lloyd's after 1720. The Sun Fire Insurance Company first started work in 1706. Bills of Mortality had begun in 1603, two years after the foundation of the East India Company. Elizabeth the First's Council had passed the first Act on Marine Insurance. The Royal Exchange and the London Assurance companies both emerged after the Great Bubble in 1720.

One commentator had written in 1747:

> Other Arts, Crafts and Mysteries live upon one another and never add one Sixpence to the aggregate Wealth of the Kingdom; but the Merchant draws his honest gain from the distant Poles, and every shilling he returns more than he carries out, adds so much to the Natural Riches and Capital Stock of the Kingdom.

Here, again, the seed had been sown at least a century before. Some time between 1620 and 1630 a certain Thomas Mun, himself a merchant, a director of the East India Company and a member of James the First's Standing Commission on Trade, had written a famous book, *England's Treasure by Foreign Trade*, which, when published in 1664, long after his death, became famous. In it he set out a defence of the export of capital (in the form, as it then was, of bullion) to the East India Company. He showed how this 'treasure'—in the terminology of the time—yielded profits through the sale of the Company's produce, and indeed through the latter's re-export by English merchants, through English ports. Thomas Mun three centuries ago thus expounded the principle of overseas investment and its invisible returns, and indeed painted a broad picture of the country's invisible account as a whole.

So it was that after centuries of formative effort, Britain came upon the ripening scene of the late eighteenth century with her invisible incomes highly developed and in full flood. She was ready to begin the construction of the modern British economy and to shape its balance of payments.

So far in this chapter, we have seen the basic elements in the situation as the eighteenth century ran towards its close. There was, briefly; large new production; a large population shift from the rural areas; new high imports; a larger visible gap; a counterbalancing invisible surplus. These were the static elements, so to speak, of the time. What happened now was that a fascinating economic dynamic came into play, leading to great strains and pressures, to one of the most acute political crises this country has known, and finally to the shape and spirit of the economy and British society as we know it today.

Firstly, the demographic shift. As has already been said, industrialisation swept farm labourers into the manufacturing towns, where they earned more. There they multiplied. The old pastoral order under which Britain's population lived mainly off its own resources in the country therefore broke up; and, moreover, the population vastly increased.[20] In Great Britain the growth between 1811 and 1841 was no less than 54·8 per cent and between 1841 and 1871 it was again 40·7 per cent. This should be compared with a growth of some 12 per cent between 1950 and 1970. A rate of 12 per cent was about the equivalent of the growth in a single decade from 1831 to 1841. When we consider that the rise between 1950 and 1970 is currently described as a 'population explosion' the force of the early nineteenth-century expansion can be imagined. From two angles a strain therefore came to bear on the food supply: there were fewer people to produce food at home, and there were many more people to eat it. Let us not fall into the error of assuming that British agriculture declined. On the contrary, even with less labour, it expanded because demand for its products was so much higher and it became more efficient. But even with this, food supplies became short and when there were bad harvests, grievously so. Food prices in the depression year of 1826 were 29 per cent above those of 1823. The price of the standard 4-lb loaf of bread was 10*d* in London during the years 1838–40. In 1836 it had been only 7½*d* and in 1834 it had been 6¾*d*.[21] This shortage of food led to dire consequences. It caused severe hardship for the population; there being starvation for some, and a loss of living standards for all. Equally, there was damage to the economy. At times of high food prices, a major part of the national income went to paying for these basic commodities. Less was therefore available for the purchase of other goods. The makers of these, and in particular, of the new manufactured goods, suffered. Their home markets declined, and they were less able to produce efficiently for sales abroad. Imports diminished simultaneously, and, with them, the ability of markets to absorb British products. Thus there was, not passive resignation to the need for higher foodstuff imports, but active pressure, both from the working population and from the new manufacturers, for wholly new, liberal, volumes of imports. Said Colonel Torrens in his *Essay on the External Corn Trade*:

> It is obviously impossible that manufacturers should continue to flourish in a country where restrictions on the importation of corn raise the value of raw produce in relation to wrought [*manufactured*] goods and thereby depress manufacturing profits . . .

In this they were opposed by the residual farming community and the traditional landowners. In the crucible of this contest lay the future of British society.

Secondly, the claims of economic growth. As has been said, there was not passive acceptance of imports as a means of relieving deficiences at home, but active pressure for them for reasons of industrial trade and expansion. Imports were not a stop-gap; they were a vital element in the processes of growth that were coming into being.

Consider the results if, regardless of their function as a source of supply, imports had not sharply increased when industrialisation took place. Although the visible gap, as we know, enlarged, we should not think that British exports of merchandise were small. On the contrary, they grew very rapidly and achieved most substantial levels. Britain, as was remarked in Chapter II, dominated the world market and provided at one time little short of half the manufactured goods in trade between the nations.

Now, as we know, the export effects of the Industrial Revolution grafted themselves on to an existing mercantile community which was already deriving a high net income from its invisible trades. What, then, would have happened if the new wave of machine-made exports had added themselves, without dilution, to the wealth of invisible exports already in being? The world would have been swamped with British goods and services; foreigners would have surrendered all their holdings of sterling and their reserves of gold in the process of paying for these overwhelming purchases. They would quickly have exhausted their power to buy more. British exports, visible and invisible, would have come to a standstill.

International trade is, above all, a balance. It is the exchange of one country's goods and services for another's. It can only go on if all the purchases equal all the sales, i.e. if there are as many importers in the market as there are exporters.

Thus, the purchase of great quantities of food and raw materials abroad was vital to enable industrialised Britain to go on selling her manufactures and machines. The effect was of course, progressive. The mere expansion of Britain's imports brought new pressures on her to increase her exports; new exports necessitating further imports. Invisibles undoubtedly had a share in this; quite apart from the cross-fertilisation of opportunity with visible trade, invisible transactions tended upwards with the general movement. Invisible exports, excluding investment earnings, grew from some £10 million in 1825 to about £75 million in 1880.

Finally, of course, it was essential for Britain to import if she was to realise the objects of industrialisation, which were, at the end of the day, no more and no less than the increased comfort and wealth of her people. As already seen, she could have kept out foreign food if she had left her population on the land; but then she would not have had her manufacturing output, and the railways, textile clothing, better housing, machinery and household conveniences that this brought in its train. Similarly, she could have made sufficient manufactured goods to meet only her home needs. But it was intrinsic to the purposes of industrialisation that the implicit added wealth this brought should be translated into actual new acquisitions. In other words Britain was bound to export a surplus of manufactures so as to buy in return all the goods and materials that could not be had in this country. She gained access to the fine timbers of the tropics, the rich fruits of the Mediterranean, the wines and liquors of the Continent, the perfumes, silks, precious metals and *objets d'art* of the East. These were luxuries hitherto beyond the reach of any but the very wealthy in England. To bring them within the grasp of the average man was part of the wealth-creating process of industrialisation.

Thus, to resolve the varied economic factors into a single formula: if the new weight of British exports was to be absorbed by the outside world, and increasing outlets were to be found, imports would have to rise; if British industry was to function and prosper, a great stream of raw and semi-processed materials was henceforth to pour into the country; if the new urban and industrialised population was to be fed, or at the minimum, if the cost of food was not to strangle the growth of the economy, foreign food had to arrive henceforth in quantity. If the British economy was to expand, if Britain was to take full advantage of the Industrial Revolution, and if she was to attain the standard of living which was, after all, the purpose of industrialisation, then she would have to become a heavy visible importer. This Britain did.

The decision was one, however, which had to be taken by a country which at the start was pastoral, socially static and protected by high import duties. There were high and controversial debates in the 1820s, 1830s and 1840s.[22] The landowners, farmers and traditional classes argued, with some reason, that British agriculture was efficient and deserving of indefinite expansion, and that the national security demanded self-sufficiency in food; moreover, that the national revenue could ill afford the loss of the customs duties by which imports were restrained. The opposing faction, cited the arguments quoted above. As the decades passed advances in one direction were made, and then in the other. Protection was stiffened by the introduction of the Corn Laws in 1815, which were added to the charges on other foods, materials and manufactures. In 1817, the then President of the Board of Trade, Frederick Robinson, pointed out, ineffectually, that restriction of imports was depriving the foreigner of the means to pay for British exports. A successor, William Huskisson, more determined, persuaded Parliament to reduce import duties by the substantial total of £6 million between 1824 and 1826. But there were no more large tariff disarmaments for nearly twenty years. However, over this period, the debate swayed up to the top of the nation's counsels. William Gladstone was put by Sir Robert Peel into the Board of Trade. Every day spent at the office he said 'beat like a battering ram on the unsure fabric of my official protectionism. By the end of the year I was far gone in the opposite sense.' And in the great Parliamentary encounter which began in 1842 he was to argue:

> Suppose that 50 000 head of cattle were to be annually imported, such importation would produce but a small effect upon the prices of meat, but it would create an import trade to the amount of half a million of money, a trade which, in its nature, would lead by a smooth, certain course of operation to an export trade in return of equal amount; which would contribute—I do not say in a moment, but in the course of years—to an increased demand for employment and labour.

In 1840 the House of Commons set up a Select Committee on Import Duties. The members—among them James Hume, John MacGregor and George Porter, all of them with Board of Trade experience—together with a number of businessmen invited as witnesses, came down strongly in favour of freeing imports:

. . . the attempt to protect a great variety of interests is at the expense of revenue and of the commercial intercourse with other countries. . . . And the witnesses concur in the opinion that the sacrifices of the community are not confined to the loss of revenue, but that they are accompanied by injurious effects on wages and capital, they diminish greatly the productive powers of the country, and limit our active trading relations.

Clearly mindful of the international nexus of trade to which Britain could strongly contribute, they declared slightly unctuously that freeing of imports would

give an example to the world at large, which, emanating from a community distinguished above all others for its capital, its enterprise, its intelligence, and the extent of its trading relations, could not but exercise the happiest effects and consolidate the great interests of peace and commerce by associating them intimately and permanently with the prosperity of the whole family of nations.

Sir Henry Parnell, an eminent authority of the day, in his book *Financial Reform*, published in 1831, sharply attacked the restriction of imported raw material, food and finished manufactures.

As the power of the manufacturing capital of a country to purchase raw materials is in proportion to their cheapness, and as the extent of manufactures is in proportion to the quantity of materials that are purchased, every particle of duty laid on them lessens the amount of industry and of annual productions.

Lord Althorp, the new Whig Chancellor, announced in 1831 that his 'general view of finance' would be based on Parnell's book, but his resolve fell down when it came to the test of actual measures.

Finally Sir Robert Peel, in the mounting clamour of the Chartists—for the demand for trade liberalisation had begun to swell into a demand for social and political emancipation—won the election of 1841 and in the following year presented a budget which began the momentous process of dismantling all the obstacles of the free inflow of food and raw materials to this country. The repeal of the Corn Laws which completed the process in 1846 was little more than a symbolic finishing touch. And it was left to Peel to put the issue, one of the greatest in the nation's history, in a nutshell:

If you had to constitute new societies, you might on moral and social grounds prefer corn fields to cotton factories; an agricultural to a manufacturing population. But our lot is cast; we cannot change it and we cannot recede.

The stage was then set. Thenceforth the chronicle of the modern British economy unfolded. The balance of payments fell into its present-day pattern. Once blended together the invisible and industrial trade streams went on feeding each other into the modern epoch. Visible imports and exports attracted more shipping, merchanting, insurance and banking services. The growth of the entrepôt and financial services, the spread of British shipping offices, banking and insurance establishments across the continents revealed new opportunities for the export of manufactures. Above all, investment played a decisive role. These investments, in that they generated profits, dividends and interest in due time, further swelled the inflow of invisible receipts, and so built a multiplier into our overseas' accounts. A most impressive mechanism evolved. Our overseas investment came to control foreign assets of thousands of millions of pounds, throwing up yearly incomes of hundreds of millions, and this mechanism is still with us today. But apart from the overseas finances created, investment had a strong industrial purpose. For a country dependent, as Britain has been, on foreign resources for the great bulk of its industrial raw materials, it was in many ways merely common sense to invest in the control, or at least the operation, of those overseas points of supply; British ownership of mines, plantations and forests overseas thus came into being. But also, in due time, British manufacturers, carrying on production as they were in a small congested country, where tons of raw material had to be moved in from abroad to make much smaller quantities of finished products, saw the economic logic of siting their new factories on top of their raw materials, and also of gaining the advantages of lower freight costs as well as lower labour costs and lower taxation where available. This became an increasing tendency as time went on and today is the main purpose of overseas investment.

In the life of a national economy a hundred and fifty-odd years is a passing moment. The economic geography of Britain today is what it was at the time of the Corn Law debates. We are still a small island, under-endowed with natural resources and more densely populated, than in those far-off days. The population is concentrated in the towns and engaged in manufacture, with only 4 per cent left on the land. Our agriculture is, technically, still highly efficient; we are a leading exporter of breeding stock, seedstock and farm implements. But our home produce is still insufficient to meet our overall food needs. Our economy, as the evidence of the years has shown, is geared to imports; we cannot produce without them, and we cannot export without them. The Board of Trade guessed, in May 1969, that for 1 per cent extra of GNP, we attract $1\frac{2}{3}$ per cent extra of imports. The input–output tables for the United Kingdom suggest an average import content of industrial output of 17 per cent, i.e. every £100 worth of goods produced needs £17 of imported raw or semi-finished material. The import content of exports alone is estimated at 19 per cent.[23] Thus, if you increase production, you increase imports, and if you increase wealth, you increase imports further. In our economy there is a calculable relationship between our activity and imports and an econometrician could no doubt produce an absorbing formula. It is to be hoped this will be done one day.

And so to the second question posed at the end of Chapter IV. If Britain's external payments are sound, why has the opposite impression prevailed so strongly?

VI A Century-old Error

The answer makes an extraordinary tale, reflecting many ages of British history, and at times having almost the qualities of a detective story. In short, it is that until the last decade, the true facts of our overseas trade had not been discovered. There are three things, let it be remembered, to explain: why it was not known that a deficit on merchandise was natural and constant to our economy; why it had not been noticed that in fact we run an overall commercial surplus; why it has not been realised that we share with America the only two significant Government deficits in the world and that this is the trigger of our national deficits?

The belief that this country is, or was destined to be, a natural net exporter of goods is immemorial. It is an axiom of national faith. The British have believed three things in their time: that they rule the waves, that they are a nation of shopkeepers, and that they export or ought to export more goods than they buy. The last, at least, is wholly wrong. However, it is a human error; practically every nation makes it.

Although this belief was nurtured early—witness the admonition of the great Cecil[24] of Elizabeth's reign:

> It is manifest that nothing robbeth the realm . . . but when more merchandise is brought into the realm than is carried forth

or the Restoration Council of Trade of 1660:

> England hath of its own growth, manufacture and produce always enough to oblige the importation of money and bullion upon all occasions, beyond any nation whatsoever in Christendom

—there is no doubt that the belief really flowered from the great series of trade returns which between 1697 and 1854 showed constant and enormous merchandise surpluses. We know now, as mentioned in Chapter II, that these were simply the result of statistical error. The fact is that this extraordinary and long-lived clerical aberration presented, over a period of no less than 157 years—from the earliest beginnings to an advanced stage of our industrial trade—apparently unquestionable evidence that we enjoyed a persistent net surplus of exports. This left us an inextinguishable piece of national folklore—the conviction that we were a natural exporter of merchandise.

The first question to be resolved, then, is how and why this statistical error went on so long, and why its true significance was not realised. As remarked in Chapter II, we shall probably never know the full answer, and this will remain one of history's mysteries. However, one explanation may reside in the fact that the trade records were really wrong because the official values ceased to represent the true value of money. It must be remembered that the constant preoccupation with inflation, that is the hallmark of present times, was not known in the eighteenth and nineteenth centuries. Temporary debasing of the value of money, and its harmful effects, had been known since Tudor days and before, but the idea that money slowly inflated as a natural event over centuries, simply was not there. If one were to ask, therefore, why the authorities of the eighteenth century did not decide that the official values must be revised to avoid distortion of trade records through inflation, the answer must be that the question is misplaced. They were in no position to suspect that there was inflation and that it was affecting the quality of their figures.

In 1854, the official figures were in fact discarded, and real valuations substituted. But, again, it would be wrong to think that this was done because the authorities of the time realised that inflation had eroded the values of the series and that this long record of imports and exports was misleading throughout. Far from it. The Victorians had no especial concern with eighteenth-century statistics. Their only observation was that the *current* official values were different from the declared values of traders. The latter they considered reliable, and so the changeover was effected. Moreover, it should not be thought that this modification was the subject of much research and discussion at the time. There were many administrative improvements in progress, of which this was considered only one. It is perhaps worth remembering that this period, and the one in which the trade figures were actually started, were phases of peculiar activity. They followed the two major constitutional turning points of British history; the Revolution of 1688 and the Reform Act of 1832. Each of these led to several decades of dynamic action unrivalled in the country's lifetime. Some of the events of the 1690s have already been described. The Reform Act of 1832 led, as we have also seen, to the mighty reversal of British economic policy, the abolition of import barriers, the repeal of the Corn Laws and the Navigation Laws, and much else besides.

More important, the sudden change from surplus to deficit in 1854 was not apparent at the time. There were several statistical series going simultaneously. Firstly, a record of exports according to declared values had been started in 1798 and this had continued up to 1854. The year 1798 was the year in which naval convoys were first organised, for this was the middle of the Napoleonic Wars. The Admiralty of the day, providently, decided to charge merchantmen for the Navy's trouble, this charge being made in the form of a tax on the value of the goods carried, which the shippers had to declare. The latter were under no temptation to exaggerate the value of their cargoes; the Admiralty, equally, was not inclined to accept an underestimate. A very accurate statistical series resulted, and when the wars were over, they were continued. They were always looked upon as of lesser standing than the 'official' figures and although they were published alongside these, they were not seriously studied. Those who did study them—like G. R. Porter, a former chief statistician in the Board of Trade, who commented on them briefly in his book *The Progress of the Nation* (1847)—noticed that if the declared values for exports were compared with the official values for imports, then the surplus showing in 1798 slowly resolved into a deficit by the 1830s. Since he, and others like him, were precisely at that time engaged in the furious battle for free trade, he was delighted. He believed that England's development had been held back by import restrictions, and that a rise in imports was what the country most needed. He was not to know that the changeover he saw was fictitious, and caused by the fact that the official import figures needed correction. If the true import figures had been available, he would of course have seen a continuous deficit back into the past. But most people, of course, had not inspected the record as closely as George Porter, and simply read the official figures for both imports and exports, which showed a standing surplus.

As against this preceding export series, the existing system of official values, although formally superseded in 1854, was not in fact dropped. It continued to be published by the Board of Trade, alongside the new series, until 1869, no less than 15 years later—and they still went under their title of 'official' values. Most people continued to read them as the correct figures. Thus the changeover of 1854 was carried out in circumstances most likely to obscure the view of the contemporary observer. It was not until the statistics of the period had passed into historical record that the old and the new series were read together.

By the 1880s scholars and men in public life had what seemed a continuous public record of the country's trade. They had the official values published by the Inspector-General for Imports and Exports extending from 1697 to 1853; and they had the statistics of foreign trade, based on declared values, published by the Board of Trade in the Annual Statement of Trade, from 1854 onwards. These presented an unbroken history of British trade figures collected by Government agencies from 1697 to 1880, and they showed surpluses until 1854, and deficits thereafter. Those who thought the switch from one to the other seemed somewhat abrupt, would have reflected that the change had been foreshadowed in the earlier line of declared values for exports, as Porter had shown, or, alternatively, they would have noted that the official values still suggested surpluses in 1869. They would have concluded that the economy was in process of change between the 1820s and 1870s and that, making allowances for statistical aberrations, British trade slipped from net exports to net imports somewhere around the middle of the nineteenth century.

This, then, became the textbook version of British trade history. When did it finally become generally known that this version was incorrect? Improbable though this may seem, not until 1967.

From the 1880s until the 1930s the dust of history was scarcely disturbed. Scholars and men of action alike were content in their use of the two series as the standard national reference on the subject. Just before the Second World War two scholars, one English and one German, threw a ray of light on the position. In the same year, 1938, Professor G. N. Clark published a book, *Guide to English Commercial Statistics, 1696–1782*, and Dr Werner Schlote wrote for Kiel University a study entitled *Entwicklung und Strukturwandlungen des Englischen Aussenhandels von 1700 bis zur Gegenwart* (published in English under the title *British Overseas Trade from 1700 to the 1930s*). Professor Clark's work illustrated in masterly fashion the deficiencies of the official values in the eighteenth century, and his book is still the essential departure point for any study of real values in British trade. However, Professor Clark could not offer a correction of these figures. Schlote compiled a single, new, set of trade figures from 1697 right through to 1933. This is no longer accepted as an accurate revision, but Schlote's contribution was both bold and illuminating. A number of historians, among them Ramsay, Ashton, Maizels and Carus-Wilson, took a hand in further researches.

Meanwhile, in America, a great body of work was going through. At some time or other in the 1950s many American historians and economists of distinction, Schumpeter, W. W. Rostow, A. J. Schwartz, A. H. Imlah, were engaged in research into the real state of British trade in the eighteenth and nineteenth centuries. Finally, in 1958, came the breakthrough. Albert Imlah published his work *Economic Elements in the Pax Britannica* in which a complete reconstruction of the trade figures on an accurate basis was presented from 1853 back to 1796. To do this, some means of substituting real values for the official figures for the half-century involved was needed. Imlah realised, where most others had failed to do so, that the declared values begun in the naval convoy service in 1798 provided the real export figures he wanted. For the import figures, an acceptable price index was needed, which could project the values of 1854 back to 1796. After examining those of Irving and Marshall, and many others, Imlah constructed the coefficients he needed. With these he converted the official import series into actual current prices for the whole half-century. With Imlah, therefore, the hump of the problem was overcome. True figures for both exports and imports were now available for the whole of the nineteenth century, and they showed a continuous deficit balance. The notion that there had been a basic change in Britain's trade position at the half-century mark was seen to be misfounded. Back in England, Deane and Cole in their *British Economic Growth, 1688–1959* came to the same broad conclusion, and produced their own schedule of trade figures for the eighteenth century, which also showed an invariable deficit. With the incorporation of Imlah's figures in the *Abstract of British Historical Statistics* (published in 1962 by the Cambridge University Press and edited by Mitchell and Deane), the corrected statistics received their accolade, and became the standard reference.

So far, however, these were labours confined to the relatively tranquil world of universities and academics. They were not known to, and had no part in, the hugger-mugger of balance of payments debate that was seething in the British Press and Parliament at this time. Few economists outside the circle of those specialising in trade history at the universities were aware of these researches and their results. Then awareness began to break through. Lord Cromer, in a speech to the Overseas Bankers Club in 1966 when he was Governor of the Bank of England, directed his audience's attention to the fact that the country's trade history was a long line of trade deficits, punctuated by only a few surpluses. Then came the Report of the Committee on Invisible Exports, which appeared in October 1967 under the title 'Britain's Invisible Earnings'. This contained, in its Chapter II, an 'Historical Analysis' supported by statistical data, which concluded with the statement that 'only seven of the past 175 years have shown a trading surplus'. This, for the first time, caught on. The phrase, with the magic number—175 years—was repeated widely in the Press. The point was discussed by a variety of economic commentators, and remarked on by politicians. Reginald Maudling,[25] Chancellor of the Exchequer in the previous Conservative Government, said:

Table A—General balance of payments
£ million

	1957	*1958*	*1959*	*1960*	*1961*	*1962*	*1963*	*1964*	*1965*	*1966*	*1967*
Current account											
Imports (f.o.b.)[1]	3 538	3 377	3 639	4 138	4 043	4 095	4 362	5 003	5 049	5 244	5 660
Exports and re-exports (f.o.b.)	3 509	3 406	3 522	3 732	3 891	3 993	4 282	4 466	4 777	5 108	5 023
Visible balance[1]	−29	+29	−117	−406	−152	−102	−80	−537	−272	−136	−637
Invisibles											
Services											
Debits—government	175	199	188	233	260	278	290	314	316	324	305
private[2]	1 065	1 010	1 058	1 183	1 212	1 231	1 298	1 397	1 478	1 515	1,603
total	1 240	1 209	1 246	1 416	1 472	1 509	1 588	1 711	1 794	1 839	1 908
Credits—government	85	54	43	45	46	39	40	45	46	42	36
private[2]	1 242	1 247	1 285	1 372	1 433	1 472	1 492	1 577	1 668	1 754	1 941
total	1 327	1 301	1 328	1 417	1 479	1 511	1 532	1 622	1 714	1 796	1 977
Interest profits and dividends											
Debits	334	389	396	438	422	420	444	491	555	568	603
Credits	583	682	656	669	674	753	838	904	1 025	990	1 013
Transfers											
Debits—government	75	77	82	94	118	121	132	163	177	179	184
private	110	99	100	101	102	111	128	154	167	183	197
Credits—government	21	3	—	—	—	—	—	—	—	—	—
private	90	103	100	104	109	111	113	131	135	134	135
Total invisibles											
Debits	1 759	1 774	1 824	2 049	2 114	2 161	2 292	2 519	2 693	2 769	2 892
Credits	2 021	2 089	2 084	2 190	2 262	2 375	2 483	2 657	2 874	2 920	3 125
Invisible balance	+262	+315	+260	+141	+148	+214	+191	+138	+181	+151	+233
CURRENT BALANCE	**+233**	**+344**	**+143**	**−265**	**−4**	**+112**	**+111**	**−399**	**−91**	**+15**	**−404**

Table A—General balance of payments (continued)

Long-term capital account[3]											
Inter-government loans (net)	+75	−44	−118	−92	−16	−91	−97	−101	−66	−61	−39
Other UK official long-term capital (net)	−9	−6	−6	−11	−29	−13	−8	−15	−20	−20	−18
Private investment											
Abroad	−298	−310	−303	−322	−313	−242	−320	−396	−353	−303	−424
In the United Kingdom	+126	+164	+172	+233	+426	+248	+277	+142	+236	+280	+395
BALANCE OF LONG-TERM CAPITAL	**−106**	**−196**	**−255**	**−192**	**+68**	**−98**	**−148**	**−370**	**−203**	**−104**	**−86**
BALANCE OF CURRENT AND LONG-TERM CAPITAL TRANSACTIONS	**+127**	**+148**	**−112**	**−457**	**+64**	**+14**	**−37**	**−769**	**−294**	**−89**	**−490**
Balancing item	**+80**	**+67**	**−22**	**+299**	**−25**	**+75**	**−73**	**+41**	**+67**	**−10**	**+175**
Monetary movements[3]											
Exchange adjustments[4]	—	—	—	—	—	—	—	—	—	—	−101
Miscellaneous capital (net)		−21	+10	+8	−35	+13	−41	−27	+40	−116	+40
Change in liabilities in non-sterling currencies (net)	+11	+10	−5	+60	−15	+40	−16	+218	−137	−148	+189
Change in liabilities in overseas sterling area currencies (net)	−195	+76	+126	+416	−333	+53	−6	+8	+7	−45	+24
Change in external liabilities in sterling (net)							+115	+48	+64	+128	+293
Change in official holdings of non-convertible currencies	−22	+23	+8	+2	+1	+1	—	—	—	—	—
Change in UK balance in EPU	+11	−10	+9								
Change in account with IMF	+1	−9	−133	−151	+374	−379	+5	+359	+499	−2	−318
Transfer from dollar portfolio to reserves	—	—	—	—	—	—	—	—	—	+316	+204
Change in gold and convertible currency reserves	−13	−284	+119	−177	−31	+183	+53	+122	−246	−34	−16
BALANCE OF MONETARY MOVEMENTS	**−207**	**−215**	**+134**	**+158**	**−39**	**−89**	**+110**	**+728**	**+227**	**+99**	**+315**

[1] Excluding deliveries of, but including payments for, US military aircraft and missiles.
[2] Private services are shown in detail in Table 8.
[3] Assets: increase −/decrease +. Liabilities: increase +/decrease −.
[4] See note on page 70.

Perhaps this will come as a shock to those who, like myself, always thought that in the last century it was the exports of British textiles and British machinery and British coal that built up the overseas investments from which we now draw so much of our invisible income.

The point has not yet, however, been fully taken. From the date of publication of the revised trade figures in 1962 to their general dissemination to those concerned in public life, was five years. To re-set Government policy on a basic change of facts takes much longer than that. The reaction at working level has, on the whole, been superficial. Whitehall economists, who have been giving their best brainwork for years to the task of raising exports above imports, have been inclined, somewhat understandably, to counter with defensive remarks beginning with phrases like 'Nobody ever said . . .' Whitehall officials have tended, slightly irritably, to suggest that they have enough trouble getting an export surplus this year without hearing of peoples' worries in previous centuries. Outside Whitehall it has been much more the 'Fancy that!' reaction. Industry has failed to make a surplus for no less than 175 years. 'If it had not been for those chaps in the City, where would we all be?' Even the latter, however, do not go on to notice that the invisible earnings they refer to have the effect of putting the nation into standing commercial surplus with the rest of the world.

This brings the discussion to the second major question. Regardless of the balance on visible trade, how did it happen that the favourable balance on visible and invisibles taken together, failed to be noticed? How could the impression arise that the country was failing to hold its own in its commercial transactions abroad, was buying more from its competitors abroad than it was selling to them, when in fact the reverse was the case?

One reason, of course, was that if a country is deeply convinced that its visible deficit, which undoubtedly exists, is the result of commercial impotence, it is unlikely to be on the look-out for evidence pointing in the opposite direction. Another is the remote understanding of what invisibles are, and the sparse knowledge of their dimensions. Statistics on invisible trade were not issued publicly until 1946. For most people, these earnings are the work of a few financiers in the City, a somewhat esoteric band, making a mint of money passing pieces of paper to each other. There is virtually no realisation that although the City, with its international money, commodity and other markets, earns a great amount of foreign exchange for the country, invisible earnings are equally the work of Cunard, BUA, the Grosvenor Hotel, British Rail, Cable and Wireless, Mitchell Cotts, Redland Croize, ICI, Shell, RTZ and a dozen other major enterprises; that invisibles are the earnings of great tracts of industrial and commercial activity that are not merely a part of, but more than 50 per cent of the total wealth turned over by the country each year.

One reason, however, is prominent and can be summed up in the single word—presentation. It is apparent from the Table A reproduced on pages 48 and 49. This table is none other than the official balance of payments account, as presented by the Government in its annual statement (the 'Pink Book'). The issue is the one published in 1968, showing all the balance of payments results from 1957 to 1967. Who would imagine from this collection of figures that there was a surplus on the total commercial transactions of the nation, offset only by a deficit on official spending? The visible gap is depicted clearly enough: it is shown in the three simple lines at the head of the table: for 1967, for instance: imports: £5 660 million; exports: £5 023 million; balance: – £637 million. (The figures are slightly different from those shown in Appendix Table VI for they have been revised since.) But where is the £3 028 million of invisible receipts, the £2 160 million of invisible payments, the invisible balance of £868 million? It is lost in the maze of sub-headings which follows the visible balance. When the eye has passed down the page to the 18th line, the words 'invisible balance' appear. And the figure placed in the column is, not £868 million, but £233 million. What has happened to the rest of the surplus? It has been mopped up by the entries for Government spending, part of the forest of sub-headings referred to. Not only are the items for Government spending inserted amongst the items for commercial income and payments, and counted with them, but Government expenditure is actually included as part of some of the commercial items; thus Government interest payments on official debts are added to the 'debits' column under the heading 'Interest, profits and dividends'. As a result, the balance of income from our commercial overseas investment is shown as a considerable under-estimate; instead of the figure which the table infers, £410 million, it is in fact £543 million.

Passing to the next line under 'invisible balance', we come to the main entry 'Current Balance'. This, at – £404 million, is neither a statement of the outcome on commercial visibles and invisibles, nor that of the net deficit on Government expenditure overseas. It is a composite figure, made out of a mixture of all. The real commercial position of the country, and the real impact of official activities, are totally lost.

From there, the account passes to a main section entitled 'Long-term capital account'. This, on the face of it, should show how much industrial and portfolio investment was placed abroad by the economy, and how

Table B—General balance of payments 1958–1968

£ million

	1958	*1959*	*1960*	*1961*	*1962*	*1963*	*1964*	*1965*	*1966*	*1967*	*1968*
Current account											
Exports and re-exports (f.o.b.)[1]	3 406	3 522	3 732	3 891	3 993	4 282	4 466	4 777	5 108	5 026	6 103
Imports (f.o.b.)[2]	3 377	3 639	4 138	4 043	4 095	4 362	5 003	5 042	5 211	5 574	6 801
Visible trade balance[1 2]	+29	−117	−406	−152	−102	−80	−537	−265	−103	−548	−698
Net under-recording of exports	—	—	—	—	—	—	20	40	60	80	130
Payments for US military aircraft	—	—	—	—	—	—	2	12	41	98	109
Visible balance	+29	−117	−406	−152	−102	−80	−519	−237	−84	−566	−677
Invisibles[3]											
Government services and transfers (net)	−219	−227	−282	−332	−360	−382	−432	−447	−470	−464	−462
Other invisibles											
Private[4] services and transfers (net)	+241	+227	+192	+228	+241	+184	+163	+165	+202	+328	+455
Interest, profits and dividends (net)											
Private sector	+434	+388	+379	+416	+480	+524	+523	+602	+579	+593	+654
Public sector	−141	−128	−148	−164	−147	−132	−116	−133	−163	−174	−235
Invisible balance	+315	+260	+141	+148	+214	+194	+138	+187	+148	+283	+412
CURRENT BALANCE	**+344**	**+143**	**−265**	**−4**	**+112**	**+114**	**−381**	**−50**	**+64**	**−283**	**−265**
Long-term capital account[5]											
Inter-government loans (net)	−44	−118	−92	−16	−91	−97	−101	−66	−61	−39	−6
Other UK official long-term capital (net)	−6	−6	−11	−29	−13	−8	−15	−19	−19	−18	+27
Private investment											
Abroad	−310	−303	−322	−313	−242	−320	−399	−354	−304	−457	−736
In the United Kingdom	+164	+172	+233	+426	+248	+276	+152	+237	+272	+380	+573
BALANCE OF LONG-TERM CAPITAL	**−196**	**−255**	**−192**	**+68**	**−98**	**−149**	**−363**	**−202**	**−112**	**−134**	**−142**

Table B—General balance of payments 1958–1968 (continued)

BALANCE OF CURRENT AND LONG-TERM CAPITAL TRANSACTIONS	**+148**	**−112**	**−457**	**+64**	**+14**	**−35**	**−744**	**−252**	**−48**	**−417**	**−407**
Balancing item	**+67**	**−22**	**+299**	**−25**	**+75**	**−72**	**−13**	**+15**	**−80**	**+176**	**−130**
Monetary movements[5]											
EEA loss on forwards[6]	—	—	—	—	—	—	—	—	—	−105	−251
Miscellaneous capital (net)	−21	+10	+8	−35	+13	−44	—	+38	−93	−67	−24
Change in liabilities in non-sterling currencies (net)	+10	−5	+60	−15	+40	−16	+220	−125	−146	+213[7]	+53
Change in liabilities in overseas sterling area currencies (net)	+76	+126	+416	−333	+53	−6	+8	+7	−45	+24	−46
Change in external liabilities in sterling (net)						+115	+48	+64	+132	+175[8]	+166
Change in official holdings of non-convertible currencies	+23	+8	+2	+1	+1	—	—	—	—	—	—
Change in UK balance in EPU	−10	+9									
Change in account with IMF	−9	−133	−151	+374	−379	+5	+359	+499	−2	−318[9]	+525
Transfer from dollar portfolio to reserves	—	—	—	—	—	—	—	—	+316	+204	—
Change in gold and convertible currency reserves	−284	+119	−177	−31	+183	+53	+122	−246	−34	+115[10]	+114
BALANCE OF MONETARY MOVEMENTS	**−215**	**+134**	**+158**	**−39**	**−89**	**+107**	**+757**	**+237**	**+128**	**+241**	**+537**

[1] Excluding allowance for net under-recording of exports.
[2] Excluding deliveries of US military aircraft and missiles.
[3] Details are shown in Table 8.
[4] Including public corporations.
[5] Assets: increase−/decrease +. Liabilities: increase+/decrease−.
[6] See note on page 78.
[7] Excludes revaluation to sterling equivalent of official liabilities in foreign currencies (+6).
[8] Excludes increases in sterling balances resulting from revaluation payments at the time of devaluation—liabilities to central banks denominated in sterling (+119); liabilities to European Monetary Agreement (+2).
[9] See footnote[a]—liabilities IMF (+75).
[10] Excludes revaluation to sterling equivalent of reserve assets (−131).

many loans the Government made to other governments. Although items are shown for all of these, the account again marries the two together, and the figure of −£86 million at the bottom of the section is a mongrel born of public and private activity. Most important, the important distinction between current and capital transactions of the private sector, on the one hand, which are in credit balance, and the current and capital transactions of the public sector on the other, which are in deficit, is lost to view.

This was the form in which the accounts were published up to 1968. A good deal of pressure, it happens, was put on the Government in that year, mainly as a result of the publication of the Report of the Committee on Invisible Exports, and some modifications were made when the Pink Book was published in 1969, showing the results for the years 1958–68. The appropriate table (Table B) is reproduced on pages 52 and 53. In separating, this time, Government interest payments from private investment receipts, and in showing Government expenditure at least on a line separate from private transactions, the table is somewhat more explicit. However, the invisible balance (11th line) shown is still a jumble of public and private figures, as is the current balance. How was it shown years ago? Table C on page 55 shows how the visible and invisible balances were reflected for the years immediately following the war. The method used is yet more damning for the private side, since the current balance is summed up in the first three lines, all on the mixed public and private basis. Thus, for 1946, the total balance is first shown as −£344 million, and this is broken down in the ensuing two lines into 'visible' −£176 million and 'invisible' −£168 million. No hint of the fact that the private invisible outcome was plus £165 million in that year, and the net Government spending minus £333 million.

It is important not to reproach the official statisticians on this score. The British balance of payments figures are a model of accuracy, and of concision. The layout of the figures, disregarding the particular point being made here, is neat and logical. The fact that Government figures are submerged in others is not particularly the choice of the British statistical services. This is the analysis favoured by the International Monetary Fund. Government figures must go somewhere. They are invisible in the sense that they are transfers of funds, and the invisible section of the table seemed to IMF the sensible place to put them. The vital point is, of course, that for all countries except the UK—and the USA, who use a different layout anyway—Government net expenditures are in fact negligible, since they are self-balancing. In the case of the UK, however, the item is large

Table C—Balance of payments

Balance of payments of the United Kingdom: Current account

£ million

	1946	*1947*	*1948*	*1949*	*1950*
Balance of current transactions					
Total	-344	-545	-29	+21	+221
Visible trade	-176	-425	-206	-151	-159
Invisible	-168	-120	+177	+172	+380
Debits					
Total	1 691	2 171	2 263	2 508	2 922
Imports (f.o.b):					
Total	1 081	1 560	1 790	1 973	2 382
Food and feeding-stuffs	520	719	826	909	974
Tobacco	71	30	36	49	58
Raw materials	318	509	606	690	960
Petroleum	60	77	127	121	149
Machinery and vehicles	20	84	50	55	54
Other imports[1]	92	141	145	149	187
Shipping[2]	137	165	174	190	199
Interest, profits and dividends[3]	83	94	102	104	114
Travel[4]	42	76	66	73	81
Migrants' funds, legacies, private gifts (net)[5]	-15	46	44	26	6
Government transactions:					
Total (net)	363	230	87	142	140
Military[6]	374	209	113	110	98
Administrative, diplomatic, etc.[7]	20	25	29	30	36
Relief and Rehabilitation	83	37	15	11	11
Germany (net)[8]	40	81	16	9	3
Colonial grants (net)	10	7	10	16	18
War disposals, settlements, etc. (net)	-164	-129	-96	-34	-26
Credits					
Total	1 347	1 626	2 234	2 529	3 143
Exports and re-exports (f.o.b.)	905	1 135	1 584	1 822	2 223
Shipping[2]	166	198	250	273	314
Interest, profits and dividends[9]	154	174	179	189	237
Travel[4]	13	21	33	44	58
Other (net)[10]	109	98	188	201	311

[1] Including silver, diamonds, parcel post and animals not for food.

[2] Tankers' disbursements and oil freights are included in 'Other (net)' credits.

[3] Excluding, so far as possible, payments through London agents on account of investments outside the United Kingdom held by non-residents.

[4] Including business travel.

[5] Excluding migrants' personal belongings.

[6] Including the f.o.b. value of food and oil shipped direct from the country of origin for consumption overseas by the Armed Forces. (*continued at foot of p. 56*

and all-important, and it matters very much how it is shown. The official statisticians will point out, rightly, that everything is in the Pink Book, and that it is just a matter of seeking out the particular analysis that is wanted. This is true, but it does not cover the issue fully. To get out the respective private and public balances mentioned above, the student of the tables must know what he is looking for, engage in a great deal of addition and subtraction, be aware of subtleties such as the hidden deduction in the investment income figures, and generally be an experienced analyst of the balance of payments before he starts.

The table, as it is presented, conveys an impression of the British external trade position that could not have been more misleading if deliberately contrived. Running his eye down the columns the observer without special knowledge will first remark on the large visible deficit, the figures confirming to him the impression generally held. He will then see a small balance or an actual deficit for invisibles, and a figure for the Current Balance which is flatly in the red. Moving on, he will see a negative sum for long-term capital. His reaction will be: that the country fails to pay its way on the exchange of physical goods; it then makes a small surplus, at most, on invisibles, which does not cover the merchandise gap, and thus falls into overall deficit on current account. It then compounds this loss by exporting capital. (Last September the Government produced another, and entirely different presentation. However since it is so recent and still perpetuates much of the misapprehension, it does not affect the point being made above, and need not be gone into here.)

This leads to the next, and important stage in the present exposition. We have seen so far what, in a passive way, prevented those concerned from realising that the merchandise gap was unharmful and unremarkable, that the country's commercial balance was healthy, and that such deficits as arose were on official and non-commercial account. But what, so to speak, put the sex into the situation? What produced the systematic, urgent plunge in the other direction? What inspired the tocsin phrase

[7] Excluding Colonial grants. Including pensions and contributions to international organisations other than for relief.

[8] Identifiable net cost to H.M. Government of supplies and services to the civilian population of Germany. Excluding occupation costs and reparations.

[9] Excluding overseas earnings of United Kingdom insurance, shipping and oil companies. Represents, in general, total earnings remitted for the payment of interest and dividends, taxation and management expenses in the United Kingdom and for re-investment.

[10] Including the overseas transactions of oil companies (other than capital expenditure), insurance, civil aviation, commissions, royalties and other services, net remittances in respect of films, etc.

'export or die' and *The Times* leader 'It *is* a moral issue'? What produced a 20-year-long national mood of self-vilification, bitter disillusionment, and hope for redemption?

For explanation we must go back to the 1880s. As earlier remarked, it was just about then that the changeover in recording of 1854 had receded into historical perspective and an apparent 200-year long trade record was available for historians and administrators. This record showed that England was a natural net exporter, since she had been such for one and a half of the two centuries involved. Now the 1870s and 1880s were also years of particular travail for economists and politicians. The end of the 1870s ushered in the Great Depression, which lasted several decades, the traumas of which still reverberated behind the pledge to endless economic growth made in as late a period as the 1950s. World trade dwindled, prices fell, industry stagnated.

> Approached from whatever point of view we may choose to adopt, the retrospect of 1878 is, in almost every respect, one of great gloom and depression. It was generally believed, at the end of 1877, that it would be difficult, if not almost impossible, to pass through another [year] equally marked by trouble and disaster; but during the last twelve months manufacturers have found in the lowest depths a deeper still. . . .

So spoke J. S. Jeans,[26] Secretary of the Iron and Steel Institute, in 1879.

There was, therefore, a keen apprehension that all was not right with British industry. Couple this with the fact that other countries—although almost equally hard hit by recession—were now beginning seriously to move into the world market, and there was ready ground in which the seed of doubt over Britain's economic powers could be sown. Of course, as is now known, the balance of payments was perfectly sound; Table V in the Appendix shows this. But those involved in the contemporary scene could only see a large and growing merchandise deficit, falling profits on British manufacture, and international competition in the international markets which Britain had formerly dominated. The combined exports of Britain's closest rivals, France, Germany and the USA, were now greater than those of the UK. This country was no longer the sole practical supplier. Again, all that was happening was that the world was growing up around the UK. Other countries, having industrialised themselves, were contributing their quota to the ever expanding total of world trade. The British share was falling, but this was the inevitable arithmetical result, and had nothing to do with Britain's performance.

> Mature consideration of the case cannot fail to carry the conviction that England has for many years been labouring under a very unhealthy deficiency of exports.

It was by her export trade that Britain rose to her position of influence and wealth, and she is not maintaining that trade at all in proportion to her increase of population or her necessities. The only remedy that appears to me is that in some way we must . . . increase the export trade. . . .

In such terms, Bourne,[27] a member of the Council of the Royal Statistical Society, expressed the typical view at a meeting of that body in the summer of 1882. And this, after the reading of a particularly brilliant paper by Sir Robert Giffen,[28] in which the prevailing gloom was opposed. Giffen, though, sophisticated as he was, remained hogtied by the statistical methods of the day. Although he clearly had strong suspicions of the surpluses recorded before 1854, he was confused by the changes of the statistical base which, as he said, had occurred not only in 1798, but in 1869 also. He could only show that there had been import 'excesses' back to 1854, and had, perforce, to begin his argument with a near concession.

The imports into the United Kingdom as recorded have in late years shown a great excess over the exports from the United Kingdom, as recorded.

It little availed him to show—as few had done since Thomas Mun, and few were to do until Imlah—that earnings on shipping, banking, insurance and overseas investment counteracted this trade imbalance. Indeed, with the imperfect knowledge of the time, he could not even show that invisible earnings equalised the trade deficiency. Much later Sir John Clapham, writing in the 1920s, was to say, however sceptical he might have been as to the gravity of the position:

The ordinary Englishman was worrying about the balance of trade in the late seventies as he had not done for many generations. He was alarmed at the steadily growing 'adverse' balance, the arithmetical excess of imports over exports; and there was much wild abuse of statistics . . . but many fancied it must be met by the sale of securities [*i.e. by disinvestment abroad*] . . . There was probably a little bringing home . . . [*in fact, of course, the increase of investment abroad went on apace*] Clumsily, ignorantly and with much misunderstanding, the balance of trade controversialists were pointing to a real change in Britain's international position.[29]

Thus, as the nineteenth century went out the myth of the 'golden age', the bygone days in which Britain had exported a surplus, was born; and its sister myth, that of the decline in Britain's economic capacity, was born with it.

Giffen's theories of an invisible offset were not accepted, as has been seen. Fairly soon, therefore, people began to wonder how the country had existed since the middle of the century, apparently earning nothing—in fact making a year by year loss. Said Giffen:

Statements have been brought to me that this country has become indebted to foreigners in twenty years to the extent of 1 000 million pounds.

The first explanation favoured was, that the deficit was being financed by the sale of British investments abroad. As Giffen, however, somewhat scathingly pointed out, this notion could be dispelled by a passing glance at the foreign bonds being floated every year in the country.

During the last two or three years a ghost has been going about England, alarming the busy people with statements to the effect that we are living on our capital. . . .

Glover, at the Royal Statistical Society debate, voiced the earliest tremors of a suspicion that in fullness of time became conviction. England was balancing her payments simply with the yearly income from the investments she had laid up in the 'good times' of export surpluses.

So the misfit of evidence to which all, through no fault of their own, had fallen victim, was rationalised into a system of economic thinking. As generation followed generation, economists and politicians perfected this into a fully-fledged analysis of British economic history, which became standard textbook practice. The great Alfred Marshall in his 'Memoranda on Fiscal Policy of International Trade' (1903–8) referred repeatedly to the changed competitive position of the UK compared with '60 years ago'. A. L. Bowley in *England's Foreign Trade in the 19th Century* (1905) stressed that Britain was no longer in 'the first class' having run a trade deficit since 1855. Taussig, in his *International Trade* of 1927 explained at length:

An inspection of the course of the imports and exports for the entire period of roughly a century from 1830 to 1914 shows that a striking change took place about the middle of the nineteenth century. During the first half of that century, until 1853, the recorded exports regularly exceeded the imports. After 1853, however the contrary relationship appears: the imports exceed the exports. The excess of imports is moderate at first. . . . Beginning about 1873 it becomes more marked . . . and towards the end of the century rises to extraordinary dimensions. . . .

Taussig was under no illusions that the method of recording had changed in 1854, but took the view that the change of statistical base did no more than explain the apparent abruptness of the transition from net exports to net imports:

None the less, the general trend of the figures for the middle years of the century indicates a change in the current of trade which in fact took place. Under the new and more accurate computation, imports not only exceeded exports at once, but continued to do so at an accelerating pace as the years went on. It is probable that in the second quarter of the century exports were greater than imports: it is quite certain that thereafter the imports were greater than the exports. . . .

Taussig then elaborated the theory of an investment cushion:

The excess of imports which developed during the second half of the century is easily explained. It was the natural result of two circumstances. One was the stage which Great Britain had reached as an international lender—the stage of maturity so to speak. The process of making loans to foreigners had been going on for many years and had been on a large scale from 1830 to 1850. . . . A growing stream of payments and income was setting in towards the lending country. . . . Capital export in its early stages . . . causes the lending country to have an excess of merchandise exports. As this goes on the growing remittances . . . come to exceed the fresh loans, and the lending country begins to have an excess of imports in place of the previous excess of exports.

Taussig then goes on to give, as his second reason, the growth of shipping and other receipts in the latter part of the century, which helped to offset the emergent deficit on merchandise.

As the twentieth century progressed, the date of the supposed change in trading abilities became a little blurred:

A generous income from foreign investments and apparently inexhaustible supplies of cheap food and raw materials concealed from the general public [before 1939] the slow but steady loss of strength that had occurred over the previous four decades.

This was said by Anthony Crosland in *Britain's Economic Problem (1947)*, and later Andrew Shonfield in his *British Economic Policy since the War* (1958) set out this uncertainty most lucidly:

There is no doubt that in the nineteenth century British overseas investment was an enormously fecund force in the expansion of world trade. . . . But all this presupposed first, an absolutely dominant position in world export trade—ensuring that the extra purchasing power in the new countries was spent on buying goods from Britain—and secondly a willingness . . . to import more and more cheap food and materials in the place of costlier home supplies. Neither of these conditions exist today. . . . There has been much discussion in recent years about the date when the decline in Britain's tempo of expansion set in. At one time it was fashionable to point to the First World War. . . . But closer analysis showed that the 1900s were a period in which Britain's industrial performance showed up particularly badly. . . . This led certain historians to propound the theory of the great slowdown of the 1890s. . . . The very latest investigations, however, suggest that the original source of the trouble must be pushed back even further into the nineteenth century. . . . It seems that after several decades of extremely rapid expansion of British output during the early and middle parts of the nineteenth century, something happened in the 1870s, and the whole process was slowed down sharply. We have never again recaptured this early élan. . . . The explanation of the drop in the tempo of British industrial expansion at the end of the nineteenth century offered by Professor W. A. Lewis is that it was the direct consequence of the slowing down of world trade, after the free trade movement of the 1850s and 1860s had expended itself. Britain stood completely exposed to the fluctuations of world trade—it deliberately bared its breast to these forces, as a matter of principle—whereas other countries proceeded with the expansion of certain crucial industries, under the shelter of tariffs and other forms of protection.

By 1960 therefore the doctrine was fully set. In the face of the statistics handed down to them, economists had really no choice in their interpretation of British history. Only the explanation which they developed fitted all the known facts. It was sensible and coherent; it explained much that otherwise seemed mysterious. It fitted the postwar presentation of British balance of payments figures, and was the standard theory set out in economic textbooks. It is the one on which any economist worth his salt, who had specialised in Britain's foreign trade, had been reared, and is the one which any ranking economist *today* will have absorbed, for the results of the new researches of Imlah and the others are barely 10 years old. It is, in the highest probability, the version of British economic history still being taught at the majority of British universities. But it is wrong.

The last word can perhaps best be left to Imlah, writing in 1958.

. . . There can be no escape therefore from the conclusion that Britain's new industrial system did not create export surpluses. Her phenomenal accumulation of overseas credits in the nineteenth century cannot be explained by the time-honoured assumption that machine-made exports supplied the credits. . . . In this first half of the century as later, Britain's invisible credits, the earnings of the merchant marine, the international commissions, the savings of her experts and technicians and colonial officials abroad, and the income from her foreign investments—made up the deficit on her invisible trade and supplied whatever new capital was invested overseas.

Now comes the final instalment of the tale. How did the standard economic doctrine of Britain's trade deficiency come to be enthroned as the lasting policy target of British Government, Labour and Conservative, since the war?

The years immediately after the war were the first in the country's history in which a real and dangerous imbalance of payments arose. We know now that this was because Britain emerged from the war with, for the first time in her history, a large burden of Government overseas expenditure. In 1946, this was the enormous contemporary sum of £327 million, and it easily outweighed the combined surplus on goods and services of £97 million. This adverse change was compounded by the great run-down of overseas investment assets that had been sustained during the war—and consequently of the incomes that derived from them. By 1945, or shortly after, £2 000 million of Britain's prewar overseas assets of £4 000 million had gone, and in the already inflated prices of that time, the remaining £2 000 million was worth only a part of what it had been before.

However, this was not recognised in the years running up to the devaluation of September 1949. On 6 August, 1947, the Government had to announce that the American and Canadian loans, obtained the previous year, had run out. A two-day crisis debate ensued. Attlee led off with a thumbnail sketch of the overall economic events leading up to the crisis:

> We had quite an artificial position before the First World War . . . increased industrialisation abroad pressed heavily on us and we found, instead of having a large export surplus after the First World War, that our balance of payments was only achieved with great difficulty. . . .

R. G. W. Mackay, a known economic authority of his day, followed him:

> Ever since 1931 we have been in a bad position in regard to the balance of payments. . . . Prior to 1913 this country was able to buy whatever it wanted with its exports and other services. . . . At no time from 1920 to 1939 was this country able to pay for its imports with its exports and services. . . . We are faced today by the fact that the development of the twentieth century is very different from that of the latter part of the nineteenth century . . . when we were the workshop of the world. By the end of the century we could afford to buy a lot of imports, process them and export them. . . . For 50 years this country has lived on the fat which has come from its external investments.

By the end of the debate there hove into view the immense and impressive figure of the Chancellor of the Exchequer, Dr Dalton. Dalton was one of the most colourful personalities of any age in our Parliamentary life. Hugely extrovert, with a booming voice that, as Samuel Brittan recalls, could be heard saying 'Between you and me' sixty feet away, he had tremendous powers of exposition and dominated his subject matter and his audience in any debate in the House. Now, Dalton was an economist. For years before the war he had been an inspiring university lecturer, particularly at the London School of Economics. He had written a highly esteemed book on public finance. Dalton was quite confident that he knew what was wrong with the balance of payments and the British economy. He needed no advice, he was the expert. And he lost no time in clearing the mind of Parliament.

> For a very long time past—for at least a generation, if not more—this country has never paid, under any Government or in any economic conditions, whether of boom or of slump, for its necessary imports by exports alone. . . . These are platitudes to all who study the subject, although they may surprise those who have not. The change which has come upon us is that, in two world wars, a great part of our overseas sources of means of payment for our imports has been destroyed: that is to say, the foreign investments which we slowly accumulated through the nineteenth century have been dispersed through the war effort twice undergone by us. Therefore the period of living on our nineteenth-century investments is over and that chapter in our history has come to an end. . . . By far the greatest and the gravest of all the immediate economic problems that are now facing us is the question of how quickly we can close the gap between our exports and our imports.

Thus put, vividly, cogently, and with all the immense authority imparted by the speaker—this statement of our economic situation convinced the country and Parliament, and reigned supreme in the policy-making of every successor government. Britain had, for long, escaped bankruptcy by drawing on her income from the overseas assets laid up in the times when her export strength was at its height. However, these assets had now been lost. Henceforth England would have to work for her living like any other country.

There is more than a tinge of Labour principle in this moral tale. Investments, whether at home or abroad, are not things that Labour politicians particularly love. Ploughing back industrial profits into new factories and mines is one thing. But living off dividends from share portfolios—which is what overseas investments were mistakenly supposed to comprise—is altogether another. The Labour Government was as much against the 'rentier' class among nations as among individuals. Then, again, the notion of expanding physical exports was much more to the socialist taste. Labour party members really did not like our apparent dependence on invisible exports, particularly in the form they were then imagined to take. If they were the product of financiers' paper-pushing in the City, the profits of men 'making money out of money', then socialists would rather do without them. Lloyd's, the Stock Exchange, merchant banks, discount houses, and the like, had high places in the roll of Socialist demonology. Much better to base the country's international solvency on the healthy product of sinewy labour in the mines or factories. In the old aphorism: 'If it doesn't hurt when you drop it on your foot, it isn't an export.'

Little in this has changed in Labour Party mythology ever since. Some sophistication has been forced in by the pressure of real life, but even recently Harold Wilson could not praise the achievements of invisible exporters without apparently suffering a wry taste in the mouth. Transport House has not moved on the issue. But such was the force of the early postwar statement of policy and the apparent economic logic of the need for exports, that you will hear views little different in Conservative Central Office either.

VII Confidence

The visible deficit, then, is natural; the commercial payments of the nation as a whole are in surplus; when we fall into overall deficit, it is because of the over-riding expenditure of Government. There is one more thing to add.

The words used above are 'when we fall into overall deficit . . .'. The 'when' is all-important. The notion that this country is always, or even invariably, in deficit, is mistaken. In all the years since 1946 there have been on the whole balance of payments—current and long-term, private and public—fourteen deficits and ten surpluses. Of these deficits, five in a row took place in the period 1964–68. All the peculiar misadventures and mismanagements of that era cannot be compressed into a book of the present size, but it is self-evident that this was an untypical piece of British balance of payments history. Something more will be said about this later. Meanwhile it is worth noting that if the period since 1964 is left out of the reckoning, then in the postwar period up to then, Britain had exactly nine deficits and nine surpluses. Equally important as the simple count of surpluses and deficits is the actual financial position of the country. The following table sets out the accumulated surpluses and deficits of the country over the whole postwar period. For the purpose sought here, the 'balancing item' has been included. This is, in the balance of payments account, no more than an 'errors and omissions' figure. Although much of it represents purely monetary flows, some of it at least consists of under- or overcounting of current and long-term capital transactions, and for that reason it is right to include it here.

As will be seen, the surpluses totalled £1 973 million by 1969, the deficits £3 309 million. If the years 1964–69 are knocked off, then surpluses at £1 404 million and deficits, at £1 410 million, were in balance; the tiny net deficit of £7 million remained. The country was solvent; there was no debt of any material size on the cumulative total of the 18 years of trading, investing and Government spending since 1946. This state of equilibrium was broadly held throughout the period and not merely at the end. Cut the table at almost any point in the spread of years 1946–63, and a near balance between surpluses and deficits will emerge.

	Surplus £m	*Deficit* £m
1946	18	—
1947	—	84
1948	305	—
1949	—	48
1950	353	—
1951	—	689
1952	95	—
1953	—	17
1954	—	17
1955	—	156
1956	63	—
1957	207	—
1958	215	—
1959	—	134
1960	—	158
1961	39	—
1962	89	—
1963	—	107
1964	—	757
1965	—	237
1966	—	128
1967	—	234
1968	—	543
1969	569	—
Total 1946–69	1 973	3 309

And yet, throughout that period, there were repeated sterling crises. Again and again, the alarm bells rang; the country's external position was declared in danger. Money was flooding out of the country, it was said; the reserves were being drained; the solvency of Britain was at risk. But our payments were in balance; the total cash flowing out of the country to meet our purchases was equalled by the cash coming in as a result of our sales. What money, then, was flooding out? What was leaking from the reserves?

Another question arises from study of the total debt position reached by 1968. As was shown by the Table, this amounted, after the griefs of 1964 onwards, to £1 905 million. But the notorious external debts of the country in 1969 were not of this order.[30] They amounted to no less than £3 360 million. Where had the rest of the money gone? Clearly some force other than that of the current payments on goods and services, of overseas investment and of Government expenditure, was at work. And, given the size of the figures and pressures involved, it was a very powerful one.

The other force was what we know as 'monetary movements'. What are these? We have a further and final segment of that comprehensive national account book, the balance of payments, to consider.

The balance of payments is the record of all money entering and leaving the country. It falls into two essential parts. The first part comprises all the elements so far considered: the sale and purchase of goods and services (visibles and invisibles), made both by the private sector and the Government; and the receipt and despatch of capital for industrial and portfolio investment and for official economic aid. These are flows of money generated by the practical activities of business and Government. This part of the balance of payments might therefore be termed the money flows on transactions.

The second part concerns the flow of money, as money. It is the in- and outflow of cash simply deposited in the United Kingdom; held purely as a financial asset and removed at will from the UK; and not at any time used to purchase goods, services or physical assets. It is accordingly, and properly, designated 'monetary movements'.

Who deposits money in the UK in this way? Firstly, the central banks of overseas sterling area countries; and, secondly, overseas private banks and financial institutions, international companies and trading concerns and foreign private citizens. In the last quarter of 1969 the total holdings of sterling area central banks stood at £1 990 million, and other holdings stood at £1 575 million. They were therefore very large.

Why are these funds held in the UK? The official deposits, held by central banks, are the central monetary reserves of the countries in question. There are two reasons for the other, or commercial holdings. Firstly, 25–30 per cent of the world's trade is settled in sterling.[31] Those engaged in this find it convenient to leave deposits in sterling in London. Secondly, London is the most efficient centre in the world for the handling of large amounts of short-term capital. International companies with working balances to place, will tend to resort to London. Overseas banks and financial institutions, with inferior local short-term facilities, also turn to London.

In Switzerland, for example, the banks, insurance companies, and business holding companies together hold more than £8 000 million of capital resources, equal to more than twice the gross national product of the country. Further, capital is attracted to the country from abroad. Owing to the conservative fiscal policies, and the traditional Swiss dislike of discount business, there is an almost total absence of short- and medium-term government obligations, and no short-term money market of any significance. The Swiss banks are therefore 'forced to re-invest those short-term funds which are entrusted to them abroad in order to earn a fair return', as Hans J. Bär,[32] partner in Julius Bär & Co. of Zürich, said in

London on 16 November, 1966. The money, as is known, comes very largely to London.

Moneys held in the UK for these various purposes are more popularly known as 'short-term capital', 'hot money' or the 'sterling balances'. They are funds held on short call (current or deposit account) with British banks, or with finance houses and local authorities, and funds held in easily encashable 'paper', i.e. Treasury bills, British Government stock, and commercial bills and promissory notes.

The sterling balances are not new. Short-term money deposits have been held in London ever since the rise of that city to financial pre-eminence, probably for a century.

What does this mean, in short? It means that Britain is not only a trading and investing country; she is also a banking country. Up and down the world, there are governments, people and companies with cash on their hands which they do not need for the moment, but which they expect to call on—probably quite suddenly—in the reasonably near future. For that reason, they will not commit it to long-term investment; obviously the nature of the funds is such that they cannot be put into new factories and the like. Since they could not be retrieved at short notice they will not go into long-term stock and shares either, which might not be easy to sell at the same price at any given time. They will go into the forms described above. And they will go to London, as the remark by Hans Bär testified, because the sums involved are very large, and there are not many places in the world where they can be handled. London is one of them.

The merits and otherwise of being a banking nation will be examined in Chapter XV. It suffices for the purpose of the present chapter to recognise that that is what Britain is, and that very large sums belonging to foreigners are kept in the nation's capital city.

What are the abiding characteristics of this short-term capital? These are that the funds are, by definition, highly mobile, i.e., they can be moved by their owners very quickly and they are 'safe' funds; that is to say they are not, as remarked above, investment or risk capital, they are the current working cash of institutions and companies, and they cannot in any way be hazarded or watered down.

In these circumstances it will be seen that the most drastic event that can occur to these funds is devaluation. The threat to the foreign holder is evident. Consider the case of a Swiss merchant banker who placed 120 million francs of his liquid assets in London, securing a counterpart of £10 million at the pre-1967 rate of exchange. Suppose he left the money there throughout the devaluation crisis. His £10 million, after November 1967, was worth only 104 million francs. He had lost, forever, 16 million francs of his client's money. Commercial prudence and, indeed, ethics, demand that risks of losses of this sort should be avoided.

Now comes the disadvantage for Britain. The Swiss banker in question would normally switch out of sterling whenever a dangerous situation appeared to threaten the pound. His would be an individual case. But there are thousands of foreign holders of sterling, and their total deposits, as we have seen, attain huge levels—about £3 500 million. When the pound seems in danger, whether or not it is in the event devalued, many hundreds of these depositors, perhaps as many as half of them, shift their money out of London. Not only do they remove their money, but they do so, obviously, very swiftly. Thus very large amounts of money cross the exchanges, and they do so at a tremendous pace. In 1960 and 1961 some £400 million came into and went out of the country again. In the last quarter alone of 1964, £400 million, again, was removed.[33] The Bank of England lately has, understandably, been chary of vouchsafing too detailed figures; but we can look at other financial centres, and get an idea of the volumes of money involved. Obviously, when money enters or leaves the City, it goes to another international financial centre. The Bundesbank published figures showing that about £510 million entered Germany between October and November 1968, and about the same amount left again in the following month.[34] This was when a devaluation of the dollar was in fact expected. When a revaluation, or up-grading of the D-mark was expected in May 1969 no less than £1 500 million passed into Germany, and then left again. Once again, before revaluation actually occurred in October 1969, the Bundesbank reported an inflow of £2 000 million, and in the two short months between revaluation and the end of the year, the whole amount went out again. France's short-term capital losses during the May 1968 episode were concealed, but they were reported to be not less than £650 million in the period from the beginning of May until the middle of June, and £1 300 million between May and November.[35]

Reverting to the UK, we know from Mr Jenkins's Budget speech of 1970 that no less than £1 000 million of short-term cash came into the country, after the restoration of confidence in the pound, in the first quarter of 1970.

This then is the answer to the question posed at the beginning of this chapter. The 'money' which flooded out of the country in the earlier sterling crises, was these short-term capital funds of foreigners; similarly the difference between the accumulated deficit on ordinary balance of payments transactions, between 1964 and 1968—amounting to £1 905 million—and the actual debts we owed then—£3 360 million—was the amount of these funds which had left the country and not then come back.

Why, it might be asked, does it matter if these funds go? They were, after all, all along other people's money. We had lost nothing belonging to the UK, and their loss does not put us into debt, in the way that a deficit on our trade does. But this is to forget that we are committed to a fixed parity for the pound. When these great sums of money surge out, the laws of supply and demand apply. With everybody selling the pound, the price of the pound, i.e. its exchange rate or parity, would, unless something were done, drop through the floor. What is done is that the Bank of England buys pounds against the stream. To buy pounds they only have the nation's reserves of gold and dollars for their use. When the buying has gone on long enough, our reserves, unrestored as they still are after wartime losses, begin to get very low. It is at this point that cries of alarm come up from the Bank of England; and very real alarm it is. To have no reserves is national insolvency with a vengeance. When reserves fall in this way, then, we borrow—or devalue so as to end the selling of pounds.

It is worth noting, once again, the very large size of these short-term flows. As was remarked, £400 million moved out in one quarter of 1964, and £1 000 million moved in in one quarter of 1970. These are rates of £1 200 million and £4 000 million a year. Or, if we take the figures reported by the Bundesbank, the money can move at the phenomenal annual rates of £10 000 to £12 000 million. Beside these, the annual deficits on normal balance of payments transactions pale into tiny proportion. The British and German basic balances run at a deficit of some £300 million. Even the largest single aggregates, like the UK visible deficit of £534 million in 1968, are relatively minute. Short-term capital flows therefore dwarf the rest of the balance of payments. They are, unless held steady, a formidable and immensely potent force.

At this point it is important to notice that movements of short-term deposits are not the only kind of monetary movement that arise in the situations described. The other major movement is that of 'leads and lags'. The meaning of this slightly occult term is simple enough. When the parity of the pound appears to be in danger, British importers owing money abroad cash pounds for foreign currency as soon as possible, both because they do not want to be caught out by devaluation with a higher sterling bill to pay, and because—where the sale may be denominated in sterling—they are under pressure by their overseas suppliers to do so. These are 'leads'. Conversely, British exporters will be slow to repatriate their foreign currency earnings, for fear of losing the additional margin in sterling which devaluation would provide; more important, foreign customers delay their payment in the hope of a reduction of the bill in their own currency through devaluation. These are 'lags'. A change of one week in these, i.e. an advance in payment for imports, and a delay in receipts for exports, of a week, alters the cash flow on account of annual trade by just about 2 per cent. The total cash flow on trade in goods and services now amounts to some £20 000 million annually. A variation of 2 per cent accordingly means a loss of £400 million. An extension of leads and lags for a fortnight means a loss of £800 million.

It is now time to examine the confidence factor more closely. What makes short-term holders decide that the pound is unsafe?

It will be apparent that the pattern of the movements is somewhat peculiar and by no means closely related to the fortunes of the basic balance itself. To go back to the events of 1964 again: of the notorious balance of payments deficit of £744 million for the year, £565 million had accumulated by the end of September. However, all through those first three-quarters short-term capital was coming in—to the tune of £452 million in fact. The two flows offset each other and there was no strain on the pound. In the last quarter of the year, there was a deficit of only £180 million, but short-term capital flooded out, to the amount of £402 million. Hence the great sterling crisis of 1964.

A sterling drain in 1949 was sufficient to bring about devaluation, even with a current and capital account deficit as little as £48 million. In 1951, with the postwar record visible deficit of £689 million, and an overall deficit of the same figure, there was no comparable strain on the sterling balances. There was a run on the pound at the end of 1954, a year in which the basic deficit was £17 million. There was a run on the pound, requiring recourse to an IMF drawing, at the end of 1956—the year which witnessed only the fifth visible surplus since 1800. There was pressure on sterling in the autumn of 1957, when there was an overall payments surplus of £207 million. Sterling balances remained steady during 1959, when there was a deficit of £134 million, and rose in 1960 although there was a deficit of £158 million. They fell in 1961, a year of a surplus of £39 million. There was no devaluation in 1964, with an overall deficit of £757 million, but sterling pressures forced a devaluation in 1967, when the overall deficit was £234 million. Similarly, there was grave sterling strain in the summer of 1966, a year when the overall deficit was £128 million (p. 66).

Movements of the sterling balances could not be a reflection of the balance of payments account as a whole, for the simple reason that this was not known at any time when short-term funds were flowing. The full account for a given quarter is not published for at least two months, and the full division between commercial and government activities in any one year is not available until the following August. The damaging movements in the sterling balances took place within periods much shorter than this. Nor is it likely that the short-term outflows were reflecting a technical weakness in the exchange market caused by the real cash flows in the current and capital account, since these were, as has been shown earlier, consistently more favourable than had been thought.

It seems apparent that the overseas managers of the funds in question could not have been taking their decisions on the basis of the detailed and comprehensive appraisal of the underlying balance of payments that would have been needed to make an accurate judgment. Few of those concerned would have had the necessary expertise, and, more important, none of them would have had the necessary information. Apart from the time delays mentioned, it is highly improbable that they regularly consulted 'Economic Trends' and 'Financial Statistics', and, moreover, made the necessary subtractions and re-calculations themselves to arrive at the net figures for the commercial transactions of the country. Indeed, some of the data required for this type of analysis was not collected in this country before 1958, and in some cases not before 1962.

The fact remains that overseas fund managers had as their only consistent guide to the British payments situation the monthly publication of the visible trade gap, and recurrent Government statements on the condition of the economy. Bearing in mind that they were foreign nationals, not necessarily experts on economic analysis, and always short of factual information—and that, moreover, they were concerned only with the plain conjecture as to whether or not the British Government would decide to devalue—it is apparent that their decisions to remove funds were made on the basis of fairly superficial economic and political assessments, tempered by market 'feel' or sentiment. Given the insistent condemnation of their own economy by the British themselves, it is not surprising that overseas short-term creditors were poised throughout to discard their sterling holdings at any signal of impending devaluation. Thus the 1956 run on the pound was triggered by an entirely non-economic event—the Suez war, and the 1957 run was caused by a devaluation in France. Similar sterling strains have arisen more recently in conjunction with difficulties encountered by the dollar and the franc, and with the events surrounding the Deutschemark.

In summary, it can be said that the instability of the sterling balances since the war has been due to fundamental distrust of the British economy engendered by British governments themselves; and actual sterling runs have been triggered by a variety of economic and political events, none of them directly related to the true state of the balance of payments.

In other words, we have no one but ourselves to blame. Foreign sterling holders have merely been infected with our own fears. Taught by the British themselves that the visible gap was a weakness, that the country was in fundamental balance of payments deficit, and that the economy was seriously defective, they have suited their actions to our words, and taken their funds elsewhere. In so doing they have precipitated sterling strains far greater than the balance of payments developments could ever have done. As we have seen our payments were in balance up to 1964, and up to 1968, only half as bad as our debts made out.

VIII The Cure: A Summary

The exposition of Britain's balance of payments history and structure is now complete. In turn, each aspect of Britain's external payments, the trading, the investing, the Government and the banking role, has been presented to view.

The picture conflicts with much that has hitherto been taken for granted. In many ways it is both simpler and more complicated than the balance of payments conventionally outlined. The visible balance may now seem much less perplexing; on the other hand the whole array of forces at work appears a good deal more complicated—particularly the inter-action between the visible and invisible accounts, between the current and the capital accounts, and most particularly, between the transactions and the banking role. None the less, some fairly simple solutions will no doubt already occur to the reader. While these now fall to be considered, it is however, clear from all the foregoing that some much broader issues now arise for examination. There is scarcely room for doubt, in the light of the facts that have been surveyed, that some of the most fundamental axioms of British postwar economic policy are now open to question.

What must follow with inescapable logic is that there is no fear for Britain's commercial viability. The UK balance of payments on commercial account is in surplus and has been in surplus throughout the whole period of postwar anxiety on the point—and indeed throughout Britain's economic history. And yet the whole of British balance of payments policy, and indeed her economic policy as a whole has, since the war, been based on the opposite proposition. Enough has been adduced in the foregoing to explain why this mistaken conclusion should have been drawn, and to show that it was an understandable error in the circumstances. The fact remains that it is radically at variance with what are now known to be the facts.

Put at its briefest, the governments of postwar Britain have set themselves the task of turning this country from a visible importing to a visible exporting nation. Clearly they have had to assume that there are some special disabilities lying on the nation which have prevented this transformation so far. These disabilities have been defined in several ways, but they fall into two categories; the 'structural' theory, i.e. that the British economy is inherently inefficient or unbalanced; and the inflationary theory, i.e. that Britain's trade is weakened by her degree of inflation. Accordingly, the effort of modern times in this country has been to change an economy supposedly uncompetitive with any other.

It is important to recognise how total has been the dedication to this aim. 'Getting the balance of payments right' has been the cardinal aim of every government from Attlee to Wilson, including the serried ranks of Conservative Prime Ministers in between. It has inspired every major turn of policy: the setting of Bank Rate, the changes in taxes, the control of hire purchase, the regulation of incomes, the re-structuring of industry, the introduction of export rebates, import surcharges and import deposits, the control of the money supply, the level of Government expenditure. It has been the intended effect of every major institution of the quarter century: the National Economic Development Council, the British National Export Council, the Export Credits and Guarantee Department, the Export Services Branch, the Prices and Incomes Board, the Commercial Diplomatic Service, the Industrial Reorganisation Commission, the Industrial Relations Commission. It has above all been the purpose of the repeated, and indeed almost continuous, succession of curbs and restraints on the economy. It has affected every aspect of the life of the private citizen—from his chance of buying a villa in Spain to the price of his breakfast egg.

In the light of the data sifted in the foregoing chapters, the very gravest doubts must be entertained as to whether these policies were right. In being directed towards removing the visible gap and achieving a commercial surplus these policies were seeking two goals, one clearly misconceived, the other superfluous. Looked at in another way, the policies have assumed that there is a commercial deficit—where there is a surplus—and have encouraged the official deficit to grow continuously; can this be correct? The question can be phrased in a different way. If, at the close of the Second World War, there had not been an established body of economic doctrine to the effect that the UK had been declining in international competition since the nineteenth century; had it been known in fact that the visible gap was a standing and normal economic feature, would post-war British governments then have decided that the latter was the principal, or even an important, cause of the country's difficulties? It seems established, beyond a shadow of doubt, that British economic policy since the war has been based on a mistake about our trading propensity and a misunderstanding of the make-up of our balance of payments.

This conclusion must necessarily extend to the two defects, structural inefficiency and inflation, by which the British economy is thought to be distinguished. These two failings disappear with the problem to which they are supposed to have given rise. Structural inefficiency and inflation were assumed to have been the cause of our commercial deficit. But there was, it now emerges, no deficit. There was no surplus. What, then, was the structural inefficiency and the inflation which caused a non-existent deficit? The answer must necessarily be that there was none. This country, like any other, must be vigilant to detect and assiduous to cure economic failings—above all inflation, the bane of the modern age. But she is not subject to a special need to eliminate them on account of her commercial balance of payments. Her commercial balance of payments is indistinguishable from, where it is not manifestly superior to, that of other countries. There is in short no special allotment of these vices to this country.

Consideration of the above leads to some understanding of the contradictions that have seemingly dogged British economic affairs since the war. Clearly, it explains why the balance of payments problem itself has not been overcome. Also, it explains why the visible gap has not disappeared. It explains why all have come to be impressed with the apparent truth that there is a conflict between growth and a healthy balance of payments. If the latter term has been taken to mean a visible surplus, the proposition is of course true. It is impossible for this economy to proceed normally, let alone to expand, without a deficit in the merchandise account. This also explains why it has been possible, at rare intervals, to obtain a transient surplus in the visible account, at the expense of a complete standstill, if not a decline, in the economy. It explains the mounting tension and indeed obsessive preoccupation over the balance of payments problem; and why successive governments have felt themselves obliged to double and redouble their corrective efforts.

It also throws light on the failure to diagnose in exact terms the reason for Britain's shortcomings. Obviously, if a visible deficit is read as an overall commercial deficit, regardless of what the true figures are saying, an explanation can never be forthcoming. Consequently, no one has been able to narrow Britain's failings down to a specific cause. Despite the strong conviction that it must be the case, there has been no conclusive proof that the British economy is a high cost one in relation to the world average, that it is more inflated, more subject to greater industrial unrest, or behind-hand in research, managerial ability, and so on. All observers have perforce had to come down to a general proposition, such as the phrase chosen by the Brookings Institution—a lack of 'residual efficiency'.

It also, of course, explains the apparent paradox that despite the absence of traceable and conspicuous economic faults, Britain has failed to grow as fast as her rivals. The answer lies in Government policy, in the continuous retrenchment of the economy in the name of balance of payments solvency. Deflation has been far more frequent and severe in the UK than in any other industrial country. Britain has failed to grow, quite simply, because she has been prevented from growing. It has been curious indeed to see Britain, in the midst of repeated and determined campaigns to reduce the pace of expansion—by taxation aimed to cut down the level of demand, to compress the market, increase unemployment and diminish the profitability of companies—continually pausing to reflect why her economy is not growing as fast as that of her neighbours.

Loss of growth was the major domestic consequence of the policies of economic repression continuously followed since the war. This will be further discussed in Chapter XI.

Thus, we need to reconsider the whole of Britain's economic policy in the light of the facts now made clear about the external balance. This will be done in the ensuing chapters, and a summary of an alternative policy will be given there. Let us start with the balance of payments itself.

We can now discern the true effect of economic policy to date. The whole country has been tuned down to a low level of activity. Low GNP, low production, low investment; all the aggregates of economic life, in short, were kept in a stunted condition. This, of course, also applied to exports and to imports. If exports and imports remained at an absolute low level—low that is to say in their actual numbers—then the difference between them was low. Thus, assuming a 5 per cent difference between imports and exports, the following is the way the formula worked. If imports were to run at £10 000 million a year, and exports at £9 500 million then the trade gap would be £500 million. If imports are kept down to say £4 500 million then exports, at say, £4 250 million, would leave a gap of only £250 million —half the size produced in the £10 000 million import case.

Now, there is the invisible surplus running concurrently with the visible balance. This over the years 1958–68, for instance, has averaged about £8–900 million annually. Government expenditure mounted steadily over that period, but averaged £360 million. Thus, if a shrinkage of the trade gap brought about a situation where visible deficit and Government expenditure were less than the invisible surplus, averaging as seen about £8–900 million over the period, then there was surplus. And if this, in addition, was a surplus large enough to contain the average annual outflow of capital, around £2–300 million, then the overall payments were in balance. Government measures acted only on visible trade, as we know, and, to a rather lesser extent over the whole time span, on private capital exports. The others were fixed in the sense that the Government did not endeavour to change them. Official expenditure was slightly restrained right at the end of the period, but otherwise it pursued a straight-line course upwards. Invisible services must have been affected to some extent by the general blight laid at regular intervals on the economy, but the invisible balance was never the direct preoccupation of the Government—some might say to its good fortune. The mechanism therefore, was very simple. The economy was so regulated, in practice, as to keep activities at a low enough momentum to ensure that the scale of visible trade did not grow too big.

There was, of course, a built-in discipline, or watchdog, for the system. Overseas holders of short-term sterling, well-trained as they were to regard a large visible deficit as a sign of economic weakening, and of future jeopardy for the exchange rate, began to withdraw their funds as soon as a deficit showed its head. This they had no difficulty in recognising, since over most of the period the visible balance was published each month, unaccompanied by any other indication of the balance of payments, and with great blasts of adverse comment from the press. When the signal went, the leakage of funds out of the country brought stress on the exchanges in short order; this required immediate action, in the most severely practical way, by the authorities, for in the absence of generous reserves, the Bank of England could support the pound only for so long. At that point, then, the Government would step in and order a general deflation of the economy. Overseas sterling holders, satisfied that the situation in the UK was now under control, brought their money back, and calm was restored.

By and by, this became so much a convention that a Pavlovian reaction set in. When capital departed for entirely non-balance of payments reasons, such as during the Suez war, or on French devaluation in 1957, when the country was in fact running either a visible surplus, or at worst a very small deficit, the only method of inducing them to return was a clamp on the economy.

This then, is how the equilibrium was maintained, year in and year out. Impelled by the cries of stricken manufacturers and trade unions, the Government would relax controls until the economy was expanding. Trade would grow, and the gap between imports and exports would broaden, in absolute, if not relative numbers. This would go on until sterling withdrawals halted matters and expansion was put into reverse.

Then the process would begin all over again. Of course, this is a *grosso modo* description of the sequence of events. There were many subtleties in the broad picture. For instance the invisible surplus tended to expand in inverse rhythm to the visible deficit. This follows not surprisingly from the fact that all trade runs to balance. When visible trade falls into deeper deficit, i.e. when sterling is passing in greater volume into the hands of foreigners, invisible trades tend to close off at a larger surplus, because the sterling available has gone into greater purchases of British services. Thus, over the period, the economy was able to run slightly larger visible deficits than it could otherwise have done, before running into check. The chart in the Appendix illustrates the roughly complementary movement of the visible and invisible sectors.

World trade tended to rise and fall in a tide, the origins of which are not certain, but this certainly moved the British visible balance with it. This interesting effect was fully described in a recent paper by the Economic Research Council, and it goes far to explain how British exports appeared to do well or badly over the period regardless of the Government's endeavours at the time. However, the basic principle remained the same. The economy was held in such a state of activity as to permit a certain level of trade and no more.

Three comments arise on this mechanism. Of course, it was not that intended by the Government. The Government's sublimely single-minded purpose was to secure an excess of visible exports over imports. Its actions were in its own estimation calculated to increase the efficiency of the economy and to drag out into the open the country's dormant export capability. It wholly accepted the implied rebuke of short-term sterling holders who withdrew funds when the visible deficit widened. Its repressive measures were in its view a salutary treatment for disorder. Enough has been said in the foregoing to show that this treatment merely weakened the economy. But the true balance of payments effect was to restrain, where not to reduce, imports. It did not increase exports—indeed, over the long term, as will be shown, the ability of manufacturers to export was impaired. But the reduction on the import side, even with some faltering on exports, was enough to reduce the gap between the two. The treatment except when brutally intensified, never of course, brought about an actual surplus on visible trade.

Secondly, this was an unhappy equilibrium. It was based on a low running economy. It involved persistent discouragement to enterprise and to industrial expansion. It involved a degree of unemployment. It also involved a sacrifice of living standards, a lower degree of economic attainment, personal development and general effectiveness than might otherwise have been achieved. By 1968 the British, once proud of being the richest nation in the world, were less rich, man for man, than the Americans, the Germans, the French, the Swedes, the Swiss, the Canadians, the Belgians, the Dutch and the Icelanders.

But this was in the very nature of the operation, as economic commentators and Ministers were throughout anxious to proclaim. Britain could only afford a certain level of economic well-being. Above that, she imported too much, and got herself into balance of payments difficulties. This was the central economic doctrine of the period. Full expansion and a balance of payments surplus were incompatible. Britain had to choose between one and the other. She had to accept a lower standard of living and of employment than she would like because her resources would not stretch to more. Her rate of expansion would have to be less than that into which her inclinations led her, because this would incur a higher import bill than she could pay for.

This whole doctrine, of course, recapitulated in simple form, the very debate that the country had gone through in immense detail in the 1830s and 1840s. At that time the unanimous conclusion, after weighing precisely those considerations ventilated in 1969 and 1970, had been that to restrict activity to the level where imports were no greater than exports, would be to abandon all the fruits which the sweat and toil of the industrial revolution was intended to provide; and that if Britain had set her hand to being an industrialised, high consumption country, she should perseverve in so becoming, and should not be distracted by immaterial considerations regarding the visible balance. It seems extraordinary, that as a result of all the twists and turns of history since the 1830s, the country should now be ordering its balance of payments policy, and indeed its overall economic life in accordance with tenets the merits of which were discarded a hundred and fifty years ago.

The third comment is that it was a risky policy. It was based on keeping the economy under artificial restraint. The posture of sitting on the lid of a high pressure vessel is not normally well-balanced or dignified. The economy was continually trying to revert to its natural shape: industry strove to expand faster, exports to rise, imports to rise faster; pent-up private investment flows tried to break out overseas. The Government, like a harassed elderly nurse with a fractious patient, scurried round endlessly remaking the bed. It was based on an understanding with that formidable body of economic power, foreign short-term sterling holders, that the British economy was really rather an ugly mess, but that if they could manage to hang on a little longer, the Government would get it right. This system could not go on without innumerable upsets; these it had in plenty in the period before 1964. Equally, it could not go on indefinitely without a major breakdown, or alternatively, in the nightmare prosecution of its policy to the point of complete stultification of the economy. In the period 1964 to 1970, both happened. This will be discussed in Chapter XIII.

From the above, the form that future balance of payments policy should take is clear. Retrenchment, as a general economic precept, we need no convincing, is nonsensical and joyless. The same is now seen to be true of the balance of payments. Trade of all kinds should be allowed to expand. The preoccupation with the visible gap is manifestly a shibboleth. There are no grounds, either historical or economic, for assuming that merchandise imports and exports, in a state of free growth, will run injurious deficits. The history of the external account, from its recorded beginnings until the present day, are a standing testimony that this will not happen. Not once in the postwar quarter century, no more than twice in this century, and no more than once during the last century, has any five-year period shown a visible deficit exceeding the invisible surplus. There is reassurance enough in the simple magnitudes of the visible balance in recent years. From surpluses up to £50 million it has alternated to deficits of as much as £700 million, and at no time has the marriage with invisibles not produced a healthy current surplus. At a deficit of £700 million it was, in any case—let it be said—in fact free from Government control.

We should therefore put aside our phobia and allow imports and exports to grow in a natural manner, and allow the gap between them to evolve in step. We should release the economy from any restraint other than those reasonable measures, as are practised in other countries, to safeguard general economic health. Our economy will then grow in line with the rate of other industrialised countries.

With the economy and the various arms of our trade free to develop naturally, reinvestment overseas, if also freed of all government inhibitions, will begin to swell and return a weightier income. The overall balance will enlarge; within this greater compass Government expenditure, if not incautiously pushed ahead, will find ample room. Above all, the stability of the short-term capital market must be kept in hand. There must be a balance between the banking and the trading function of the country at all times. False warnings should not be sounded about the state of the economy, so propelling the sterling balances into flight. At the same time, external factors affecting the sterling balances should not be taken as signals to slash down the growth of the home economy. The nature of the British surplus, and the success with which the official outlays are being accommodated, should be stressed so as to invite a steady influx of short-term capital. The banking and the trade functions should be made complementary, rather than mutually hazardous.

This then, in broad brush, is the line of policy that follows from the facts of the situation that have been exposed to view. Its different parts must now be discussed in more detail.

IX Government Expenditure Re-examined

First, to dispose of a point that is bound to be uppermost in the minds of many readers at this stage. Why not simply stop Government expenditure overseas? If this is the cause of the difficulty, why can it not promptly be removed? The problem appears simple; and so does the remedy.

It is simple, of course. Without Government expenditure we should be running a surging surplus in every year. This would have mounted from a substantial £100 million in 1952, to no less than £1 300 million in 1969. Our accumulated surplus over these years would now attain the grand total of £6 000 million, enough to give us overseas invested capital of £13 500 million, instead of the £7 500 million we in fact have. Even this is a minimum calculation, since it merely adds up the private surpluses the country has made, before official expenditure was drawn off them. But those surpluses would have been invested *pro rata*, and overseas assets would have grown in geometrical rather than arithmetical progression, since they would have been continuously refortified by profits and dividends. The final result could be £20 000 million; it is not really calculable, but bound to be very great.

Better still, if we had got ourselves into a position like Germany and Japan, who have net receipts, rather than a net outflow on military account, or if we had acquired the massive civil incomes that, for instance, France derives from the agricultural payments made by the Common Market central fund, then we would have been that much better off, perhaps another £1 000 or £2 000 million.

However, it is important to maintain the issue of Government expenditure in perspective. At this point we must consider the various arguments, of no small significance, that can be advanced in favour of Government expenditure overseas. Let us begin with the economic argument. Some would contend that foreign outlays by officialdom are actually beneficial to the commercial balance of payments.

Whitehall, for instance, would no doubt say that the cost of the diplomatic service should not be shown as a pure loss, since it promotes exports; also that official spending by our posts overseas is countered by the purchases made by foreign embassies in this country; the latter purchases are listed on the private side of the balance of payments. Whitehall might also say that the earnings, for instance, of civil aviation are shown in the accounts as private sector gains, whereas of course the airlines are mainly state-owned. Telecommunications earnings, similarly, which are shown in the private sector of the account, are the earnings of a Government service. The Ministry of Defence sells military equipment to foreign currency customers. The former Ministry of Overseas Development said that 60 per cent of our grants and loans to developing countries are used for purchase of goods and services in this country.

All this is true, but it needs qualifying. Foreign governments, for instance, spend comparable sums on their diplomatic services, and aid their countries' exports, but they do not run official deficits. If our earnings in the air are mainly from state airlines, so are our payments to foreign air carriers. And what of BOAC's interest payments on its large foreign borrowings? But apart from this, the question of foreign exchange earnings and disbursements by nationalised industries and services seems to be wide of the point being made here. The distinction being drawn is between the industrial and commercial balance of the country, which is in surplus, and the non-commercial outgoings on political and military account, which are in deficit. The foreign earning activities of those industrial and commercial enterprises which are in state ownership fall into the first category. If the State bought itself into all our industries and into banking, insurance, shipping and the like services, then we would still have to make a judgment whether the balance of payments was in deficit because we were buying more than we sold in the competitive fields of business and manufacturing, or because we were paying out more than we received in political, military and administrative expenses. The fact that, if the State owned all our factories and businesses, we would with little doubt go speedily bankrupt, does not affect this consideration. It is best, then, to leave out of account the foreign exchange receipts and payments of the nationalised sector. So far, in any case, the inroads of public ownership have, thankfully, not been substantial—at least in the balance of payments sphere—and the figures would be marginal, even if added.

As regards the return on foreign aid, the Ministry's figures may well be right; so much sterling undoubtedly is used to purchase British exports. How many industries on the other hand, goaded by Whitehall to provide supplies for a tied loan, have diverted exports from some commercial destination, or from a home market customer, thus letting in imports? And what about the Reddaway Report, welcomed by Government, which said that the exports attracted by capital placed overseas would be sold anyway; and which governments used as a defence for their restriction of private capital investment? Whitehall cannot have it both ways.

Let us now make an adjustment to the 1969 figures for the official deficit, and in deference to the Ministry of Overseas Development, we will leave their claim untouched. Net outgoings were, as already shown:

Current expenditure:	(£*m*)
Military costs	250
Purchases of military equipment	61
Military grants	9
Subscriptions and grants to military organisations	7
Economic grants	86
Administrative and diplomatic costs	53
Subscriptions and contributions to international organisations	48
Interest on official debts	329
Other	4
Total current expenditure	847
Long-term capital	95
Total official deficit	942

Now for the items that offset the above expenditure. Let us assume that the full cost of the heading 'Administrative and diplomatic expenditure' is covered by exports attributable entirely to the efforts of the commercial diplomatic service. Next, the spending in this country of foreign embassies and like establishments, listed in the 1968 accounts as £89 million. Next, the Ministry's estimate of exports resulting from economic grants and loans, £110 million, and Ministry of Defence sales, £50 million, viz:

		(£*m*)
Total official deficit		942
Less:	Exports secured by commercial diplomatic	53
	Exports generated by loans and grants	110
	Foreign official spending in the UK	90
	Ministry of Defence sales	50
	Total:	303
Net official deficit		639

With all these allowances, then, the deficit remains substantially the same.

Whitehall has another line of reasoning, however, which merits careful thought. The commercial and the official balances are indivisible, they would say, because both are the work of the nation as a whole; and the nation should therefore ensure that it earns enough to pay for political and military expenditures. These outgoings are as much the choice of the nation as the purchases and sales of goods and services. This is a practical attitude, but it does raise a vital economic issue. How far is it, in fact, possible for the commercial transactions of a nation always to rise to cover official spending? *Prima facie*, it might be argued that Government expenditure is simply the purchase of foreign goods and services, or the placing of British capital in foreign lands, analogous to purchases and capital investment in the private sector. In other words, official expenditure is no more than an extension of the national import bill and capital outflow, to be covered by exports in the normal way. There is some substance in this. Clearly, supply and demand is a balance. The nation's imports, as has been pointed out in the previous chapter, provide foreigners with the sterling they need to buy British exports.

Nevertheless, there is an obvious flaw. This reasoning assumes that supply always rises to meet demand. In other words, Government expenditure can be pushed up as high as Whitehall wishes; exports must always rise to cover them. This is unrealistic. The truth of the matter is, of course, that supply and demand is a balance in both senses. Supply rises to meet demand, but demand also falls to meet supply. This, as has been seen, operates in the commercial field. An increase in production and wealth leads to an expansion of imports, an increase of exports leads to increase of production, and this again leads to an increase in imports. But if there is a decrease of production and exports, then there is a reduction of imports; or if imports fall then production must also fall. A rise or fall on one side of the balance must be accompanied by a rise or fall on the other. But none of these disciplines apply to Government expenditure. The Government payments abroad do not bring in raw material for production and conversion into exports, and are not therefore subject to the ebb and flow of output and trade. They are made to refuel a destroyer in Africa, or to pay the British subscription to UNESCO, or to finance a south-east Asian irrigation scheme. Most important of all, they are not dependent on the foreign currency earned from exports. The Government does not obtain its foreign currency through the commercial banking system, as do private importers. It raises a charge against itself through inter-governmental channels. Where the commercial surplus proves sufficient to cover the annual total of these, it pays off its official obligations. Where not, it issues Treasury Bills and similar paper. Government expenditure thus proceeds in a straight line, dictated only by military and political considerations. The fact that it is subject to no commercial disciplines is evinced by the steady year on year growth of the amount, as can be seen from the Table on page 25.

The answer, then, to the question whether it is possible for the commercial side invariably to rise to cover the official side of the balance of payments seems to be that this is intrinsically unlikely. However, this is only the conclusion that seems to arise most credibly when the available evidence is studied. It must be stressed that the proposition has never been subjected to systematic economic research. It remains a proposition simply stated by Whitehall whenever faced with the facts of the commercial surplus and the official deficit. The truth is that the problem of running a balance of payments that consists of these two sides is new and rare—as was shown at the beginning of this chapter—and this has simply not been absorbed by the public and official mind.

None the less the basic point made by Whitehall—that official expenditures are willed by the nation—cannot be denied. The commitments are incurred because they have, or are thought to have, an important national purpose which will rebound to the benefit of all in the country; and they are commitments incurred by the common accord of all acting through their elected governments. As soon as we approach the subject of Government expenditure we come into contact with issues that are no longer purely economic. As has been remarked already, Government expenditure is a political not an economic activity. There are numerous political reasons why these disbursements should be maintained; why, in fact, they should be regarded as of great utility. They are reasons of such strength that, if the costs can be accommodated within the economic sphere, they should be continued. The remainder of this book will set out to show that they can be accommodated satisfactorily.

What are these pressing reasons for the continuance of such costs? Firstly, this is international work which needs to be done. Economic aid is sought by developing countries; large areas of the world must be policed by defence forces from somewhere. If there is inequity in the fact that the burden is materially left to the USA and the UK, it remains true that in the absence of other volunteers, somebody must do it, and that if it is not done, the world will be a poorer and more risky place. To some extent the burden of economic aid is less unequally shared. British official contributions measure around the average of OECD countries, and noticeably less than some, such as France. On the other hand Britain probably contributes more in kind, through the effect of special commodity buying arrangements, such as those for sugar, tin, wheat, meat, butter and coffee, and through Commonwealth preference; and of course she does not enjoy the offsetting large Government receipts, already mentioned.

But it is in the realm of military defence that the burden is almost exclusively confined to the two countries, as was made clear in the recapitulation of overseas forces in Chapter IV. The United States acquired these obligations through her position as the dominant power of the West; the United Kingdom through being the remaining ex-imperial power with forces still deployed at the end of the war. Both are on duty through historical accident and national interest; and neither are wholly volunteers. However, this in no way lessens the fact that their forces provide a guarantee of emergency policing in the Indian Ocean, offer an obstacle to the unlimited advance of Chinese Communist influence, underpin the internal self-government of East Africa, discourage a major conflagration in the Middle East, assure the continental security of Latin America, and defend Australasia. It may well be asserted that these countries should be capable of looking after their own security; so they should, and it is to be hoped, so they will: but the point is that they are unable to do so *now*, and it is now that the action is needed from elsewhere. It might be remarked that the American opposition to Chinese aggrandisement is puny, and unavailing against political methods; the fact is that the governments of the area think otherwise and want it, and are convinced that it gives them, if nothing else, a breathing space in which to shore up their defences against infiltration. It may be that the threat from the Communist world is exaggerated, but the fact is there is a danger of over-running *now*, as Soviet activity in the Indian Ocean suggests, and as the spoken and written word from Peking still insistently proclaims; when the danger recedes, then the defenders will be glad to relax. It may also be that the US and Britain have national interests in the form of trade and investment to protect; this does not lessen the fact that the world at large has shipping, airlines, mines, plantations and factories in these areas, and they are as much at risk, and as firmly defended as the British and American. Finally, of course, it is a fact that the British Government has decided on measures of withdrawal, and that the American Government is endeavouring to disengage itself from Vietnam, and, it seems, from other areas also. The fact of this intended evacuation does not prove the inefficiency of these operations. It merely demonstrates that they do indeed constitute a balance of payments burden, and that they can eventually grow too large for the two countries to bear. That a cost is involved is illustrated by the Australian Government's public declaration that the attempt to fill part of the gap left by the British will necessitate a large increase in their defence budget. Singapore announced a threefold increase in her defence budget, and a similar situation prevails for Malaysia. The Gulf sheikhdoms are finding they will have to set up a defence force to replace the British contingent. The deep concern expressed by these and other countries throughout the area, when the British intention to withdraw was announced, is further proof of the need for such policing.

Nevertheless, more protective needs will arise in the future, either here or in other theatres, and they will have to be attended to. No doubt they will be filled by British and American contingents. Unless the Japanese, the French, the Germans or the Dutch volunteer, who else will there be?

There is a further, much more national, but no less valid, class of reasons why Government overseas expenditure should go on. This is generally referred to under the phrase 'subscription to the big-power club'. By this is meant the British aspiration to play a role in international policy—to be one of those nations whose views carry weight in international decisions over peace and war, alliance and treaty, poverty and plenty. Britain would like to be consulted, and indeed to have a speaking part, in any East–West *détente*, or in the reverse case, in any crucial East–West confrontation—in any Far Eastern settlement, or the like. To have this say, she must take some part in the work of defence and policing going on. She must, in short, maintain a 'presence'. This seems a fair rule. In a hard and costly world, those who have the major say should be those who have had a piece of the action. 'Put up or shut up' must be the unavoidable rule of international comity. It seems in every way right that Britain should bid for this kind of voice in world events, if she can. The UK has had about as much experience of international coexistence and negotiation as any country in history. She has much to offer, and the world has much to benefit, by her views in the solution of international problems. It would be a pointless loss to the world if the United Kingdom's co-operation were withdrawn, where it could still be forthcoming. Apart from this, the United Kingdom is entitled, like any other nation, to obtain for itself the maximum say in world decisions that will affect, perhaps mortally, its own population. It should not be felt that these ambitions are disproportionate to the size-scale and the times in which Britain is now living. The world long since resolved into continental units of which Russia and America are the dominant ones and in whose dialogue the UK can never have more than a subordinate part. The UK, by spending abroad on defence and aid, is buying a say as a medium power in this world. But intervention on that scale is better than no intervention at all; and other medium-sized nations might be happier for the involvement of one of their number. Thus there seems no solid case why the United Kingdom should not endeavour to get as much influence as she is able to acquire in the world at large.

To revert, then, to the main theme as we left it at the end of Chapter

VIII. There are grave reasons to suppose that British policy has got itself into a dilemma based on an economic misnomer; that in order to correct an illusory external disequilibrium it is constraining business and industry to the point of standstill, if not atrophy; and that the array of special economic failings to which policy-makers have supposed Britain to be heir to, are as much fancy as fact. Let us consider this last point.

X The Proposition that We are Inefficient

There is, it has been shown in Chapter VIII, no presumption on balance of payments grounds that we are inefficient; we do not, in short, have exclusively British structural or inflationary weaknesses. The proposition now must therefore be that the British economy is no better, and no worse, than its neighbours.

Let us now test out this proposition against the concrete evidence. The present chapter will deal with structure. Chapter XI will deal with inflation.

The first important test is a comparison of the balance of payments itself with that of other countries.

Britain is a part of the West European sub-continent and has an economic form comparable with the rest of the area. Western Europe as a whole is, like the UK, heavily populated, small in extent, short of arable and pastoral acreage, highly industrialised, dependent on imported raw materials, sophisticated in commercial, financial and maritime skills. Britain, historically, took the lead in industrialisation, and to this day is more advanced in the social evolution that followed this. She has, for instance, withdrawn labour from, and mechanised, her agriculture to a far greater extent than any of the three major economies on the mainland, France, Germany and Italy. But the Italians, the Dutch and the Scandinavians were from the earliest times rivals to British shipping and maritime expertise. Amsterdam, Frankfurt, Milan and Zürich were commercial and financial centres vying with London down the centuries. France and Germany are, historically, major overseas investors alongside the United Kingdom.

The merchandise trade of the sub-continent should not, therefore, cause surprise. It is almost entirely in deficit. The following Table shows the trade balances of all Western European countries in 1968:

	$m		$m
EEC			
Belgium/Luxemburg	-40	Norway	-713
France	-157	Portugal	-382
Germany (c.i.f.)	+4 490	Sweden	-171
Italy	+1 051	Switzerland	-384
Netherlands	-335	*Other*	
EFTA		Greece (c.i.f.)	-766
Austria	-455	Iceland	-50
Denmark	-436	Ireland	-363
Finland (c.i.f.)	+25	Spain	-1 574

Unhappy mortals: they are nearly all in deficit. Where do they find the wherewithal to survive? We have already seen the answer in Chapter III and in Table VII of the Appendix; it is in their invisible balance, i.e. their net earnings on services and overseas investment. For convenience, the figures are shown below.

Current Balance of Western European Countries—1968[36]

	Visible *$m*	*Invisible* *$m*	*Current Balance* *$m*
EEC			
Belgium-Luxemburg	-40	+124	+84
France	-157	-81	-238
Germany (c.i.f.)	+4 490	+144	+4 634
Italy	+1 051	+1 302	+2 353
Netherlands	-335	+469	+134
EFTA			
Austria	-455	+318	-137
Denmark	-436	+199	-237
Finland (c.i.f.)	+25	+40	+65
Norway	-713	+873	+160
Portugal	-382	+162	-220
Sweden	-171	+24	-147
Switzerland	-384	+1 187	+803
Other			
Greece (c.i.f.)	-766	+290	-476
Iceland	-50	+3	-47
Ireland	-363	+210	-153
Spain	-1 574	+725	-709

As will be seen, they fall into precisely the same pattern as the UK. A visible deficit, offset by an invisible surplus.

One year, however, is not necessarily conclusive. Table VII in the Appendix shows the visible and invisible balance for all these countries back to 1960. The evidence this table provides is clear enough. Western Europe as a whole is in most years a net importer of merchandise, and a net income receiver on invisible account. Going back a little further, the following analysis by the Economic Commission for Europe, contained in its 1948 Survey of the European economy, is significant:

Balance of Payments of Europe as a Whole

	1938 $m	*1946* $m
Visibles		
Imports f.o.b.	−5·8	−9·4
Exports f.o.b.	+3·7	+4·3
Balance	−2·1	−5·1
Invisibles		
Investment income	+1·4	+0·5
Other	+0·7	−1·2
Current Balance	0	−5·8

The Economic Commission for Europe commented:

Throughout past decades long ante-dating the First World War, these 'invisible' receipts had permitted, and, through the interplay of economic forces, had produced, a substantial excess of [visible] imports from overseas countries. The economic structure of Europe had become adapted to the inflow of income from investments and services and to the attendant [visible] import surplus.

The Economic Commission then went on to draw the moral that Europe would henceforth have to increase her visible exports. This, as we know from events in the UK, was fashionable thinking at the time.

As the tables in this chapter and the Appendix show, Europe does not seem to have followed this advice, any more than has the UK economy.

Not only is the UK balance of payments structure indistinguishable from that of the continent to which she belongs, but the particular problems that have beset her since the war have been shared by her neighbour countries. In particular they have had to overcome the loss of invisible income caused by war-time disinvestment abroad, as the table shows. Once again, add to these the official burden borne by the UK, but not by the others—together with the particular British vulnerability to short-term capital flows—and the continuance of balance of payments troubles in the UK is explained.

What is the historic structure of trade and payments in Europe? The long-term balance of payments history of Europe presents a field ripe for research. Little has been published, although there is probably much data available in national archives. Even a cursory search shows that both France and Germany developed some time ago into net importers of merchandise. The Direction-Générale des Douanes in Paris, the repository of French trade statistics, has a continuous record of imports and exports back to 1827 and this is reprinted in Tables VIII and IX of the Appendix. France went into invariable visible deficit around the year 1880, where she has remained ever since. Throughout she has been a net investor abroad, sometimes heavy; the proceeds for this coming from favourable current balances underwritten by invisible receipts.

The following is Germany's record, derived from Moulton and McGuire's *Germany's Capacity to Pay* (McGraw-Hill, New York, 1923).

Germany's balance of payments, 1894–1913 (*annual averages in RM million*)

Selected intervals	*Favourable balance on invisibles*	*Adverse balance on trade*	*Net payment balance*
1894–1898	+1 000	−987	+13
1899–1903	+1 260	−1 073	+187
1904–1908	+1 350	−1 472	−122
1909–1912	+1 490	−1 842	−352
1913	+1 600	−1 008	+592

Again, an invariable visible deficit, and an equally invariable invisible surplus, comes to light.

Thus we have, after only the briefest investigation, solid evidence that the three major economies of Europe—France, Germany and Britain—were already geared in the nineteenth century to the same mechanism of trade imports, service exports and foreign investment.

Apart from what has emerged so far, two main points of interest in the European payments picture call for comment.

The first is that, of all the national accounts, that of the UK seems by far the most consistent. Other countries have tended to wobble in and out of surplus and deficit on both visible and invisible accounts, although the prevailing pattern of visible deficit and invisible surplus is evident. In the UK on the other hand, the relationship between the two sides of the current balance has been constant. Save for the 1930s and a bad patch in the late 1840s an invisible surplus has unfailingly arisen to cover the merchandise gap.

The second point is that postwar Germany, with her much lauded visible surpluses is a clear deviant from the normal. In the postwar evolution of the German economy there is again scope for some fascinating study. One reason for Germany's present visible surpluses is the massive annual deficit on invisibles which Germany, contrary to her pre-war habit, has run since 1945. This does not emerge clearly from the figures as they are set out in Table VII of the Appendix; the following[37] will show the position:

	1968 ($*m*)
Visible balance	+4 490
Invisible balance	
(Services and investment income)	−4 770
Transfers	−3 047
Total	−7 817
Private current balance	−3 327
Government	
Receipts from foreign troops	+5 347
Other (transfers)	−4 137
Balance	+1 210

On every item of services, in which she formerly made handsome earnings, Germany is now a net importer—shipping, travel, insurance, patents and licences, contracting, professional services, and others; this apart from the heavily adverse burden of transfer movements. On foreign investment income, Germany has throughout been heavily in the red. Owing to the wartime loss of overseas assets, the failure of the country to re-invest afterwards, and a continued flow of foreign capital into Germany, payments from Germany to foreign investors between 1960 and 1968 exceeded receipts from German capital placed abroad by some £120 million annually. If Germany were not running a great visible surplus, she would be insolvent.

Another important reason must be the low level of consumption in postwar Germany. It is axiomatic, as has already been seen, that full expansion of the European industrial society is accompanied by high imports. With the massive inflow of food and raw materials required, European countries must become net importers of merchandise. It is clear that postwar Germany has subscribed to the opposite model. The massive loss of population due to wartime casualties and territorial sequestration alone was a contracting factor. Secondly, the inclinations of a nation that had survived into the wreckage of immediate postwar Germany were not those of high mass consumption. Nor was the mood of trade unions predominantly turned towards high wage achievement. Until very recently the German standard of living, measured by any of the normal comparison—household equipment, calorie consumption, telephones, motor cars, etc., was below that of other West European countries. In a recent report, the OECD has pointed out that German trade surpluses are as much due to low imports and domestic consumption as to high exports.

What is interesting is that there are ample signs that this era is now passing. Perhaps the rejection of Erhard, the architect of the 'economic miracle', marked the change. The German is now no longer grateful just to be alive, intent merely on rebuilding rather than on expanding. The war ended 25 years ago and 25 years sees a generation out. The generation moving up was nurtured on years of stability and industrial success. It is no longer content just to see the wheels of industry turning and its wealth flowing out of the country. It wants prosperity as well as success. The German of today wants to consume. By most measurements now, the German standard of living is soaring.[38] In 1962 there were 95 cars in Germany for every 1 000 inhabitants, as against 114 in the UK; now there are 199 against Britain's 196. She had 131 television sets per thousand, as against Sweden's 217. She now has 231, against 282 in Sweden. German trade unions are demanding and restless. German workers want leisure, amenities, comfort. In German cities the typical concomitants of the consumer society have appeared—scarcity of household manual workers, delays in services, traffic jams, overfull shops and restaurants.

The German industrialist also is looking outward again. His disinclination to move his production abroad is subsiding. Whatever the reason for the earlier reluctance, be it the trauma of wartime losses, the fear of revaluation—and therefore of loss of the value of assets in terms of marks—or sheer doubt as to the acceptability of German capital abroad, the flow of foreign investment has begun. It is mainly in portfolio form at the moment, but the share of direct investment is growing. 'It is a remarkable fact', said the Bundesbank in 1968, 'that the Federal Republic of Germany . . . became an important capital exporting country in 1967.' Two years earlier the Bank had referred to the need for 'a certain surplus, which would permit the financing . . . of the capital export which is indispensable on economic and political grounds.' Private long-term capital flowed into Germany in every year up to 1967. In that year the net flow reversed from £170 million inwards to £160 million outwards. In the following year it was no less than £1 000 million outwards. In 1969 it climbed to no less than £2 000 million. This must inevitably affect the net flow of investment income, and with it, Germany's deficit invisible account. Indeed Germany's net outflow of investment income, fell from £175 million in 1967 to £84 million in 1968 and to £35 million in 1969.[39]

Is Germany reverting from a home-oriented, low consumption, merchandise-exporting, capital-importing country, odd as that is in an advanced industrialised region, to a high consumption, high importing and capital exporting country, in keeping with its neighbours and with its own economic history? On a short view, it is impossible to say. But there are signs that it may be.

On the score of the balance of payments alone, then, there is little to support the theory that the British economy has structural weaknesses peculiar to itself. To turn to the economy itself, various specific charges have been made. These should be examined in turn. The British, it is said are old-fashioned; they are tied to traditional ways; they have failed to adapt themselves to the modern world of technology and trade. It is worth looking at a few of the facts.

Presumably 'old-fashioned' industries might be deemed to include coal, steel, textiles and shipbuilding. Like many other economic *obiter dicta*, this categorisation is something to beware of. Whilst the Japanese can make a mint of money out of selling steel and textiles, the Americans can clean up the international coal market, and the Swiss do handsomely out of the old world industry of clockmaking, it is well to recognise that all trades can be useful and profitable, regardless of their age. However, the industries mentioned are those that the UK first developed, and it might be fair to say that in a British economy that had not evolved, they would be as preponderant now as they were in the past.

In 1910 coal, iron and steel output in the United Kingdom accounted for 13 per cent of GNP;[40] in 1968 the share was 5 per cent. Between 1910 and 1966 the economy as a whole, as measured by GNP, grew roughly two and a half times in real terms.[41] Within that overall growth, industry as a whole grew four times. Within the growth of industry, again, the production of chemicals expanded over eight times; motor car output went up 180 times; gas, electricity and water supplies increased 15 times. Coal actually fell: 264 million tons were extracted in 1910; only 175 million in 1966. Steel grew just under four times—from 6·4 million tons to 24·3 million tons. Textile fabric output fell—from 640 million square yards to 302 million square yards. Shipbuilding remained static—1·2 million gross tons were commenced in each year.

The UK has the only independent computer industry outside America.[42] She leads the European field in the aerospace industry, particularly in aircraft engine and fuselage construction. British European Airways is the biggest international air carrier after Pan American. Heathrow is the biggest interchange airport in the world. The UK first developed commercial nuclear energy and is ahead of any other country other than the USA. The UK also first invented or discovered—and did so in recent times—penicillin, radar, the hovercraft, the vertical take-off aircraft. She has the largest oil refining industry outside the United States. Of the 200 largest companies in Europe, as at December 1968, 107 were in the UK. The following,[43] according to an OECD study made in 1968, is the percentage of total research finance spent on the aircraft, chemical and electrical industries—the 'research intensive' industries, as the OECD calls them:

US	46·4
UK	41·3
Belgium	40·9
Germany	39·7
Netherlands	35·7
France	33·7
Japan	33·7
Sweden	33·6
Italy	28·7
Canada	24·6
Austria	23·2
Norway	16·8

These data do not seem to point to an inert or inadaptable economy.

Perhaps, if the UK appears to be as progressive in industry as other countries, her trouble is that this does not show in her trade? Does she still export to old, slow-growing markets—or is she still attempting to sell outmoded goods, rather than the products of modern technology?

The concept of what is a 'fast-moving' and what is a 'slow-moving' market is another of those economic truisms which do not bear too close examination. Developing countries are generally classed as slow-moving, but as the name implies, they may well be the best place to establish your exports. Nevertheless, have British exports followed what has been at least the vogue in overseas sales? Taking the customary division of the world into the 'fast-growing' European market, the 'slow-growing' Commonwealth markets, with the US as a constant bonus area, then British sales have progressed as follows:[44]

	1955	*1965*	*1968*	*percentages*
To:				
EEC	14·0	19	19	
Commonwealth	42·0	28	23	
USA	6·4	10	14	
Rest of World	37·6	43	44	

Britain increased her exports to the 'Six' at a fast pace; the proportion allotted to the Commonwealth was nearly halved, and that to the United States was doubled.

Some regard to history will, here again, improve the perspective.[45]

The immemorial destination of British exports has been Europe. When this country first began trading in any volume, towards the end of the eighteenth century, the adjacent land mass of Europe was overwhelmingly the main outlet. Eighty per cent of all British sales abroad were sent to this market. Throughout the nineteenth century, and indeed up to the present day, 25–30 per cent of sales were consistently made to Europe as a whole. There is some irony in the present plea that we should join the Common Market in order to 'get into Europe'. We have been there for centuries. The opening up of the American economy and of the Commonwealth markets in the late nineteenth and early twentieth centuries, gave British manufacturers two new outlets, which they added to their existing custom in Europe. The advent of American protectionism, which reached its peak in the 1930s, and the rise of European economic nationalism in the same period, pushed temporarily a greater volume of British exports into the Commonwealth. Since most comparisons of trends take the 1930s as their starting point, the illusion of an historical dependence on the Commonwealth has grown up. After 1945, with the removal of the prewar factors, the balance moved back the other way. In the long perspective, UK trade can thus be seen to have moved to and fro among its outlets in accordance with the practical rewards of the time.

Analysis of the product pattern[46] of exports tells a similar story. Coal, iron and steel, and textiles dominated British export trade throughout the nineteenth century. In 1920 they still accounted for 50 per cent of our foreign sales, and in 1938 the proportion was still 30 per cent. They now account for 8 per cent. In 1938 the new industries of chemicals, electrical machinery and transport equipment (motor cars, trucks, etc.) supplied 4 per cent of British exports. In 1968 they accounted for 32 per cent. All the signs therefore are that British trade, as any national commerce must, has evolved steadily through the centuries in response to opportunity and capacity, and is now adapting and changing faster than before. This line of enquiry has in fact already been pursued by the National Institute of Economic and Social Research (Fast and Slow Growing Products in World Trade: *Economic Review*, August 1963), which came to the conclusion that

> there is not sufficient evidence of a relative failure in one field rather than in the other, nor is there evidence of any great handicap from an initial bias in Britain's pattern of trade towards slow-going products.

What of other countries? Taking 'fast-moving' products as chemicals, electrical and other machinery, and transport equipment ('Standard

International Trade' Classification, 6, 71, 72 and 73), the following[47] was the percentage to total exports in two recent years for the UK and other countries.

	1953	*1965*
Fast-moving		
UK	43·4	52·0
France	24·0	30·0 (1964)
Germany	50·0	57·5
Japan	20·0	37·0 (1964)
USA	40·0	45·0 (1964)
Canada	—	16·0
EEC	—	48·0
EFTA	—	33·0
World	20·8	24·5

Clearly world exports, given the number of primary producers, must be strongly weighted towards products other than highly developed manufactures. The USA does not show so high a percentage as the UK because of its large exports of agricultural produce; France is in the same case. Japan ranks low because of dependence on sales of textiles; these alone accounted for 21 per cent of her total. Does this show an unprofitable orientation of their export effort? At the end of the day, probably the only proposition that could be carried would be that it suits the UK alone to switch to 'fast-moving' products, and this, as the Table shows, she has done.

A natural further aspect to consider is that of prices. This is, by any measure, a rich field for economic surmise, and for confusion. Countless graphs have been drawn of the rise and fall of British prices, compared with other countries; innumerable studies have been made of the 'price elasticity' of this or that export or import. Yet no generally received doctrine has emerged. Many researchers have found data explicitly suggesting there is no relationship between prices and sales. Many have found evidence that British prices are out of line, many have not. The then Prime Minister went out of his way to say, when introducing the July 1966 package of restraints that British products 'are competitive in price'. There was a presumption at devaluation in 1967 that British export prices were too high, but nobody made out the statistical case. The plain fact is, British prices may be higher than those of other countries, or they may be lower; nobody knows.

It cannot be too often stressed that the actual prices charged in international trade are unknown; they cannot be, and are not, collected by the statistical services. There are millions of individual prices in international trade, for there are millions of individual articles. Thousands of manufacturers produce thousands of goods, in thousands of variants, all at different prices. Prices for the same article vary according to inland region, according to whether they are sold at home or abroad, according to the importance of the customer, according to the size of the order, the quality of the material incorporated, the divergence required from standard, the freight cost involved, the ancillary equipment ordered, the services bought or not bought with it, and a hundred, or a thousand, other conditions. They also fluctuate rapidly in time in accordance with changes in costs, taxes, regulations, and so on. They are also, let it be remembered, often secret. Prices are a piece of the action at the point of sale. Manufacturers do not necessarily hawk them abroad. Outside the realm of consumer goods, and such other goods as come to be publicly valued, the original price data, then, is often incomplete, or non-existent.

An actual case history is of use in this context. Steel, before nationalisation, was a commodity subject to Government price control, and these prices were published. In comparison with most, steel is a highly homogeneous material. Its prices, one might well have thought, would be simple and easily appraised. But in fact, though the metal is the same, steel is sold in thousands of different forms, from solid two-ton slabs to microscopically thin steel strip. The prices of each of these variegated products fluctuates according to quantity, the quality of the rolling, forging or casting operation concerned, the degree of alloy admixture in the metal, the deviation from basic specification, and according to whether the product is coated, bright-drawn, galvanised, sheared or perforated, etc. The list of controlled prices issued by the supervisory body, the Iron and Steel Board, ran to twelve demy-quarto booklets.

For Britain's nearest and greatest competitors, the steelmakers of the European Community, the arrangements were very similar. Prices were supervised, and published. They were every bit as copious, and the High Authority's prices schedules occupied a thick, stiff-cover volume. Community export prices, like the British, were, however, unregulated and unpublished.

Consider, in the face of this, the problems of a researcher sitting down to work out whether British steel was competitive with Community products in the world market. The short answer is that he could not tell, for the export prices he needed were not available. All he could do was to study the published home prices in the hope that they might reflect in some way export prices. This in itself was a mountainous task. He had to find, amid the welter of sheer numbers, and of different measures—feet and metres, metric and long tons—qualities, processes, discounts, rebates and taxes, an assortment of precisely identical products, sold in exactly the same circumstances and on exactly the same conditions. Here, he was in a sense lucky, for a very broad outline of the price structure on each side was compiled, after diligent research, by teams of officials each year from the High Authority and the Iron and Steel Board. A specimen of this is shown on p. 103. This was not really suitable for intensive price comparisons.

But the researcher had a further, more fundamental difficulty. Completely rigid published prices in the UK and inside the Community would have been administratively tidy, but hardly a spur to inter-company competition—and competition is a frequent casualty in any regulated industry. Accordingly a loose link was pieced in. In the UK the published price was made to vary from district to district. In the Community, 'alignment' was allowed, i.e. Community makers could, at the point of sale, move up or down to the price of a competitor. The result of these two devices was that the actual home price of British or Community steel became virtually unknown. No one knew what quantities of British steel were sold into the different zones. No one knew how much Community steel was sold on alignment. A broad comment by the British Iron and Steel Federation, referring to Table D (opposite) is significant:

> The prices shown are published prices for the particular quantities and qualities shown and actual prices may diverge from these . . . in certain circumstances. Indeed, in really weak market conditions, the situation becomes such that it might be more meaningful to put that footnote as the main item on the page and show the published prices as a footnote. What actual, as distinct from published, prices are in any of the countries concerned at any given moment is very difficult to assess. In Britain where the deviations have tended to be only marginal, the authorities have a reasonably adequate volume of confidential data on deviations; but in the ECSC, they are only just beginning to get round to the problem of measuring alignments on Community prices . . . and in Japan I understand there is virtually no data available to anyone. I am afraid, therefore, that I cannot attempt to go beyond the table of published prices as it stands. Indeed, we should like very much to know the answers ourselves.

This was the position for steel, a homogeneous product in the overall spectrum of merchandise, publicly supervised on both sides, subject to price control, and to the publication of prices. How much more difficult then is the task confronting the researcher needing to decide whether Britain is internationally competitive in the rest of the vast miscellany of things she sells abroad. How does this country compete with the international price of fork-lift trucks, self-opening die heads, carboys and

Table D—Comparison of home trade prices in the main producing countries, June 1967

Product	Size	Quality of a size, tons	United Kingdom	United States	Germany		France		Belgium		Japan
			Open hearth steel		Steel to specification						
					Group 1	Group 2	Basic bessemer	Open hearth	Basic bessemer	Open hearth	(See note)
			£ s d	£ s d	£ s d	£ s d	£ s d	£ s d	£ s d	£ s d	
Billets	4-in. square	50	34 1 6	41 5 0	33 5 0	37 7 6	29 16 0	34 0 6	33 10 6	38 12 0	
Angles	5 by 5 by ½ in.	5	44 2 6	55 17 0	40 17 6	45 4 6	39 2 0	43 0 0	36 18 0	43 1 6	£47 7*s* 0*d* (6 by 6 in. by ½ in.).
Joints	12-in web	5	43 18 6	56 13 0	37 8 6	41 6 6	38 0 6	41 19 6	35 0 6	41 4 0	£56 9*s* 0*d* (14 in.)
Plates (structural)	20 ft. by 60 in. by ¼ in.	10	47 15 0	56 13 0	43 16 6	46 16 6	44 10 0	48 11 0	47 19 6	53 15 6	£36 6*s* 0*d* (8 by 4 ft. by ¼ in.).
Plates (ship)	20 ft. by 6 in. by ⅝ in.	10	49 7 6	54 13 0		50 12 6		53 13 0		57 16 0	
Rails	90 lb./yd.	500	44 3 0	50 8 0	46 15 0		42 6 6		45 16 6		
Bars	1½-in. diameter	50	43 1 6	55 13 0	38 17 6	43 4 6	38 4 0	42 2 0	35 19 6	42 3 0	£50 8*s* 0*d* (2 in.)
Reinforcing bars	⅝ in. diameter	50	43 19 0		34 5 0		37 9 0	41 7 0	35 16 6		£38 6*s* 0*d* (¾ in.)
Strip, hot rolled	3½ by 0·104 in. coil	10	47 0 0	57 9 0	45 8 0	48 0 6	42 8 6	46 19 0	43 11 0	47 11 0	£49 18*s* 0*d* (4 by 0·06 in.).
Sheets, cold reduced	6 ft. by 36 in. by 20 g.	25	58 14 6	62 17 0		56 19 6		59 12 6		60 17 0	£45 17*s* 0*d* (6 ft. by 36 in. by 20 g.)
Tinplate, electrolytic (per s.a.t.).	33 by 26 in. E. 50 0·0099 in.	100	9 19 1	10 7 3½		10 12 4		10 9 7		10 16 1	

This table was published in Professor Weidenhammer's Report to the US Senate on the world steel situation. The following note accompanied it.

The general basis of comparison is tested steel delivered to consumer's station.

The German prices include 4 per cent turnover tax (on German pricing system this is included in the basis price). Specification group 1 is equivalent to basic bessemer steel and group 2 to open hearth steel.

Owing to the operation of alignment the actual prices obtained by producers in the ECSC countries may be lower than those shown.

Japanese prices: These prices are from the Japan Metal Daily and are described as wholesale prices. Because of the complete lack of detail available from Japan they must not be taken as comparable with sizes, qualities, etc., shown for the other countries.

tubular containers of glass, microbial vaccines, plastic bobbins, vacuum flasks, perambulators and imitation jewellery—to quote only a random selection from the UK Trade Accounts? Are our export prices higher or lower? Nobody knows.

The economist, then, when he is judging the international competitive ability of this country, is not using prices at all as a reference. What does he do? He compares export performance by calculating 'unit values'. A 'unit value' is simply the result of taking the whole value, in pounds sterling, as recorded by the Customs, of a great slice of export trade, and of dividing it by the total number of 'units'—number of articles, or total number of tons—also recorded by the Customs. To take a random example[48] from the iron and steel field:

Year 1954	*Quantity*	*Value*
Item	(*tons*)	(£)
Ingots, blooms, billets and slabs; sheet bars and tin-plate bars of steel other than alloy steel	2 906	164 033

'Unit value', then, as calculated from this data, is £56 2*s* 0*d* (a quite unbelievable figure, at least twice any credible price for any of the products contained in the item).

There is no need to emphasise to what extent unit values must be a rule of thumb estimate, subject as it is to discrepancies in Customs recordings and invoicing, the overlap of official and private definitions, and, above all, to the movement of volumes and prices of individual products within the item. Practical economists are too wary, having worked out unit values for one item in UK trade, to proceed to work out another unit value in the Custom tables of another country and set one alongside the other. Quite apart from the improbability in many cases of there being a comparable item, the scope for inaccuracy is obvious. What is done is that the unit value in one country is put into index form and the growth over years is measured against the growth of another index in another country: viz., £56 2*s* 0*d* in 1954 is called 100; and if the unit value in 1960 is £84 3*s* 0*d*, i.e. half as much again, then the index for that year amounts to 150. Again, there is no need to emphasise the boundless hazards in this method. It suffices only to point out that, since the starting point in real prices is never shown, different upward movements of indices in different countries can give an entirely false impression of their real competitive relationship. The diagram on page 105 is reproduced from an Annual Report of the High Authority. It shows the movement of published home prices in the

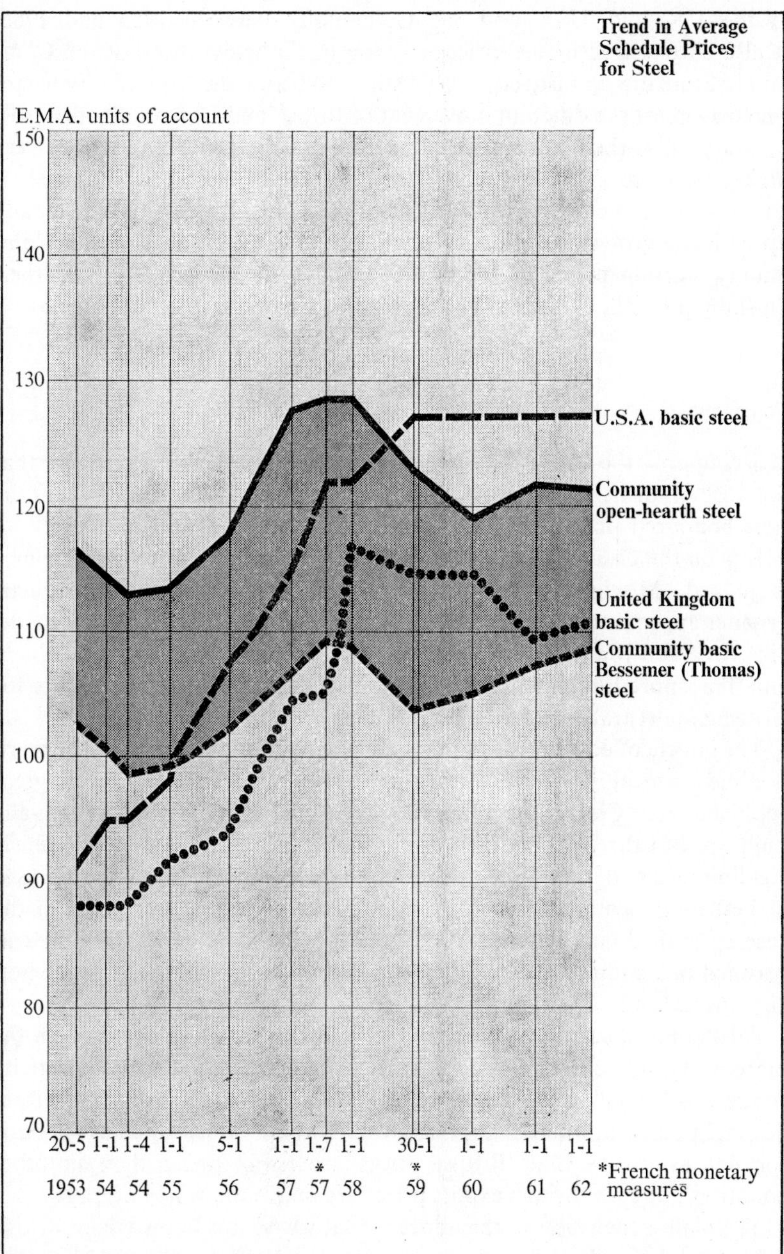

Figure 3. Movement of Steel Prices

in the UK and USA and the Community between 1953 and 1962. It also shows British steel prices starting much below those of the Community, moving up fast, but ending still well below the Community mean. The reason for the different movement of British and Community prices is, of course, that the latter shortly after the war were producing steel at very high cost from dislocated and damaged plant. Their prices tended, if anything, to come down, whilst those of the UK and USA moved steadily up with the growth of prices as a whole. Now, taking British and Community starting prices in 1953 as $88 and $109 respectively, and their finishing prices in 1962 as $111 and $115, one can construct an index:

	1953	*1962*
UK	100	126
Community	100	106

Seeing only the above index, the observer will immediately assume that the cost of British steel products soared uncontrollably, and that, in the time-honoured phrase 'Britain priced herself out of world markets'.

It is on the basis of such methods that British export price performance is judged. Moving on from these estimates for individual products, broader approximations for great wedges of British export trade are made, viz., for 'Non-Manufacture', 'Chemicals', 'Textiles', 'Metals', 'Machinery and Transport Equipment' and 'Other', and finally, vast assessments for British export trade as a whole.

The efforts of economists in this sphere should not be decried. The work is done painstakingly, and within its conceptual framework, with great sophistication. Clearly the effort should be made, and a science gradually built up. But there is very little doubt that it is as yet a primitive science, yielding results of a high degree of unreliability. Its measures can be used at best as indicating very broad movements of prices over years in the case of individual countries. As a guide to the state of actual prices as between one country and another, it can only be viewed with the greatest circumspection.

All the more surprising therefore to find these unit values used as the ingredients for charts, models, scatter diagrams, and price elasticity studies, often of great complexity and giving conclusions to within decimal points. Still more surprising to find these values taken as the basis for flat assertions that 'British prices are rising faster than in other countries', or that 'British export prices are above the world average'.

The plain conclusion to the above is that we do not know where British prices stand in relation to those of other countries but that we have no reason to suppose that there is an innate, unique disposition in British industry to push its prices up.

Much better would it be to take due note of such real indicators as there are for the state of prices in various countries. All industrial costs work through necessarily into the consumers' pocket. Do we in Britain feel ourselves higher priced in our shops and restaurants than elsewhere? If so, why the anxiety about the high living costs which membership of the Common Market will bring? And why the continuing shuttle of Continental shoppers across the Channel to London, where, it is understood, they buy not only food, but clothing, household goods and other necessities so much cheaper than at home. When international companies and organisations under pressure from their staffs, provide local cost of living allowances, they do not grant the highest rates for personnel stationed in the United Kingdom; rather the contrary. Harold Wincott, in his famous 'shopping basket' articles of the late 1960s, reviewing the cost of a normal day's activity in London, Paris, New York, Rome and other capitals, found London rated steadily below, rather than above, the average.

All of this discussion of the level of prices pays no regard, of course, to the question whether prices are a predominant, or even a major factor in export sales. Suffice it to recall here that they are generally conceded not to be decisive. The force of this point does not lie merely in the well-known additional factors in sales—quality, services, packaging, promotion, etc.—all these have been rehearsed often enough. What is also true is that in consumer goods sales, the price itself is very often part of the sales package: one goes for the 'top end' or the 'lower end' of the market, and one does oneself no necessary good by moving out of it. Hard though this may be to imagine for anyone who has not actually engaged in the job of selling, a firm making a luxury suitcase worth 30 guineas would not necessarily sell more if they offered it for 15 guineas. Furthermore, in capital goods the decision as to whether or not a sale goes through depends increasingly on whether credit is available, and in what currency, at what rate, and for what term; and on the political orientation of the seller's country.

All in all, the contention that Britain has 'priced herself out of the market' is so unspecific and ill-substantiated as to be of little practical help.

From prices to the other field of selling, marketing—advertising, salesmanship, packaging, delivery. Here one is altogether out of the field of measured and recorded fact. There are no statistics for salesmanship and packaging; although, here again, what there are on delivery times do not suggest a British standard perceptibly different from any other. The verdict we have in this field is an amalgam purely of value judgments, hearsay, indirect speech. More often than not it is based on what is said overseas to visiting British VIPs, of Parliamentary or higher origin, or to Ambassadors, Chamber of Commerce, BNEC and other semi-official missions. What is rarely divined by these visitors is that a customer will always complain about his supplier, given the chance, whatever the nationality of the latter. If the Duke of Edinburgh went to the USA in the name of France or Italy, rather than of Britain, he might well hear harrowing accounts of the peccadilloes and sins of Pechiney, Olivetti or Rhone Poulenc. These people who are spoken to abroad are men in business, in the real world of cash gain or cash loss, concerned with real problems of financing a new retail chain, opening a second shop, paying the mortgage, or sending their children to better schools. They are not interested in awarding praise, or helping to decide who is top of the world export league, or in adding to Britain's prestige. They are out to get better goods from their supplier for less money. They complain. Every tyro salesman is taught first to listen sympathetically to his customer's complaints, and then to take his order.

What is the true answer? Are the British better salesmen or worse than the others? Again, the mere stating of the question reveals its naïveté. One might as well ask: are the British better whist players than others? The answer is, individuals vary, but the average is probably no better and no worse than anybody else.

One straw in the wind. Anyone who travelled Pan-Am to America a year or so ago could have picked up on his seat a little booklet advising American salesmen on how to approach their European customers. There was much intelligent and objective observation of national selling habits in this booklet. It brought home clearly how methods differed and yet were equally efficacious. However, it advised, when dealing with the British, to be brisk and concise, and above all, to be sincere. This perhaps touches a vital nerve. Be it hard sell, soft sell, or any other technique, the basis of a sale is always the establishment of confidence between buyer and seller. The British, it seems, at least have the reputation of knowing this.

And so to another large area of concern. The British, it is felt, are hogtied by their poor industrial organisation. Bad labour relations, strikes, pay demands, obstructionism by trade unions, have slowed up technological advance, raised costs and prices, and impeded deliveries of export goods. Of course British trade unionism is in need of reform; the collapse in mid-1969 of the Industrial Relations Bill was deplorable, but can so great an onus be placed on labour organisation? Is it so much worse than elsewhere? The British are reputed internationally for their civic behaviour; has this broken down uniquely in the sphere of labour relations? The burden of complaint under this head has certainly been inconsistent. The fear was first that Britain lost more working days than any other country through labour disputes. The faint voices pointing out that this was not the verdict of the only international authority equipped to say, the ILO, finally broke through. The theme then became that, though British unions did not strike for as long as other nationalities, they struck more often. This was taken up, particularly by the Conservative Party, as the new key to the riddle of Britain's 'failing' trade; but the paper 'Is Britain Really Strike-Prone?' produced by H. A. Turner, Professor of Industrial Relations at Cambridge University, for the Cambridge University Department of Applied Economics, cast some sober doubt on the statistical basis of this belief. In particular, Professor Turner showed that international data on strike frequencies was so inconclusive that the ILO had continuously disregarded it.

Indeed, it was just because of the inadequacy of such figures for comparative purposes that the ILO (which supplied them in the first place) has never itself used them in its quite frequent reports and papers on the trend of industrial disputes, and that the Ministry of Labour in this country was—until recently—most reluctant to publicise them or to see any inference drawn from them.

Professor Turner's analysis of the actual experience of separate countries in the field of industrial stoppages suggests here again that no hard facts can be assembled in support of any view other than that Britain's place in the league is average, or slightly above average.

This review of the major charges made against the 'structural' efficiency of this country's economy implies only one conclusion. Britain must acknowledge many imperfections in her economic system; she can count herself no better than average in the world league table of performance; she will need unceasing effort and vigilance to preserve the standards that she holds. But the notion that she suffers from some congenital deficiency, peculiar only to herself, simply does not stand.

XI Inflation

The word has many connotations, but refers essentially to a state of affairs where the price of everything continuously rises, and the value of money therefore falls. This is a malign condition, eating accumulated wealth, re-distributing real income, and diverting the energies of the economy. Some of the ways in which this happens will be pointed out as this chapter proceeds. But what we are principally concerned with here is whether Britain is peculiarly susceptible to this ailment.

Britain is inflating. So is the rest of the known world—industrialised countries and agricultural countries; advanced countries and developing countries; capitalist countries and Communist countries. The phenomenon is commonplace and universal. The theory, however, is that Britain is in some special way 'inflationary'. The exact form of the inflationary diagnosis is somewhat ambiguous. In part, it is a derivative of the 'structure' theory, i.e. Britain's trade is in deficit; this is because of a fundamental imbalance in the economy; this imbalance takes the form of an excess of demand over supply; an excess of demand over supply creates inflation. Alternatively it is just felt that, for whatever reason, probably unknown, Britain has fallen foul of the vice of inflation and that this has led to her trade difficulties. The theory about inflation takes two main forms. The crudest, and unfortunately the most common, is that inflation is purely a British sickness and that this is why she has fallen behind her sounder neighbours. The second is that Britain has inflated *faster* than her trade rivals.

A really long-term look at Britain's record is firstly necessary. Since we are in this, as in other cases, dealing with a supposedly ingrained British fault, a cursory view of the past few years is insufficient.

The pound is historically one of the most stable currencies in the world. As a matter of historical interest, its par rate with gold did not materially change between the reign of Elizabeth I and 1931, when it was taken off the gold standard. Since then there have been two devaluations only, one in 1949 and one in 1967. In France there have been six devaluations since the war, in Italy nine. Going back further in the eighteenth and nineteenth centuries, European currencies were very much on a par. The franc, the mark, the lira and the schilling were all of very similar value and they all roughly equalled a sovereign. Where are they now? There are (if one disregards the 'new' franc) about 1 400 French francs to the pound, about 1 800 lire, about 60 schillings, 10 marks, 12 Swedish kroner and 17 Norwegian kroner.

The weight of long-term inflation has certainly been outside and not within the borders of the United Kingdom.

Let us now measure inflation, not indirectly by the relative values of national currencies, but directly by the actual rise of prices within each country.

Taking the postwar era alone, the movement of retail prices, between 1952 and 1968 in the Community and in the UK was as follows:[49]

1958=100

	Ger.	*Fr.*	*It.*	*Ne.*	*Be.*	*Lux.*	*UK*
1952	94	83	83	86	93	94	81
1960	102	110	102	103	102	101	101·6
1964	114	129	124	119	111	108	115
1968	125	146	139	141	119	117	137

There is little in the above Table to suggest that inflation had run away with the UK leaving Europe as a whole untouched. There is also a significant point to be drawn from the Table. The year 1964 was allegedly the year in which all Britain's past sins were visited on her, and the accumulated overheating of years at last boiled up an immense balance of payments problem. But as will be seen, the growth of British prices up till then was on a par with Germany, and substantially less than that of France, Italy and the Netherlands. It was only after 1964 that prices began to rise at a rate at least comparable with the European front runners. In other words, inflationary impetus coincided with Government deflationary zeal.

This leads into a wider and very important field of consideration. Inflation, as has been seen, is measured by the level of prices. The theory of inflation, very crudely expressed, is that what we pay for goods in the shops is decided by how hard we want them—how many people are asking for them; if there are too many, then the goods run short, and the manufacturers put up the price. They put up the price because they themselves come under pressure for supplies of the wherewithal to make the goods: raw materials and labour, and the price of these goes up. Thus, if overall demand in an economy grows too great, overall supplies become more expensive, and inflation, or high prices, is the result.

Like many theories, it is seen to be less obviously working in practice. Clear extraneous causes, such as devaluation, which raises the price of imports across the board, play a part. The devaluation of 1967 raised import prices by a nominal 17 per cent. Then there are taxes. Whether levied on goods as they leave the factory, like purchase tax, whether levied directly on the company, like corporation tax, or whether charged more indirectly, like death duty, income tax and local authority rates, all taxes and charges soak through into retail prices. The combined effects of devaluation and the Budget tax burden of 1968, for instance, are supposed to have raised retail prices by 4 per cent. Next, and not least, there is Government expenditure;[50] i.e. there is, besides the purchases of commercial goods and services by the population at large (rather oddly entitled, in economic language, the 'private sector') the expenditure of the Government and local Councils for things like education, roads, hospitals, agricultural subsidies, defence, public libraries, museums, Civil Service pay, housing, and the capital needs of the nationalised industries. These expenditures are large. They amounted to £19 000 million in 1968, as against £46 000 million for the public and private sectors of the economy combined; in other words, they equalled nearly one half of the entire nation's spending in the year. If the Government is a big spender, then this is a further pressure exerted by demand on prices.

However, as soon as the Government comes into the field of analysis, there is, as always, more to the problem than has so far been apparent. 'Inflation', as has been said, is a monetary concept. It means there has been a movement upwards in prices. This is, in principle, caused by excess demand. Now how, in theory, can this happen? How can excess demand actually change prices? It might have been thought that since no more goods can be sought than are actually made, demand would end when, so to speak, the manufacturers had sold out. Moreover, since people are self-evidently both makers and buyers, they can in practice only buy goods with the proceeds of what they have made. In the nation at large the total income from production is the total income for buying, and there is no more. Why then higher prices? This observation incorporates a basic truism of economics: supply and demand must balance. However, there is an intermediate stage in which inflation or rising prices can occur.

Money, in the first instance, is of course only what is earned from production. But having got the money, a man does not have to spend it right away. He can refrain from buying. He can save it, or, which in the overall economy is the same thing, he can invest it. All savings, whether they go into the Post Office, the bank, or stocks and shares, are invested. In other words, the man in question, or the economy as a whole, can, as a producer, add to his plant and thus create capacity to produce more goods in the near future. If a reasonable degree of this investing goes on, the same amount of money begins to chase more goods. Dividing one into the other, obviously the price will not rise; it should fall. In the opposite case, more money is available to chase the same goods, and clearly, prices will rise. Crudely explained, this is the mechanism by which excess demand causes prices to rise. The effect of this for the nation and the balance of payments is evident. The nation grows poorer in a real sense, because it has fewer goods than it might have, and since its prices are rising, it sells less in the international market. Of course, there is an inbuilt discipline. With too little investment, insufficient goods eventually come on offer to absorb the money available, and funds are channelled back into savings. With too much investment, producers' current earnings fall, and they release more goods. This is a *grosso modo* description of the process which takes place, and which is of course immensely more complicated. The essence of the function is that through a miscellany of relationships, and of causes and effects, the pressures of supply and demand are brought into balance.

What is important is that this evening-out effect is achieved through the intermediary of money, the 'veil' as Pigou called it, or the 'servo-mechanism' of the economy, as others have described it. The circular flow of money round the economy, in and out of the hands of producers and consumers, brings all the pressures into juxtaposition and embodies the balance between them.

This is where Government diverges from the rule. The Government is of course a spender, and not an earner. It derives the wherewithal to spend—its revenue—from taxation. In other words, the 'private' economy, before making its decision as to whether to spend or invest its money earned from production, surrenders a certain sum to the Government. When the Government spends, however, it can only buy goods and services from the producers in the private economy, and so it feeds the money back into the pool. The level of taxation is determined by a number of political factors, some of them remote from the equations of supply and demand. Thus, if Government, the spender and non-earner, is over-active, inflationary tendencies are necessarily reinforced; and in a way that supply and demand pressures cannot control. But the real danger is not here. Since the end of the war, Governments have habitually spent *more* than they have received in revenue. This has implications that are serious though not necessarily bad. After all, the Government can borrow, and has done for centuries. Since the war, however, the Government has gone on from overspending income, to borrowing funds, and finally to *creating* the extra money required. This is inflation with a vengeance.

To take this analysis farther would require a detailed examination of monetary theory as a whole, and of Exchequer practice, credit control and public debt management. But the broad point seems clear. Of course money must be created, merely to keep pace with the growth of production. If the economy this year makes 1 million articles for £1 each, and next year makes 1 100 000 articles, as it should, then there will have to be £1 100 000 if the price of each is still to be £1. Also, as Keynes has taught us, in different circumstances the Government may have a role to play in creating consumption. But a Government that creates money outside these functions, in order to finance expenditure that is not subject to any outside control, is clearly inviting consequences of a serious order.

Let us then sum up the effect of Government activity on the movement of money or inflation.[51] Firstly a large quantity of money is siphoned out of the private economy, where it might have been put to investment. In 1968, over £15 000 million was withdrawn in this way, or just about half the national income. It is only a small mitigation that about £4 000 million of this went into state-owned investment, partly in the nationalised industries. When it is considered that about £4 000 million came forward for total private investment in 1968, it is clear that Government activities have eaten substantially into the national cake. This imbalance is aggravated when the Government, having decided that the economy is 'over-heating', applies a squeeze to the private sector. The curbs that are then placed on the market for goods, the added costs inflicted on investment by high interest rates and the credit ceiling, then further discourage private investment. To an extent, the public is forced to save in order to support the Government's expanding activities.In October 1967 Sir Leslie O'Brien, Governor of the Bank of England, observed:

> The more inexorably the public sector marches upwards, the more we have to disturb the rhythm of the private sector, where most of our prospects of growth lie.

Figure 4 demonstrates this only too well.

Secondly, having drawn off the funds quoted above from the private economy and distorted the balance of resources, the Government, as has already been seen, then drives a sizeable wedge of it back through the consumer sluices of the economy by spending on goods and services, as we have seen, and so adding an inflationary pressure.

Thirdly, in going beyond even this point, in overspending its income and artificially bringing new money into being in order to finance the extra expenditure, the Government is injecting the purest kind of inflation into

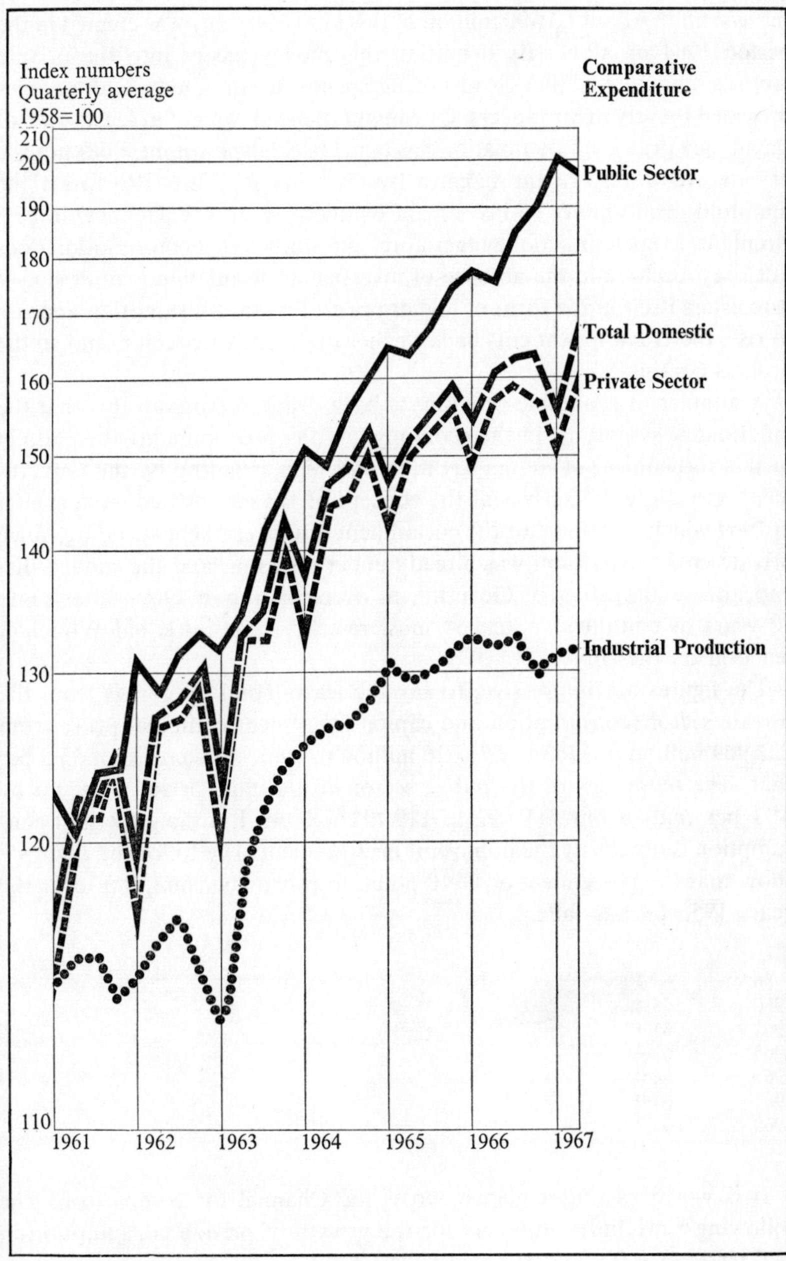

Figure 4. Public and Private Expenditure

the system.[52] About £3 400 million of this kind of money was created in the period 1964–68 alone. By definition this money passes into the private sector's hands, for the Government spends it on goods and services provided by private producers. One might then ask why, if at least some of the money drawn off by taxation has come back as new mint, does not the private sector restore the balance by investing it? This is to forget the manifold disincentives to investment enumerated above. The new money circulates as spending money therefore, and since actual consumption does not rise—because in the absence of investment, production is not rising—it registers itself in the form of higher prices. Private consumption appears to rise, the Government cuts back further on the private sector, and so the process continues.

A number of reputable economists have deduced from all this that the inflationary symptoms in the economy are due predominantly or entirely to this mechanism of money creation and high spending by the Government. Certainly the arrival of the concept of Domestic Credit Expansion in 1969 which really meant the curtailment of Government spending, since private credit expansion was already under restraint, and the sudden disappearance altogether of Government overspending in 1969—after some 30 years of continued practice—must re-echo some intestinal Whitehall reaction on the subject.[53]

The figures are impressive, to say the least. Total outgoings from the private sector (consumption and capital investment combined) rose from £22 909 million in 1963 to £31 046 million in 1968, an increase of 35·5 per cent. The outgoings of the public sector in the same period went up by 61·1 per cent—from £11 692 to £19 122 million. But the growth of consumption is obviously the important measurement. The following figures[54] show that the percentage of GNP going to private consumption over the years 1956–68 has fallen.

1956	64·1
1960	65·4
1962	65·4
1965	63·9
1966	64·0
1967	64·0
1968	63·7

It is worth casting a glance across the Channel for comparison. The following[55] are index numbers for the growth of private consumption in real terms over 9 years, as against the UK:

Private consumption 1968 (1959 = 100)

UK	121·4
Germany	151·7
France	162·4
Italy	164·6
Netherlands	166·0
Belgium	142·7
Luxemburg	133·6 (Base 959)

Rising wages are considered to be a valuable measure of inflation. The following[56] is a comparison of the average gross income of individual wage and salary earners in the UK and the Community in 1967.

	$
Belgium	3 323
France	3 516
Germany	2 873
Italy	2 415
Luxemburg	3 329 (1965)
Netherlands	3 270
UK	2 716

The following[57] is an index figure which shows how average hourly wages have risen in Community countries and in the UK between 1953 and 1966. Taking 1953 as 100 for all, the following is how matters stood in 1966.

Belgium	218
France	275
Germany	265
Italy	250
Luxemburg	217
Netherlands	312
UK	225

This is as far as we need go on the subject of inflation, within the confines of the present study. Clearly, the view that this country as a whole is inflating faster than other countries is without foundation.

However, the above analysis has thrown light on two crucial aspects of the central notion of inflation. Firstly we have once again seen, and this time in the larger context of the home economy, the detachment of the Government from the ordinary commercial pressures of the economy at large. The Government is not a producer; it is a spender and a consumer. It derives its income, not from earnings, but from a levy charged on those who do produce, and from money of its own creation; its expenditure is regulated, not by income limits or by a need to save, but by non-commercial, social and political objectives. It is thus divorced from the supply and demand equation at both ends, free to pursue its resource-using activities in straightline fashion according to the dictates of policy.

We have seen this happen in the lesser field of the balance of payments, where the Government is similarly emancipated from the constraints of foreign exchange availabilities—in other words from the need to possess earned money. This is the equivalent of the money-creating mechanism at home. Indeed it is part of the same thing: imports and exports are only part of the global supply and demand interchange of the whole economy, and the roles of Government and private sector in both will be the same. There is a distinction between the home and external payment system in that, because of the inter-connection with autonomous foreign economies, and of the divisions between national currencies, any debt incurred abroad must eventually be paid off by a surplus in the foreign sector of the economy; but in the disciplines bearing on their activities public and private sectors retain their essential differences. In respect of the balance of payments, we wondered whether the non-commercial incursion of the Government actually disturbed the economic equation of forces within which it was operating. The portrayal of the process in the home economy perhaps answers this. It can be seen that undue arrogation of resources by the Government can unbalance and weaken the private sector, and it is perhaps in exerting this effect at the heart of the system that the Government inflicts injury on the balance of payments.

With all this it remains inevitable and not necessarily wrong that Government financial activities should be ordered in this way. Indeed, it is difficult to see how, unless the Government owned all the means of production and became synonymous with the economy, any other system could prevail. What the Government does is intrinsically good; it maintains, defends and regulates the community pursuant to the wishes of its electorate. However, it is essential that the Government should be conscious of its method of operation, and should be aware that it is working within an economic framework, but not subject to its laws. It should be aware of the zones of harm into which it can move, failing due circumspection, and it must be ready at all times to adjust to the economy, rather than disregard the latter's susceptibilities. Most of all, it must not so misunderstand its own impact on the economy as to ascribe the harm it may do to deficiencies on the part of that economy. As we have seen, the intrusion of Government spending has slowed down the growth of consumption and investment resources in the private sector. It is wrong for the Government to descry in the inflationary symptoms of its own making, a sign of over-expansion in the private economy, and then to depress the latter still farther. What, basically, has to be recognised, is that the historic change of financial base that occurred a broad half-century ago has diametrically changed the character of the monetary system. The move from gold-related to managed currencies removed all objective disciplines and placed the supply of spending power in the sole hands of Government. The implications of this infinitely more flexible and sophisticated system are still emerging and requiring recognition. It is clear that there is much in the field of money supply and its own effect upon it, that Government has to learn. Meanwhile, it shows every sign of judging the movement of the economy and the balance of payments by simple criteria applicable to the gold currency era.

Necessary admonitions aside, it is worth remembering here also that monetary inflation has also served a political objective espoused by every government of the United Kingdom since the war and by virtually every government elsewhere. This is the objective of full employment and constant economic expansion. However contradictorily the British Government at least has viewed the economic expansion that has ensued, there is little doubt that this is the product of the dynamic monetary policy that has been followed. Advantages thus must be weighed with disadvantages. Inflation in support of sectarian political goals must be eschewed; some inflation in pursuit of a universally approved social and economic aim is perhaps inevitable. Provided its pace is not immoderate, and the necessary cushion is made ready for those likely to suffer from it—there are no fixed income classes any more, but there are pensioners and the like whose incomes move sluggishly in response to inflation—there is no reason to assume it a thoroughgoing evil. Perhaps, in this light, the most obnoxious evil it has conjured up, in this country, is the conviction of governments that the private economy has created it, and should therefore be restrained. The internal examination of the economy, then, identifies inflation as the product of basic economic aspirations in the post-war period, and as the practical result of Government rather than private doings; it does not isolate any worthwhile evidence of true inflationary over-consumption on the text-book model. It certainly lends no support to any view that the British economy alone among others is preternaturally disposed to inflation.

This then concludes the inspection, begun in the last chapter, of Britain's economic data in the light of the inference, drawn from a view of her trade performance, that some congenital defect was at hand. The concrete evidence does not substantiate this inference. The various suspicions that have been raised—that our trading pattern is wrong, that our prices are too high, that the economy is structurally oriented to excessive consumption, that it is a unique victim of inflation—for none of these can substantial evidence of any objective merit be found. The UK economy is no worse than and no different to the other economies of the world. It suffers from the errors and failings of all human enterprise; it will be exempt from none of the efforts needed to maintain progress. But it has no inherent vice, not shared by any other country. And continuous retrenchment, in order to suppress a supposed unique deformity in our economy, runs the risk of so upsetting that fundamental balance of money supply and goods supply—mentioned earlier—that inflation may in fact be enhanced.

XII Contraction

But, of course, there has been more economic retrenchment in the UK. Very considerably more. In fact, viewing the post-1945 period as an historic whole, it might be said that restrictions have been continuous. There were the controls and rationing of the immediate postwar period. Then there was the slashing budget of 1951, brought in by Gaitskell, and imposing a burden of tax only exceeded by the truly desperate exactions of Jenkins in 1969. '. . . so far as fiscal policy can do,' said Mr Gaitskell, referring to his Budget, 'it will protect us from inflation.' There was an increase in Bank rate, cuts in capital investment and in hire purchase after the Conservative victory in October 1951. There was a period of restraint in 1955 and 1956 and again in 1957. After another breather the same cycle began in January 1960 with 'crisis' measures in July 1961. In the autumn of 1964 came the deluge, with virtually continuous suppression until 1970, more than half a decade.

What happens to a country kept under repeated or continuous restraint? Not surprisingly it does what the measures intend it to do. It becomes restrained; it fails to grow.

We have already seen how the mere force of high Government activity draws off much needed resources from potential investment and growth in the private sector. Now one must visualise the effect upon an economy, already retarded in this way, of high company taxation, high interest rates, a credit squeeze, price control, hire purchase controls, and the many other weapons of deflation. Investment is the key to growth, as has been seen; the flail of deflation slashes at this in two ways, one deliberate and recognised, the other, one suspects, inadvertent or plain willy nilly.

The intention of policy is of course the restraint of the home market, the slowing down of consumption in the classical aim of switching resources to investment. However, it has been seen that private consumption in the UK has not been rising excessively; in fact the data suggests that it has been less than desirably buoyant. Now, a due level of consumption is vital to investment. Manufacturers must be assured of the sale of their goods, before putting in capacity to make more. Consumption and investment run, in normal economic circumstances, in natural balance.

The consequences of postwar deflation show the pitfalls of arbitrary policy intervention in these matters. With consumption reduced still further by these measures, manufacturers have less, not more, incentive to invest. Private investment in manufacturing was running at £299 million quarterly in 1961.[58] After two years of Selwyn Lloyd's compression of the market, it had sunk to £241 million (both in the prices of 1958). The respite of 1963 allowed it to revive and such was the impetus achieved that it managed to struggle up to £303 million by the third quarter of 1966. After that the forces of repression engulfed it, and by the first quarter of 1969 it was still at £319 million. Such was the experience of eight years of industrial life in this country. It is important to recognise how essential this field of private manufacturing investment is to the growth of the country's economy. Other investment of course takes place. Houses, roads, docks and bridges are built, coal and limestone pits are excavated, electrical and generation plants are installed; money put into these is investment, since it is providing essentials for the production of the future and not consuming goods running off the production lines now. Some of this investment is done by the Government, and, as we know, Government investment has been rising. But it is the manufacturing sector of the economy that provides the central needs of production, the machines, tools and plant without which nothing can be made—not merely boots and shoes and other consumption items, but the concrete mixers and crushers required for roads, houses and docks, and the alternators, pylons, ovens and cables needed for power and gas stations. All of the manufacturing sector, with small exceptions, is in private hands.

A concrete case is useful at this point. The Table opposite illustrates the purchase tax and hire purchase controls applied to the motor vehicle market in the period 1950–69; it is taken from the Report by the Economic Development Council for Motor Manufacturing issued in January 1970. To these impositions might have been added the excise duty on motor spirit (petrol rose from 4*s* 9½*d* a premium gallon to 6*s* 6*d* between 1964 and 1969, and the rise in road fund licences (from £15 to £25 between 1964 and 1969). The motor-car industry, one of the most crucial to the onward progress of the economy, has consistently been picked out for deflationary pressure by successive Chancellors, for their own good reasons, and on that account it has perhaps suffered more than the generality of industrial endeavour in the country. However, its experiences by the same token illustrate more aptly the common lot. The home market for passenger cars, which had reached a total of nearly 300 000 in 1964, fell to 218 000 in the second quarter of 1969—a drop of more than

Past rates of purchase tax and hire purchase restrictions on cars and light vans

Purchase tax on cars: changes in rates from 1950 to 1969

Year	*Month*	*Change in rate*	*Rate %*
1950	April	Higher rate removed, all cars	33⅓
1951	April	Increased to	66⅔
1953	April	Reduced to	50
1955	October	Increased to	60
1959	April	Reduced to	50
1961	July	Increased to	55
1962	April	Reduced to	45
1962	November	Reduced to	25
1966	July	Increased to	27½
1968	March	Increased to	33⅓
1968	November	Increased to	36⅔

Hire purchase restrictions on cars and light vans: 1958 to 1969

Year	*Month*	*Change*	*Minimum deposit* %	*Repayment period* (*months*)
1958	October	Restrictions removed	—	—
1960	April	Restrictions reintroduced	20	24
1961	January	Repayment period extended	20	36
1965	June	Restrictions	25	36
1965	July	Further restrictions	25	30
1966	February	Further restrictions	25	27
1966	July	Further restrictions	40	24
1967	June	Relaxation	30	30
1967	August	Relaxation	25	36
1967	November	Restrictions	33⅓	27
1968	November	Further restrictions	40	24

25 per cent. Figure 5 pictures most vividly the state of the British car market. As we entered 1970 car registrations were just about back to the point they had reached at the start of 1960. So much for a decade of commercial effort. The Report can best take up the tale at this point.

Investment plans conceived in the mid-sixties with expectations of steadily rising home demand based on projected rapid growth of the economy were met with five years of stagnation in demand for vehicles, due primarily to (albeit necessary) [*sic*] government deflationary measures, and returns were accordingly well below expected levels. With this experience, companies are likely to take a cautious view of future trends, and weigh the probability of various outcomes of a project accordingly. The greater the degree of uncertainty, the lower is

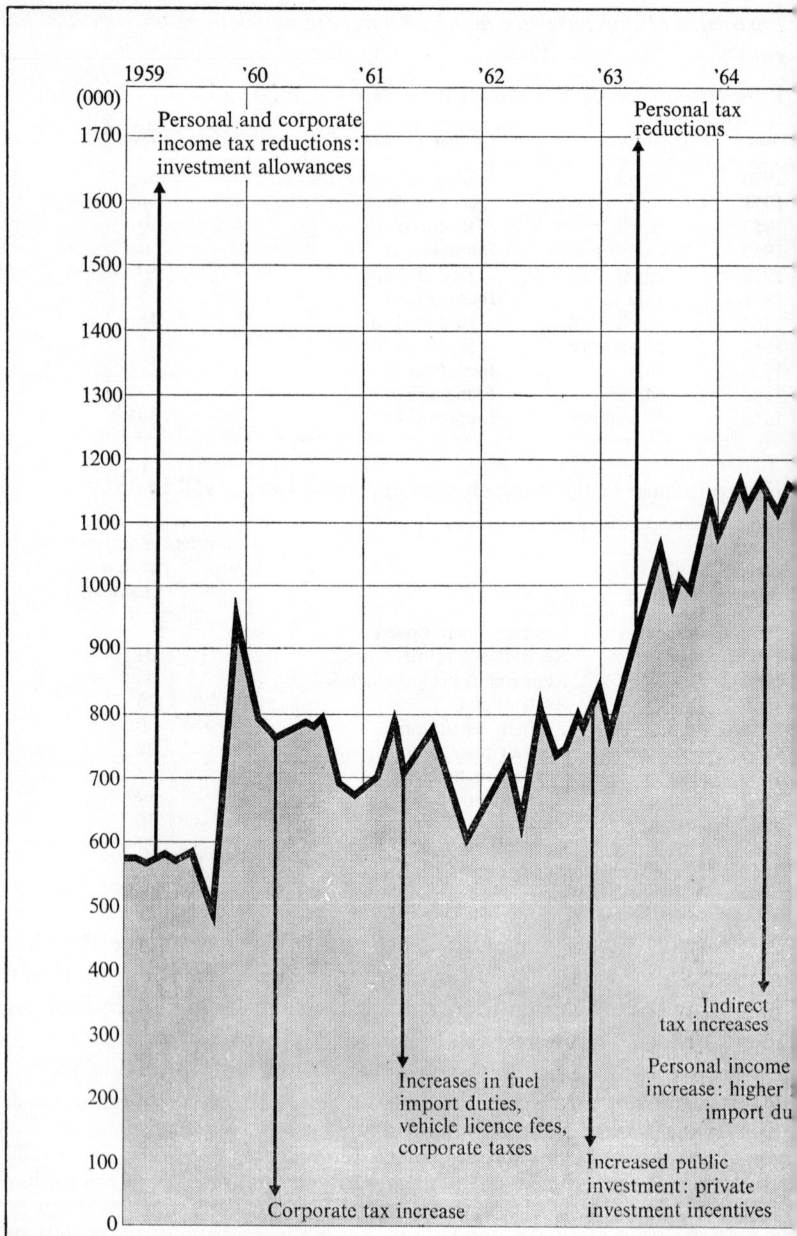

Figure 5. New Registrations of Cars

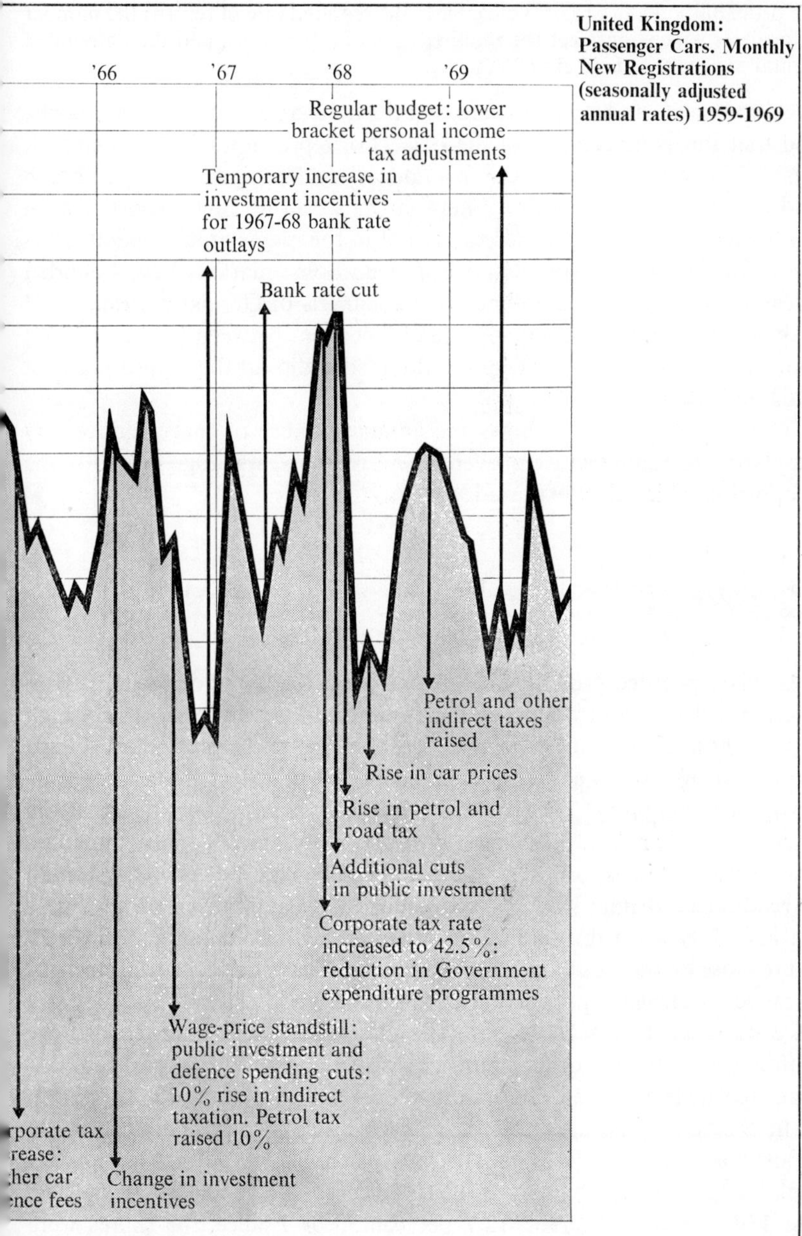
United Kingdom: Passenger Cars. Monthly New Registrations (seasonally adjusted annual rates) 1959-1969
'66
'67
'68
'69
Regular budget: lower bracket personal income tax adjustments
Temporary increase in investment incentives for 1967-68 bank rate outlays
Bank rate cut
Petrol and other indirect taxes raised
Rise in car prices
Rise in petrol and road tax
Additional cuts in public investment
Corporate tax rate increased to 42.5%: reduction in Government expenditure programmes
Wage-price standstill: public investment and defence spending cuts: 10% rise in indirect taxation. Petrol tax raised 10%
Change in investment incentives

the probability that a project will achieve the required rate of return; the number of projects which can meet the required rate of return falls, and the amount of capital expenditure is likely to fall.

Of course, it can be argued here that the industry should turn to exports, and that this is indeed one of the objects of repression of home demand. One is bound to wonder where this notion of a free option between home and export sales came from. Where in the world do high exports spring from a lean home market? Certainly not in the major motor manufacturing countries. The Japanese and European home markets have bounded ahead explosively. The combined home markets of Germany, France and Italy grew at an average annual rate of 9 per cent between 1960 and 1968; that of Japan doubled itself, and redoubled again, in the period between 1962 and 1968.

The following Table[59] shows the annual number of cars produced by the Japanese manufacturers over a few recent years, together with the proportion which they exported:

		%
1962	268 784	6
1964	579 660	12
1966	877 656	17
1968	2 055 821	20

Is this export-led growth? It looks very much like the opposite. If production is driven up by exports, then one would expect to see a very high export ratio, about 50 per cent at least, in the early years; and then a tailing off of exports as home demand begins to reflect the added prosperity of the country. The Table shows a very small export figure at the start but a slow rise as production grows. Clearly, the trigger for Japanese growth was not in exports at all—the share of which even in 1968 was small in relation to Britain's 37 per cent—but in the mightily growing home market. Only when this had raised Japanese car makers' annual throughput to close on the 2 million mark did the latter have the industrial strength to move a noticeable proportion out into the world market. But they still have far to go to reach the export level attained by Britain. Indeed the notion, generally, that other countries storm along on their export momentum, that their economies boom on 'export led' expansion does not seem to fit the facts. The data can be very easily compared. Total Japanese exports of all commodities equalled 9·1 per cent of GNP in 1968; as far back as 1965, it was higher, at 10·1 per cent. The Italian share in 1968 was 13·6 per cent, in 1965 12·7 per cent. For France, the shares were 10·0 per cent and 10·7 respectively. Canada 20·1 and 16·8. Germany, for

1968, 18·8, for 1965, 15·9 although for 1960, it was slightly higher, at 16·1 per cent. These figures[60] hardly substantiate the theory of growth induced by the single factor of exports. Real events in the world of trade and production are more complicated than that. Economic growth and exports have moved up hand in hand. Basically, a country's home market provides the mass, standard sales; the export market is more variegated, more uncertain, and more costly to feed. A national economy builds itself up on its own strength, then spreads its exports abroad; when its exports reach a certain level, then it is more profitable to invest abroad. Such is the sequence of events demonstrated by history and implied by industrial logic.

The second, and inadvertent, reason, is the increase in the purely financial deterrents to investment. A company wishing to expand its production must build new factories and plant, and for this it must raise money. It obtains the money in three major ways. First and foremost it raises it from its 'internal resources', i.e. it pays for new plant and buildings by saving from its annual profits. The amount obtained in this way varies, but it might be fair to say that about 60 per cent of all new investment is financed from internal resources. The second way is to borrow. A company can float a loan, or a 'debenture' which means that it will receive from a variety of lenders—collected together either through the medium of the Stock Exchange or a financial specialist like a merchant banker—the capital sum required, repayable over 20 or 30 years at a fixed rate of interest; or it can in some circumstances, particularly for smaller projects likely to pay for themselves quickly, borrow from the banks. The third method is to issue shares on the Stock Exchange, i.e. it raises more capital from the public, who, however, acquire a piece of the ownership of the company and must be paid dividends whenever profits allow. Now, a period of deflation militates against all these methods. Firstly, the vast increases in taxation and the rise in costs which are synonymous with a deflationary period, squeeze the company's profits. These profits have already been diminished, as has already been seen, by the decline in the home market. Accordingly, the company has smaller internal resources from which to finance new investment. Secondly, a period of deflation is characteristically marked by 'tightness of money'. This phrase means that there is less money being brought forward for lending and investing, and that it 'costs' more, that is to say, interest rates are higher. Less money comes forward because of high taxation and prices, which leave people with less cash. It also means that people take out fewer insurance policies and buy less on hire purchase (the Government curbs this anyway, as remarked earlier on). Consignment by the big insurance companies and finance houses have fewer funds at their disposal, and are therefore less ready to take up debentures or shares in industrial companies. This is a much more important factor than it might seem at first sight. The insurance companies and finance houses revolve immense capital sums which they must keep permanently at work earning interest. They, the 'institutions', are in fact the biggest buyers of shares and debentures in the country, accounting for about 60 per cent. Money is 'tight', then, and the Government assists this by placing a curb on banks' lending—the notorious 'ceiling' over which the Chancellor and the banks had many a stiff word during 1968 and 1969, and on innumerable other occasions in the postwar period. If money is tight, it becomes, by the normal law of supply and demand, more expensive. Interest rates rise generally and this again is encouraged by the Government, in that it raises Bank rate, an important determinant of rates across the market. The company finds this a further aggravation of its situation. If it does issue capital then it will be expected to pay high dividends, for if it doesn't, investors have ample opportunity to put their money where it will earn higher returns; the same applies to debentures. Now, resources for higher interest and dividend payments is just what the companies have not got, since their profits have been slimmed by the forces mentioned above. Banks traditionally charge lower rates on their loans, and companies wherever possible will turn to that quarter; but, quite apart from the fact that this form of capital lending is not really the banks' business, the Chancellor, as we have seen, has got there first, and forbidden the banks to lend above a certain amount. This is only a brief outline of the way in which company investment intentions are thwarted; the list could be extended considerably. However, as will be seen, the industrial producer is beset by difficulties on all sides.

A third major, and also inadvertent, investment deterrent brought about by official deflation, is the plain uncertainty of it all. The Table on page 123 shows that purchase tax rates and hire purchase deposits and repayment terms have in the postwar period gone up and down like a window blind. What is the average board of directors to make of this whirligig? On what basis of sober fact are they going to visualise their future sales and plan their forthcoming investment? It must be remembered that, once inside the boardroom, investment is no longer an economic abstraction. It is real money that has to be sweated and negotiated for: real money that will disappear into a green field and re-emerge as plant and buildings; real money will be lost, and lost for ever, if the new factory does not make a profit. At the back of all the cogitation and planning in private, risk-taking business, lies the threat of bankruptcy; with loss of employment and income, and break of career for all concerned. Give a firm a long enough period, then, of shrinking markets and uncertainty, and the philosophy on investment will be 'when in doubt, don't'. This philosophy will tend to persist after good times have been restored. After all, it is always safer *not* to invest. If there is no investment, no money is lost. A chance of earning more money has simply been forgone. And so, over the whole economy, a multitude of company decisions, for good business reasons, adds up to slower growth for the economy. It has long been an article of faith in this country that lean times make efficient business. All the practical facts set out above, all of our industrial history, and all the experience of our industrial neighbours suggest otherwise. An industry thrives and gears up its efficiency in the fact of an expanding market and the opportunity for gain. In business, as elsewhere, success is bred by success.

Enough has been said above to show that applying the brakes has brought the British economy, as inevitably as any other moving vehicle, to a halt. This is well borne out by any comparison with other countries. If one takes any measure of volume, of pace, of economic advance, then one finds the British at the bottom, or near the bottom, of the list. The recent survey of the British economy, produced by the American Brookings Institution, illustrates this perfectly. Firstly, the growth of the national income (a measure of the total earnings in a year of the economy, akin to gross national product or GNP) shows the following annual percentage increases:

National income

	1950–54	*1955–64*
Germany	7·1	5·6
Italy	5·6	5·4
France	4·9	5·0
Netherlands	4·9	4·3
Norway	3·8	3·9
Denmark	3·6	4·8
USA	3·5	3·1
Belgium	3·4	3·5
UK	2·6	2·8

A similar picture is shown if we take GNP itself: the annual average rate of growth for the period 1960–65 was

Japan	9·6	Germany	4·8
Canada	5·5	USA	4·5
Italy	5·1	UK	3·5
France	5·1		

Take the growth of industrial production: if the level of output in 1963 equals 100, the following[61] is the level reached in various countries in 1968–69:

	1968	*1969*
Germany	128	144
France	123	142
Italy	136	140
Netherlands	143	161
Belgium	120	132
Luxemburg	112	127
USA	133	139
UK	119	123

Output per worker has similarly flagged:[62]

Output per manhour in manufacturing, 1963 = 100

Japan	175·0
Italy	146·0
Germany	137·0
France	133·0
USA	115·0
UK	122·7

The levels of trade have followed suit, as shown[63] by the shares taken by various countries in the total manufactured trade of the world:

Share of world trade %

	1958	*1968*
USA	23·3	20·2
Germany	18·5	19·5
France	8·6	8·3
Italy	4·1	7·3
Japan	6·0	10·7
UK	18·1	11·1

A good deal too much has, of course, been made of the declining UK contribution to total exports. The world is an expanding place, full of newcomers. Those countries which industrialised first and got into the export business (and the UK was *the* first) naturally saw their own share go down as other nations added their quota to the pool. This is the mathematics of the case. One man making a hundred bricks is making 100 per cent of the output. If another man joins him at a 100-brick rate of output, then the first man, although he is still making not less than 100 bricks, is now contributing only 50 per cent of the total. The table shows that other established exporters—France and the USA—have lost part of their share. Some of the countries with a much-vaunted increase, particularly Germany and Japan, have, it will be found on examination of the recent trend, merely returned to the share they held before the 1939–45 war, a war in which they came off worst and lost much trade. Nevertheless, it would have been thought that there was a base level commensurate with her size in the modern world, to which Britain should fall, and which she should then hold. But this has not happened; she seems to be going through floor after floor. This seems another inevitable result of clumsy deflationary policies. If a country's investment, production and GNP are persistently held down, where other countries' are not, then its scale of trade will shrink in relation to other countries also. This trend is excellently demonstrated in NEDO's 'Effect of Government Economic Policy in the Motor Industry' (1968).

Curiously enough, all of the above data on Britain's retarded progress have been widely quoted as further evidence of the structural defects of the country. 'Why', the question has repeatedly run, 'is Britain a slow-growing country in relation to others?' Rarely, if ever, has the answer been 'because Government measures made it such'. There is certainly no doubt of the economy's inherent ability to grow. Left to itself, it will put on expansionary momentum with the best of them. In a well-stated analysis in the *Westminster Bank Review* of November 1969, W. A. Eltis of Exeter College, Oxford, shows the following growth rates for production in the 'squeeze' and 'non-squeeze' periods.

	%
1955 (4th Quarter)—1958 (3rd Quarter)	0
1958 (3rd Quarter)—1960 (1st Quarter)	9·1
1960 (1st Quarter)—1963 (1st Quarter)	0
1963 (1st Quarter)—1965 (1st Quarter)	8·3
1965 (1st Quarter)—1967 (3rd Quarter)	0·4
1967 (3rd Quarter)—1968 (4th Quarter)	5·6

Moreover Mr Eltis shows that total investment increased at the rate of 20 per cent a year, when it was allowed to.

However, lengthy and often intricate researches have been devoted to the abstract question why Britain is an inherent slow grower. To quote one example—no worse and in fact much better than many others—the Brookings Institution study mentioned above gives a very full chapter to this subject, which examines the potential for 'reducing waste in the use of resources in agriculture', the increase in 'residual efficiency', very briefly wonders whether 'Europeans simply work less hard than Americans' (dulce patria) and ends with the general conclusion that

To a considerable extent, conditions beyond the control of the United Kingdom were responsible for the higher growth rates in other countries.

But in the whole of this 20 000-word painstaking dissection of the British economy, the effect of deliberate and avowed Government policy is dealt with in the following cursory passage:

Many British observers [*sic*] believe that the 'stop-go' pattern of the British economy has discouraged business from acting on the basis of the longer term outlook and has discouraged needed investment as well as adoption of other means of raising productivity; its elimination, they believe, would bring improvement. There is probably some merit in this contention, but elimination of 'stop-go' would not strike at the root causes of inefficiency.

XIII The Apogee

The period from 1964 to 1970, as was said in Chapter VIII, was the one in which all our chickens came home to roost; all the perils latent in the policy pursued since the war came to fruition. This period is full of lessons for the future, and deserves study.

The story of this era begins with the hand over of the Treasury from Selwyn Lloyd to Reginald Maudling. After an inventive and capable start, Selwyn Lloyd had got enmeshed in a typical sterling crisis. The outflow of short-term capital this time had been triggered off by the revaluation of the German mark in March 1961, and a larger than usual overall deficit in 1960. The syndrome had operated; short-term money left the 'weak' British economy to go to the 'strong' German economy. Selwyn Lloyd then went into one of the fiercest deflationary onslaughts on the economy then on record, and one, moreover that concentrated more than usually on the private sector. When he was succeeded by Mr Maudling in 1962, the economy was displaying all the woes of a Government-induced recession. Production had been stagnant for nearly two years, investment had fallen by at least 20 per cent, unemployment was rising to 500 000 and over, the trade unions were soured by the pay freeze, industrial managers were wringing well-wrung hands. Maudling had some unusually suitable qualities for the job. He was firstly one of the more percipient economic brains that had come to the Treasury. Secondly he had an equanimity of temperament that was ideal for the banker's side of the Chancellor's role.

Maudling, it seems apparent, was struck by the incongruity of the policies so far pursued—the persistent thwarting of abounding economic energies because of an import/export problem. It is certain that he had not cottoned on to the heart of the matter—the fact that the visible deficit was normal and immaterial—we have his own written record for that. Nor indeed could he have been expected to appreciate so new a discovery at that date. Nonetheless he clearly decided that the way out was to liberate the economy from this stranglehold of the trade balance. From this commenced his 'dash for freedom'. Given a chance to get on a new, higher level of activity, the economy would find its own balance in the trade field. A sustained expansion would pass through a period of high imports into one of high exports; Maudling undoubtedly thought that exports would eventually climb above imports, but his effective reasoning was no worse for that. Provided heads could be kept during the import upsurge phase, the economy would come out on a new, broader plateau. He was the first Chancellor to opt for expansion as a cure in itself. As the spring and summer moved on, he handled the short-term monetary position with superb imperturbability. Confidence, he recognised only too well, perhaps more perceptively than any other postwar Chancellor, was crucial. All through the summer he parried alarms and doubts with masterly equipoise. The economy was sound, he said, he knew what he was doing; all would be well. There was no concealment of the fact that the year's end would see a deficit, and a big one, but this he said was foreseen, and the watershed would come in the following year. By the end of July short-term money had remained firm, and the reserves had actually risen. In the third quarter came the largest deficit of the year (the fourth quarter was to be much smaller) and the inflow of short-term capital, although large, did not fully offset it; he countered this with a small loan and a small drawing on the reserves.

Would his plan have succeeded? We know now that exports, as promised, grew mightily in 1963, even in the climate of growing depression that then prevailed. He would have had an improving balance after 1964. Although his particular target of a merchandise surplus would not have been attained, he might have lifted the economy on to a new plane, and might well have brought in a new balance of payments posture. But he was unlikely to have kept confidence intact right through. There would probably have been a breakout of confidence funds in late 1964, or during 1965, depending on how well he handled the figures for the year 1964, and how well he contained disquiet in the ensuing months. Probably he would have been forced to take some restrictive measures, and to borrow more. But his main strategy might have won through.

What happened of course was very different. The first two weeks of October 1964 were taken up by a General Election campaign. In the course of this, the Labour Party, as was politically legitimate—although, heaven knows, economically ill-advised—raised an enormous hue and cry about the balance of payments. We were going to have, they said, a monstrous, an unprecedented deficit. The country was about to plunge up to its neck in international debt. This was not merely the result of one year's mismanagement, they said: it was the culmination of a decade of negligence and incompetence, during which the economy had become antiquated, complacent, inert and wholly uncompetitive. The Conservatives defended themselves curiously badly against the onset, perhaps because Maudling was partly inhibited by the appearance during this time of the worst set of figures he was due to cope with. At any rate, the effect on foreign short-term depositors of this Labour onslaught was electric. What had been on the cards throughout the year was a leakage of short-term funds. What happened was a break in the dam. The sterling balances began to stream out as from the beginning of October, and then went into flood. This was to continue, except for the briefest of respites, for a full five years. As we know, no less than £1 300 million net was to leave the country. Rarely in history have electoral interests collided so violently with economic interests.

Having brought about this exceedingly perilous position, the newly invested Labour government began to compound their misfortunes in every conceivable way. Within the first ten days of their existence, they brought out, with pride, a White Paper declaring the economy to be, in effect, in a state of emergency. They brought in, without warning or prior consultation with Britain's trading partners, an export rebate and import surcharge, in violation of a dozen international treaties, including the major GATT and EFTA Conventions. They made noises about cancelling the Concorde project. They had a blistering row with the assembled EFTA ministers in which they made their view perfectly plain that internal British requirements took precedence over her obligations abroad. They produced an emergency budget which increased income tax, petrol tax and other charges to the extent of £215 million, one of the highest postwar exactions so far. At the same time they abolished Health Service prescription charges, put up pension rates and other social welfare benefits, and added a new burden to employers' National Insurance liabilities. They raised Bank Rate to crisis level at 7 per cent and ordered $1 000 million of standby credits from IMF. They put a curb on domestic bank lending. They announced, without specifying how they would act on the announcement, that they would increase—and drastically re-model—company taxation, and add a capital gains tax, and so sent the stock market into disjointure. They made innumerable speeches about the sins of British industrial management and the treatment they would mete out to them. All this in the space of a few weeks from the date of the election. The advent of any Labour government, with the anti-business, little-Englander, public extravagance label traditionally attached to it, would have sent a tremor down the backs of foreign holders of sterling. This one excelled itself. In the eyes of the world the British Labour government had inherited a massive deficit—in which all implicitly believed—and was intent on enlarging it; it seemed to lack the merest understanding of the nation's finances, and certainly the will to manage them; it appeared as impervious to foreign interests as the most pessimistic had predicted. Britain was going headlong down the path to perdition. What would the Labour government do next? Would they freeze the sterling balances and then devalue? What else might they do? Foreign holders of sterling could not get out of the currency fast enough. By the end of November the most vicious sterling crisis in postwar history had developed. As reports of money sluicing through the exchanges poured in, the new Labour government began to sink slowly into a vortex of confusion and financial ruin. Then on 25 November the Bank of England announced an enormous $3 000 million loan from the central banks of eleven other countries, which it had whistled up in front of the rapidly growing emergency, in the space of a few days. England was now in debt to the tune of £1 400 million, but she could meet the pressure on the exchanges; the parity went up, and she was saved for the moment.

But only for the moment. The trade balance certainly began to look better. As Maudling had predicted, exports moved up quite strongly—5 per cent in volume terms, 8 per cent in value. Imports moved less than 1 per cent in volume and in value. The trade gap was halved. The better rise of exports over imports was to continue in 1966. But the April budget, with its massive concentration on Corporation Tax and on the capital gains tax, reawakened fears that this was a partisan government pursuing its own hobby horses. As the months went on a medley of new contrivances added to these fears—the Prices and Incomes Board, the Land Commission, the investment dollar surrender, investment grants, the Industrial Reorganisation Commission, the Selective Employment Tax, nationalisations, present and projected. The impression grew that the new government had inherited a balance of payments problem, but, beyond advertising the fact, it was mainly concerned to do other things.

One must not carp at the Labour government's political proclivities. Much of what it did made sense in terms of its own household gods. But in the balance of payments context, which is where the Labour government squarely and voluntarily put itself, the policies were irrelevant. Then, the string of policy abortions began to grow longer. The grandiose Statement of Intent on prices and incomes, which was disregarded by the trade unions almost from the day of signature, the National Plan, described by an unkind critic as not a policy for sound development, but a photograph of a policy, and which was disowned by its own government's retrenchment measures two months before it was published, the TSR 2—F111 fantasia, Rhodesia, the oddly mistimed, or untimed, application to join the

European Community—all these gave the impression of a plausible, but ineffectual government. Above all, public expenditure grew and grew. The new boards and institutions, the new Civil Service Departments, the great increase in capital expenditure by local governments and public corporations, led to levels of official costs never experienced hitherto. The picture was that of a deflating private sector, but an inflating public sector. And so, after the big outrush, confidence ebbed and flowed, but steadily receded overall. There was a renewed outflow in early 1965, accentuated at the time of the budget, reinforced as the early summer went on, checked somewhat in May and June, renewed in late summer, eased in the autumn and winter; the pressure returned full force in the early months of 1966, continued through the summer, and was moderately abated by another credit operation with foreign lenders—one of a long line over the two years—in September.

To all this, the Government replied by piling the agony on the private sector. Taxes rose inexorably, the credit squeeze was tightened, special deposits were demanded of the banks, hire purchase restrictions were intensified, a freeze on wages, prices, dividends and salaries was declared, a surtax *on* surtax required some unfortunate executives actually to pay more than 20*s* in the £; private building controls were imposed and strengthened. The effect on growth in the private sector was self-evident. The impetus of the 1964 upsurge lingered on for some while. But the accumulation of taxes, the rise in wages, the climb in interest rates, the erosion of the home market, the multiplication of Government controls, and above all the uncertainty of the future began to take their toll. Private investment as a whole, after a rise in 1963 and 1964, levelled off in 1965 and slid gently down until 1967; it kicked up in 1968 then fell again. Manufacturing investment stagnated throughout. Manufacturing stocks slid and slid throughout 1965, 1966 and 1967. Company profits in real terms fell by 10 per cent.

The effect on the balance of payments was predictable. As has already been remarked, the trade deficit diminished throughout 1965, and this was as a result of a faster growth of exports over imports. This particular 'Maudling cycle' was, of course, bound to even out, but it ran on quite strongly into 1966. In fact there was in the final portion of 1966 a surplus on visible trade. Taking all elements of the external account into consideration—which few people did—the balance of payments was really quite healthy in 1965 and 1966. From an overall deficit of £381 million in 1964, the position on Government and private current account moved to a small deficit of £50 million in 1965 and to an actual surplus of £64 million in

1966. This of course was due in large measure to the invisible account, which moved into sharply stronger surplus in 1966 and was to strengthen substantially more in the succeeding years. The underlying indications were then that visible trade might have moved under the Maudling experiment to a position, still in deficit, but at a higher level of activity, and that this would have been covered by a larger invisible surplus. However the upward movement in the visible trade balance did not last. Under the exactions and distractions of prevailing policy, exports tapered off more abruptly than might have been expected and resistance to imports flagged abnormally. The way exports of motor cars moved, as shown by NEDO, is eloquent testimony. Imports, having dropped rather unusually at the end of 1966, moved up again swiftly in the first quarter of 1967, although they levelled and dropped slightly again in the second quarter. Exports at the same time fell away from their end 1966 peak, fairly sharply in the second quarter of 1967 and less sharply in the third. All in all there was a deficit on visible trade of £135 million, not counting payments for American military aircraft purchased by the Government, in the first three quarters combined in 1967. Against this there was of course the surplus on invisibles, now striding up at a tremendous pace (the surplus on services alone grew by 50 per cent over the previous year). This amounted to £550 million by the end of September 1967, and if one deducts Government current expenditure of £532 million, including full official interest payments, and the cost of US aircraft, and an overall capital outflow of not more than £2 million, one is left with an overall deficit of £140 million. Nonetheless, with all this, this new visible deficit was too much for the despairing holders of sterling—who had been in and out of the currency with the alternating alarums and false dawns of the preceding three years. What with this, and the Middle East war, and the rise of interest rates in New York, and the weird application to join the Common Market, made in May 1967, and the downturn in world trade, and the now open talk in London and the British press of devaluation, it was all too much. To stay was to court complete disaster. Like an army camped on an avalanche slope, they packed up and went at speed. Nobody outside the Bank of England and Whitehall knows how much capital left the country in the autumn months and particularly in the few weeks before devaluation on 16 November. But we know it was hundreds, if not more than a thousand millions. A significant enough yardstick is the further $3000 million borrowed immediately after the operation was through. This time the torrent was too much for any power to stem. Devaluation was forced on a government resisting almost to the last. But there was no way of stopping the pitiless rush. If the Government had not devalued, they would have run out of reserves and funds to defend the parity, and the pound would have dropped, out of control, anyway.

No sooner was devaluation over than it was acclaimed by the Government, as a great new opportunity. We were free of a fusty old rate that had never been any good to us. Now with this brand-new $2·40 parity we would sweep the world with our wonderfully cheap exports, and those unpatriotic Britons who insisted on buying foreign goods would now be discouraged by the higher prices they would face. Enough has been said in the foregoing to suggest that this view, whilst being forgivably optimistic, was unreal. Exports are not determined by simple price changes; imports are useful, most of them essential, to the economic life of the nation. The major effect of devaluation therefore was to increase by 17 per cent the four-fifths of British imports which consisted of food and raw materials, and which could not be dispensed with. The balance of trade in 1968 threw up another near record deficit, £534 million.

And so into 1969, with lengthening debts—another IMF loan was incurred during the DM revaluation scare in the spring—and lengthening disillusionment. True there were some relieving features. The visible balance, as it was bound to, was recovering somewhat from the impact of devaluation. The worst of the import uplift had passed, and exports, aided by a steady rise in price, and by an underlying and unprecedentedly big upward cycle in world trade, moved upward reducing the margin. The trade gap in the first half of 1969 was £214 million, still a very large sum, but better than the phenomenal £495 million for the first half of the preceding year. The invisible surplus had moved up again and brought home a sweeping £650 million as against the £550 million of the year before. Government overseas expenditure had at length ceased to rise and was still running at some £230 million in the half year. Long-term capital flows, under Government strangulation, were reversing and becoming net inward, rather than net outward movements, and for the first half of 1969 only a residual £80 million left the country. The country was thus in actual overall surplus in the first half. But this was noticed only by a few. All eyes, as ever, were on the visible balance. Month followed month in which a resounding deficit was announced by the press. The pound was intensely vulnerable. Another run could start at any time. No one knew where the resources to stem this would come from. Surely no more loans from abroad would materialise. The Government had exhausted itself in measures to depress the economy; there seemed no more armholds to apply. The country's external debts were still huge; there were at least

£3 300 million to pay. No one could see where the money was to come from.

And then, suddenly, two things happened. In August 1969, out of the blue, there was a surplus on visible trade; and it was a very large one—£42 million. The surprise this caused can only be appreciated by recalling the run of monthly deficits so far that year:

	£m
1967: Average	–46
1968: Average	–58
1969:	
January	–13
February	–65
March	–55
April	–59
May	–13
June	–22
July	–36
August	+42

The Board of Trade was vastly satisfied, but in a short but significant footnote at the end of its customary commentary on the figures there was some explanation. There had been a statistical discrepancy. Briefly, it was this. A month or so before, the Board of Trade had discovered that export returns were deficient.[64] All exports are, of course, recorded by the authorities on the basis of returns made to them by the exporters or shipping agents; they are naturally not counted individually by the Customs. Immediately after the war, the system was rigorous. Shippers were made to send in their returns *before* the sailing or departure of the ship or aircraft carrying the goods. Then shipments to the sterling area were made exempt from the 'pre-entry' requirement. Exporters had to send in their returns within six days of the departure of their goods. Finally, in 1963 all exporters were made exempt from pre-entry. In June 1969, the Board of Trade announced its discovery that some exporters, who after all had plenty of forms to fill in already, ceased from that date to send in returns at all. There were not many, but the Board of Trade calculated that the abstentions amounted to 2–3 per cent of exports in all. This may seem a small fraction, but in balance of payments terms it was large—about £130 million in 1968. Following this announcement much pressure was put on exporters to record all their shipments; not only the Government but trade associations and chambers of commerce, who had long smarted under the aspersions on Britain's trade effort, urged exporters not to go on voluntarily undervaluing themselves. The August figure was the result. Some exporters, the Board of Trade reckoned, were still failing to register, but a lot more were either digging up old returns they had failed to send in at the time, or they were sending in documents long before they needed to. Applying various corrections, the Board of Trade said the real figure should be considered to be £35 million—a smaller sum, but still a big surplus. Most people did not even look at this footnote, however. The Board of Trade must not be misunderstood on this point. Its procedures required it to announce the trade balance as it arose from the entries actually sent in. Thousands of these arrive each month; there is no practical means of segregating them by date; in normal times the discrepancies all come out in the wash. It was right then to put the revision as a footnote. Those, however, who read the fine print remained sceptical about the real balance. The Board of Trade, again, made no apologies. Its estimate of the 'over-recording' and 'under-recording' was necessarily based on a small sample. The Board of Trade was better equipped to guess well than anybody else, but it was still a guess.

Came September, and another surplus was recorded; this time £28 million, corrected in the footnote down to £13 million. October showed £+6 million, corrected to £+4 million. Then November came with a surplus of £14 million, and the Board of Trade said all the discrepancies had disappeared. December showed an exact balance. Finally, in January 1970, an enormous surprise. A surplus of £39 million! There was huge astonishment and huge delight all round. Those who had been following the figures intimately were not a little suspicious. The year's run of trade balances had now assumed a very odd shape indeed (see page 142).

But few had given it that much introspection. The country had run a surplus for six solid months. The balance of payments itself had been transfigured. The sterling balances reacted vigorously, if not violently. There had been indications of a returning stream through the autumn, as surpluses succeeded each other. Now the floodgates opened. The Bank of England mopped up foreign currency and repaid official debt hand over fist; the pound pressed hard towards its parity peg. Everybody half hopefully, half fearfully, waited for what the ensuing months would bring. The National Institute prophesied an immense surplus for the year, of nearly £1 000 million, and demanded the dismantlement of the economic squeeze—for fear of too great a widening of 'the gap between actual output and potential output'.

In this lay the second major event. By the end of 1969 it was evident that Jenkins had stopped the economy. People were arguing, not whether GNP had risen moderately or sharply, but whether it had or had not

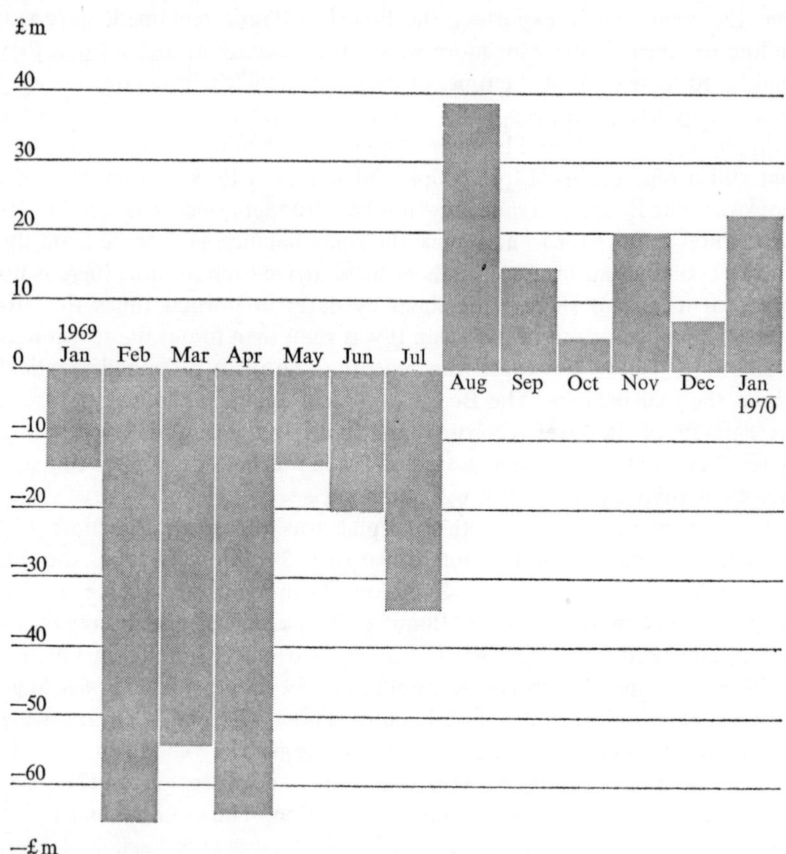

Figure 6. Shape of Visible Balance, 1969–1970

achieved a tiny ½ per cent in the second half of 1969. Industrial production had perhaps risen four-fifths of 1 per cent between the end of 1968 and the end of 1969. Stocks had fallen; import volumes had not shifted for about a year. The economy was flat, idling at nil rate of increase.

Jenkins was, as Maudling had been in his time, an out of the ordinary Chancellor. Although their policy aims were diametrically different, they both commanded respect. Both were intellectually gifted, and could tell their officials what to do. Both did what they set out to do. Before Jenkins, many a Chancellor had said Amen to the proposition that the economy's growth should be stilled, and had let expansion go on. Not so Jenkins.

With the steely-lipped resolution of the intellectually convinced, he carried the job through to the last nail and hammer blow. To his staggering load of taxation—compared with the previous postwar record of £300 million, he, in 1968, brought in taxes of £1 100 million—had been added £350 million worth of extra National Insurances charges (levied primarily on the employers), the whole array of demand and consumption constrictions mentioned above, and various novel forms of repression, such as the 'fines' on special deposit interest to clearing banks and the import deposit scheme. Lastly, and anything but least, there had been the slicing of Government expenditure. At long last Roy Jenkins had put a stop to the growth of Government spending. For the first time in thirty years there was, in 1969, an excess of Government income over expenditure. This in itself was good: the inflationary creation of money ended in 1969, and Government expenditure was halted at the point, albeit high, that it had reached in 1968. The State's grasp on the nation's resources was under restraint. In normal times this would have been all to the good; the economy would almost certainly have benefited. But the withdrawal of Government demand at a time when historically massive taxation was in force, and when huge and heavy pressures were being exerted on private expenditure and investment was a further sickening blow at the vitality of the economy.

In early 1970, therefore, there was a lull in the battle over sterling. Owing to the run of visible surpluses and to the demolition wrought by the Chancellor—which of course was applauded as sound treatment of the economy—the strain on the pound had disappeared. The foreign exchange market was unwontedly quiet.

Like the defenders of Monte Cassino after the saturation bombing had reduced the position to ruin, the British people came out to survey the debris. They saw Bank Rate staying at crisis height for longer than at any time since the Bank of England itself had been formed in 1694. They saw continuous high unemployment such as had not been witnessed since the Great Depression of the 1930s. They saw a gilt-edged market unrecognisable after five years' adversity. In mid-1970, at the time this book was written, no one could foresee what was yet to come.

Had Jenkins really contrived the nightmare vision of postwar British leadership and brought about a structural transformation of this country into a net visible exporter? If so, the country could expect, as a low growth, low consumption and low output nation, to slip gently away into the industrial fringe of the world. Or was this standstill to be succeeded, as so often before, by a reflation followed by a visible deficit, a sterling crisis and renewed deflation? This seemed the most likely outcome. Meanwhile, like the erstwhile defenders of Cassino, one could only survey with remorse the ruins of a famous victory. And in the uncanny stillness of that momentary truce, there could be heard the steady clear voice of Mr Jenkins, now far away in New York and beyond, now close at hand in the House of Commons, saying that Britain's economy was now the strongest in Western Europe.

XIV The Cure: More Fully

In the eighteenth century, healthy men with minor complaints were bled by determined physicians until they were near to dying. The comparison with the treatment of Britain's postwar economic ailments is too strong to be ignored. We are very likely to die of the present remedy.

We must change our treatment before it is too late. Like that of the eighteenth-century practitioner, it is based on a false diagnosis. Necessarily so—for prolonged and morbid repression improves neither the human nor the economic body and must be misjudged. We have mistaken the natural shape of our economy and trade for the symptoms of internal disease.

The prescription then for future policy is normal life: normal expansion as in any other industrial country.

What does this mean? How will the various sectors of the balance of payments develop in undistorted conditions; what will be the interaction between balance of payments results and a healthily advancing general economy; what will be the size of the figures we can expect to see in our balance of payments accounts in future years? To begin with the visible account.

An exact answer is impossible. It is clear that levels of international exchanges originating in this country are abnormally low; what should be the proper levels of trade in goods and services, is particularly difficult to assay. Britain's visible exports at the moment equal about 16·8 per cent of GNP. This compares with the following range:

	1968
	%
Germany	18·8
France	10·0
Italy	13·6
Japan	9·1
Netherlands	33·1
USA	3·9
Belgium/Luxemburg	38·0

Obviously the right percentage varies enormously country by country.[65] The same is true for imports, which in the UK currently amount to 18·5 per cent:

	1968
	%
Germany	15·2
France	11·0
Italy	13·7
Japan	9·2
Netherlands	36·8
USA	3·8
Belgium/Luxemburg	38·8

Import and export propensities clearly depend on the differing economic size and structure of each country. Those with large resources of primary material and a large home market will tend to trade less abroad than others. Other factors, political, historical and financial, will obviously also have a bearing.

There is thus little guide in the comparison with other countries. One would expect the UK share to be around the West European average, although on the other hand, the incomplete transfer of resources from agriculture in the European countries would suggest that the British ratio should be higher than Germany's and certainly higher than France. Japan, an ill-endowed island like the UK, would be a clear model to follow, were it not patently clear that Japan has by no means yet attained the potential it should in economic and commercial development.

Another guide lies in Britain's own history. A review of the record makes it immediately clear that only at one time in our economic history were levels of imports and exports as low as they were in the years 1945–70. In the period 1934–38 imports equalled 16·6 per cent of GNP and exports amounted to 11 per cent. This period was, however, the aftermath of the world depression when economic activities were at as low an ebb as they had ever been. In 1925–27 the proportions were 24·9 and 19·0 respectively. The whole of the inter-war period was, however, a disturbed and difficult time and the figures are unlikely to be typical of the economy in full working order. If one goes back to 1913, one has arrived at what was in fact the most recent year in which economic development was proceeding without special disturbance, either external or internal. If one goes further, to 1885, one has a year in which the economy was maturing rapidly, although under the influence of a contemporary world depression; the effects of the latter, however, were less severe than those of the 1930s episode. The following are the trade proportions[66] (1968 for comparison).

	Imports	*Exports*	*Balance Percentages of GNP*
1885	27·0	23·0	4·0
1913	29·0	27·0	2·0
1927	26·0	20·0	6·0
[1968	18·5	16·8	1·6]

There is a strong presumption in the light of these figures that trade, if allowed to run free, would rise to levels appreciably above those of today. There is one change in the essential structure of trade over the years which should perhaps be taken into account. In the period up to the Second World War, the UK was a fairly important entrepôt centre, i.e. through its merchanting houses it imported and re-exported goods intended for other destinations. This of course expanded the figures both for imports and exports. This has fallen away since. Many people think that this is mainly because a decline in entrepôt business was inevitable, and that we should therefore aim at import and export levels which would be lower than in the past, by these margins. On the other hand, it is equally feasible that Britain lost this trade, as she lost shares in other activities, because of the postwar contraction of British business generally, described in the previous chapter. It would seem right to reduce the previous trade proportions by half the margin represented by entrepôt trade, viz.:

	Imports	*Exports*	*Balance Percentages of GNP*
1885	25	20·5	4·5
1913	27	24·5	2·5
1927	24·5	18·5	6
[1968	18·5	16·9	1·6]

It is perhaps interesting to note that of the three years shown above the one in which trade may be thought to be moving most healthily and naturally—1913—was also the one in which imports and exports were at their highest in terms of GNP, although it is, significantly, also the one in which the balance between the two was at its smallest. One is tempted to take 1913 as the model for a properly functioning external economy. However, statistical prudence suggests that the mean of all the years should be used:

	Imports	*Exports*	*Balance Percentages of GNP*
Average 1885, 1913, 1927	25	21	4

Now, the important thing is to see what quantities would be involved if these were the percentages of trade today. The following would be the figures for 1968:

	Imports (£m)	*Exports (£m)*	*Balance (£m)*
1968 (on above basis)	9 171	1 704	−1 467
1968 (actual)	6 807	6 273	− 534]

Thus, if we were running our economy at historically normal levels, we could look to see a balance between imports and exports at a negative figure of some £1 500 million; tending, if the 1913 model is a real optimum to something lower, as low as £600 million.

So much for the visible account. If the economy was free to make its own progress, what would be the position of the invisible account? Historical series of invisible imports and exports are incomplete, but we do have a continuous record of the balance between the two. For the present purposes, this is the essential data. In the 1934–38 period, the invisible balance, relative to GNP, was just over 5 per cent. It has been said that the late thirties were an impoverished economic era, but this applied primarily to production and trade in goods. Although services must have been affected by the general blight, it would be fair to take these as an admissible example of pre-war earnings. In other years the percentage was: 1927, 8; 1913, 12; 1885, 10. For comparison, 1968 was 3. Again it will be seen that the 'best' year, 1913, had the largest invisible surplus. Transposing all these figures into an average, and expressing them in terms of 1968, we have:

	% of GNP	*(£m)*
1885–1938	9	3 300
[1968 (actual)	3	1 031]

Once again it would be fair to assume that the balance ought to tend in practice towards the 1913 optimum of £4 400 million.

The combination of data then gives the following:

	Visible	*Invisible*	*Current account balance*
1885–1938	−1 500	+3 300	+1 700
[1968 (actual)	−534	+1 031	+497]

The reader might look at these figures and adjudge them fanciful. Fanciful they certainly are in relation to the minute ratios and quantities of our stricken postwar years. The fact is that they are real. They are the expression, in the £ *s d* of 1968, of the kind of trade and earnings that actually occurred, year after year, in this country in other and happier times. The times in question, moreover, were not merely happier, they were not so far off. The most recent figures relate only to thirty years ago.

Nor are they so much out of line with contemporary experience. The visible trade data—25 per cent and 21 per cent of GNP—are tame compared with the 38–33 per cent clocked up in 1968 in Belgium and the Netherlands. The latter country, with its maritime and financial endowments, is not so far removed from the UK. Or, to take a country closer to the UK dimensions, the 19 per cent for German exports in 1968 is a near parallel to the 21 per cent postulated for British exports. With the

UK's greater shift from agriculture and consequent greater reliance on food imports, a greater trade propensity than Germany's is in principle to be expected. These figures, then, with the—for today—enormous trade gap are not in themselves outlandish.

Similar points apply to the invisible data. The invisible surplus for Norway and Spain, shown on page 92, equalled 8 per cent and 4 per cent of the GNP respectively. The UK is decidedly stronger in the invisible field than either of these countries. Nevertheless the reader may still boggle a little at the sheer size of the invisible surplus presupposed—£3 300 million, as compared with the £1 000 million of 1968, or £1 300 million of 1969. Where in the world, he might say, will all these earnings come from; it may be very convenient that they cover the putative great visible deficit so generously, but they are larger than today's gross earnings, let alone the balance between earnings and outgoings. What is going to happen to call forth these immense balances?

The question neatly summarises the crux of Britain's trade. One might much more aptly ask where the invisible earnings came from in earlier years. They were equally big then. Nothing special happened then to bring them into being. What it is important to remember is that trade is an expanding circle. It is a continuous flow of sales of goods and services and purchases of goods and services. One side aliments the other. If a country steadily buys more it sells more, and vice versa. The flow of sterling into foreigners' pockets by reason of their sales to the UK provides them with the cash to buy British goods, which become UK sales, or exports. The flow of foreign currency into British traders' pockets gives them the wherewithal to buy foreign products—foreigners' exports and British imports. Thus if trade in any quarter begins to push up—as it would do if the economy were free—it feeds resources into and widens the circle. Moreover, if the natural posture of visible and invisible trade are deficit and surplus respectively, then these two will both grow. As their gross components, imports and exports, grow, so the margin between them, the balance, will grow also. The reciprocal effect is obvious here. If large imports and exports close off to a large deficit balance between them, then so much residual sterling is left in the hands of foreigners. This will enable the large receipts and expenditures on invisibles to close off at a large surplus.

This is what happened over the course of British economic history. No single event magicked into place a large visible deficit and a large invisible surplus. Feeding upon the inherent strengths and needs of the national economy, a structure of trade—visible imports of food and materials, and exports of manufactures, invisible exports of shipping, banking and other services—came into existence, a faithful projection of the geo-economic character of the country.

Thus the projected pattern of receipts and payments is not as surprising as might be thought. It would in fact be rather odd to suppose that the financial and service activities of this country are not, in the 1970s, capable of maintaining the volume of trade that they recorded in 1938, 1913 or 1885. The services sector of the economy, as was seen in Chapter III, has grown faster than the manufacturing side. It in fact provides more than 50 per cent of present-day GNP. It is difficult to imagine a reason why, for example, the British banking and insurance industries, given a healthy opportunity to do so, should not powerfully extend their activities farther into the foreign markets than they are today. The Eurodollar market is the creation of the London banks. If the issue of capital in London were once again free, is there viable reason to suppose that British banking and the London capital market would not earn sums comparable to other times? Unless it is to be assumed that the country's services are smaller and less efficient than in the earlier years of the century, then it is contrary to good sense to assume that their contribution to the balance of payments should be materially smaller than at that time.

Of course, it is often remarked that a number of Britain's major invisible activities in former times—shipping, commodity broking, international bond issues and portfolio investment—are now becoming obsolescent and no longer a fruitful source of incomes. It is to be wondered how much real substance there is in these beliefs. As regards shipping, world trade is now proceeding faster than at any other time in history. World seaborne cargoes are accordingly advancing at a similarly unprecedented pace. Whereas, however, the volume of world trade[67] grew $4\frac{1}{4}$ times between 1937/38 and 1970, the volume of British exports grew only 3 times.

These figures tell a story for British shipping. There are many complicated factors involved. Here is, nevertheless, one that is basic. Most national shipping industries rely firstly on a healthy home market—and this means a high level of cargoes moving into and out of British ports. This has not occurred. British shipping has been handicapped to that extent. But there is enough shipping demand in the world at large, as can be seen, for a British shipping industry that was properly supported to make substantial revenues still. As regards merchanting and commodity broking it seems over-facile despite the rise in corporate purchases of raw material of inter-Governmental arrangements, and of direct marketing by exporters to assume that merchant and broking functions are out of date. Activity in other centres of the world does not suggest this. There is always scope, and a need, for a free market, and for a price determinant. As to inter-Governmental agreements, this seems an example of the official intrusion into commercial affairs that could best be reduced. Finally, the Eurobond market, the New Zealand government loan, the Swiss bank advance to the U.K. government, not to speak of the surge of portfolio investment into Australia, certainly do not suggest that this form of capital raising is on its last legs. Here again, Government measures rather than the declining pull of the market appears to have done most of the work of diminution. Moreover, other fields of invisible revenue have emerged to complement those which are in relative decline, for whatever reason. The whole range of contracting, consulting and professional work overseas has steadily mounted. Airlines, besides shipping companies, are now foreign exchange earners. British hotels, railways and restaurants are contributing to an unprecedented and substantial net income on tourism—one of the new industries of the late twentieth century. Alongside portfolio investment, direct investment has grown like a mammoth.

All in all, then, the kind of trade dimensions shown on page 148 seem not at all unreal. This is the level of the current balance which this country might be expected to be in, after a period of uninterrupted development. It stands to reason that, with current surpluses around the £1 500 million mark, the problem of Government net outgoings on a scale of £4–500 million would be quickly solved. These charges would be paid out of the surplus with the greatest ease. What would happen would of course be that the private sector, after making its overall net return on trade, would pass on a portion for Government use, before applying the rest to investment. The process would be the same as was described in Chapter X for the home economy. In fact it is basically the same process. The nation would save a little less for investment abroad, as it does at home, but these would be funds well spared.

Of course, this state of affairs would not come about in a moment. The kind of import/export balance on goods and services of past years that has been taken as a model was the product of decades, if not centuries, of organic and natural growth. The basic pattern is still there, but to recover the inherent strength and volume that was steadily lost over the years from 1930, and most particularly from 1945 onwards, will not be the work of a few months.

To visualise the process in practice: if the economy were released to expand naturally tomorrow, what would be the effect? To begin with, the visible import bill would not shoot through the ceiling, as is so often dourly predicted. Britain is not more given to inflation than other countries; she is not therefore afflicted with higher prices, and vulnerable to unseen floods of imports waiting only for an opportunity to get in. Moreover, it will take some years before this under-nourished and half-speed economy can generate the activity necessary to draw in the £9 000 million of imports envisaged on page 147. There are thus no grounds of substance on which to presuppose a sudden and great uprush of merchandise imports into this country. On the other hand, imports would certainly begin to rise, and exports would rise with them.

The exact rhythm and scale of this movement is difficult to foretell. It is most important to bear in mind that never in the modern British economy has there been a development of imports and exports along natural lines, unhindered and uninfluenced by outside or artificial agencies. The years between the two wars were economically still-born. Ever since 1945 the Government has waited, like an excited terrier, ready to pounce on imports as soon as they moved. We have therefore had in the postwar period some very jerky starts and stops. Trade has repeatedly risen, then been heavily sat on. Investment, consumption and trade propensities have then simmered until released, when they have boiled over. The consequences have been oscillations sharper than nature undisturbed would ever permit. A survey of the year-to-year change over the last decade may help to form a picture of trade impulses:

	Imports	*Exports*	*% Change over previous year*
*1958	1·2	−4·3	
1959	7·1	4·5	
1960	12·1	4·3	
†1961	−1·0	3·0	
†1962	3·0	2·0	
*1963	3·9	5·8	
†1964	11·2	2·8	
†1965	0·8	4·5	
1966	1·7	4·3	
1967	8·2	−1·4	
1968	10·6	14·3	
1969	2·1	10·3	

* reflation. † deflation.

The above figures all show actual quantities, or volumes, traded.

Two cycles are revealed. A period of downward pressure on the economy was ending in 1958. Reflation went on until the latter part of 1961. Deflation was then put into force until 1963. Reflation was pursued until the end of 1964. Deflation, begun then, became intense in 1966. One preliminary point worth noting is the absolute fall in exports at the end of each deflation; so much for the 'export switch' effect attributed to home-market compression.

Obviously the economy does its best to maintain an even keel despite the forays of government. None the less there is an evident ballooning of imports in the first year or so of each reflation. This is followed by a levelling off. The steadying down (1961 and 1965) can be ascribed certainly in large part to natural momentum rather than to official measures. In the case of 1961 restrictive measures were not brought in until the latter part of the year, and in 1965 the main measure operating, the import surcharge, was, by common consent, of doubtful efficacy. It is also worth noting, in passing, that as deflation was prolonged imports began to rise again.

Exports, as would tend to be the consequence of governmental preoccupation with the level of home demand and imports, were inclined to move on a more even keel, but to rise and fall, none the less, in slightly delayed response to expansion and deflation. The growth of exports tended to catch up with imports, although not quite. Thus in the years 1959–61 the average annual rise of imports was 5·3 per cent: that of exports, 4 per cent. For the period 1963–66 it was about 4·4 per cent for both. On the whole this tends to confirm the view that, if trade were left to itself, imports would first rise quite briskly, then exports would come forward; the two would then rise together, imports slightly faster than exports, until the margin between them had widened to the natural interval suggested on page 147. All in all this suggests that in 1968 figures we could look to an initial rise in imports of around £6–700 million, and of exports by some £200 million—a margin of about £4–500 million.[68] This blip in the figures would be succeeded by a narrowing of the interval, mainly owing to a levelling out of imports. This is of course regardless of price movements which might themselves either widen or reduce this gap. Following this initial ballooning and relapse, we do not know, from experience, what would happen—as has been said; the process at this point has unfailingly been halted by Government intervention. However, it follows from all that has been said earlier that the train of events would then be a natural slow growth on both sides until the large aggregates earlier postulated, and a margin between these of some £1 500 million had been established.

To turn to the invisible side. That there is a good deal of resilience in this account is evident from the way that net earnings sprang up from £708 million in 1963 to £1 300 million in 1969. Chart I in the Appendix shows how the invisible surplus broadly fluctuates in response to the position on visible account. The invisible surplus of 1970 of course fell from its recent peak because the visible deficit declined. But if the deficit remained steady, and in fact grew progressively and moderately, then balance of payments principle, and indeed British history, suggests strongly that the invisible surplus would grow with it. There would of course be a braking effect when the potential of present investment incomes had been exhausted. However, the performance of the past five years suggests that there is plenty of give in the account as yet. We do not know where the block would occur, if indeed in the real sequence of events it did occur. Under proper conditions, the reconstitution of overseas assets might proceed continuously from the start. In any case there is plenty of scope for further expansion of purely service earnings. Since these are, as we know, 40 per cent of the total figures at any time, the target surplus of £3 300 million that has been envisaged would mean that services alone must grow to around £1 500 million. Obviously there is an interaction between service earnings and investment, as has been said, but this is not to say that there is not an unused earning potential to be exploited meanwhile.

Of course, there will be interaction, not only within invisibles, but also across the whole balance of payments account. Visible and invisible earnings are inter-related, as has been seen, as the result of practical circumstances. Manufacturing, trade and investment on the visible side both depend on and create invisible activity and earnings; service ventures open the door to visible trade and investment. They are also, above all, bound together by the bond of common finance. There is thus no danger—outside the spectral visions of Whitehall—that one part of the account will detach itself and loop away out of control. Imports will not speed off into the blue, creating an even more astronomical trade gap. By the same token, invisible earnings will not soar sublimely, creating sudden vast surpluses; this is the contrary point worth remembering. The two sides will move together, as trade components always do.

The above suggests then that it might be right, in the early phases of economic emancipation, to envisage a visible gap of the order of £4–500 million and an invisible surplus around £1 500 million. Assuming no increase in Government expenditure, the position would then be as follows:

	£m
Visible gap	– 500
Government (assuming only £200 million in official interest payments)	– 675
Total	– 1 175
Invisibles	1 500

This suggests a balance of just over £300 million for Government loans and private long-term investment. Not enough, but the balance is viable. As the aggregates increased, the balance would increase also.

This point has special reference to income from overseas investment. This is one of the more important elements of the whole balance of payments. At the moment it is certainly the element which is most in need of attention. In Chapter III it was seen that net investment income of itself provides no less than 60 per cent of the total invisible surplus. This it has done consistently back through the years, at least for a century. In Chapter VI it was seen that this income has been severely curtailed in recent decades owing to the ravages of the two world wars. In 1945, unlike 1919, a political attitude held sway according to which overseas investment was bad.[69] The placing of capital abroad has been discouraged with increasing severity ever since. Some replenishment of capital holdings overseas has, however, gone on. By the end of 1968 the net stock in being amounted to £7 500 million, worth just over £2 000 million in 1939 terms as against the £4 000 million of that year. The loss to the country's incomes and assets represented by this figure must be appreciated. If 1968 overseas investment had stood only at the level achieved in 1939—or 1913 for that matter—it would have been worth in current terms at least £15 000 million, and probably £20 000 million. To find the last time our overseas investment amounted to £2 000 million in the money of 1939 it is necessary to go back to 1890. In short, the investment of British capital abroad has, through the accidents of war and the mistakes of policy, effectively stood still for three-quarters of a century.

Viewed from another angle, the £4 000 million assets of 1939 were equal to twice the GNP of the country at that time. A fund of the same proportion now would be worth the staggering sum of £75 000 million. It is in fact somewhere between this and the earlier figure that the true loss to the country must be placed.

To look at the purely income side, the overseas holdings of 1913 brought in a net income of £200 million, as again was the case in 1939. It was not until the early 1950s that this figure was again achieved, even in the much depreciated currency of that time. Net incomes had by 1968 reached the total of £654 million in current values. This compares with the £800–1 000 million which the 1913 revenues would be worth in present-day money. It ought to be pointed out, in parenthesis, that comparison of the pre-war and present figures shows that investment today is yielding much higher incomes in proportion to the assets. In other words it is much more profitable. All the more deplorable, then, is the policy which has been followed in its regard.

Comparing incomes, again, with GNP, these were equivalent to 8–10 per cent of the latter in 1938 and 1913, and to a mere 1·8 per cent of GNP in 1968. If the previous rates had been maintained in these terms, we should now be gathering in nearly £3 000 million annually from overseas.

So, over time, one of the most precious elements in the nation's economic armoury lapsed away. It is important to remember that overseas investment did not fall of its own accord. The fund of overseas assets grew into to a powerful and faultlessly running machine before 1913, imparting benefits both to capital providers at home and to the countries in which it was used. What crippled it was a series of events quite unrelated to questions of economic efficiency; the biological accident of two wars and the political hazards of sectarian thought.

In the broad perspective of the British balance of payments, as we can see it now, overseas capital and the returns it provides, stand out as a vital element. It was the impairment of this, when combined with newborn official expenditure overseas, that in fact caused the balance of payments difficulties in which we have been embroiled for this last quarter century. The harm done by successive postwar governments in not recognising this fact, in not doing their utmost to regenerate our overseas wealth—in pertinaciously obstructing, in fact, the new outlow of capital—is manifest. All the more ironic is the present claim, that the country cannot export more capital because the balance of payments is not strong enough to permit it.

We shall therefore have to await the reconstitution of overseas assets before the balance of payments can regain its former vigour. A supplementary point here is important. Besides its intrinsic income merits, it is clear that overseas investment is central to earnings in the invisible account as a whole. This is the significance of the steady percentage of 60 per cent which, as has been noted, it has occupied in the total invisible surplus, in good times as in bad. If with large as with small invisible earnings, investment income always maintains the same proportion, then, obviously it is taking the invisible account up and down with it. The relationship is in any case quite natural. There is no greater magnet for a country's shipping, financial and other services than companies owned or in shared control overseas. The string of British banks, insurance offices, marine companies and others that followed British investment across the world, and the banks legal offices, accountants, consultants and public relations advisers that have followed the latterday American investment into Europe, South America and elsewhere are proof enough of this.

Through the medium of investment, the invisible account is linked with the visible account and with the home economy. A major and growing segment of overseas investment is now in the form of so-called 'direct' investment, that is, the establishment by British companies of manufacturing and distribution subsidiaries in other countries. This is only part of a world trend, exemplified in particular by the Americans. The present-day internationalisation of markets and of technology are clearly such that many modern industries cannot survive in competition unless they match the international operations of the foremost companies. However, to invest in foreign subsidiaries again demands a healthy and expanding home economy; a fertile domestic soil from which these international growths can spring.

Another requisite for growth will be the restraint of public expenditure. It has been shown in Chapter XI that the claims of the State throttle the balanced expansion of the private economy. The balance of payments is merely one outflung arm of this economy. It will grow and remain healthy, only as the main body grows and achieves sound proportions. It is of course true that the major growth of public expenditure has occurred only in very recent times. Between 1964 and 1969, total expenditure by the public sector, including transfers, interest charges and the like, rose from £12 793 million to £19 122 million.[70] In these five short years, public outgoings multiplied themselves by more than half as much again. This is phenomenal and unsustainable. It was clearly linked with the political flavour of the time.

There is one very large corollary to the whole of the projection given above. This is that the entire development of the economy and its related trade and investment flows will be dependent on the maintenance of confidence in sterling. The task of restoring Britain's trade balance, as was seen in Chapter VIII, is twofold—each part being of equivalent importance to the other. The Government must on the one hand pursue the right economic and trade policies; on the other it must ensure the appropriate psychological environment in which this can take place. In short the Government must seek and attain in equal measure, economic expansion and the stabilisation of the sterling balances. If, failing this, foreign short-term creditors are allowed to remain in a frame of mind such that they will precipitately withdraw their holdings as soon as they see UK imports rise, then the whole venture will be abortive. It will be impossible ever to set the economy and its trade into progressive expansion and increasing profitability. A full, properly thought-out exercise in public education should be mounted. The Government will have to mobilise all the means at its disposal to generate the proper climate of opinion in which our balance of payments reform can run its course. British embassies abroad, the British Council, the Central Office of Information, the BBC, should be fully briefed on the true position of the balance of payments, and the policies being followed by the Government in its regard. Similar information should be made available to British delegations to international economic organisations—the United Nations, the OECD, GATT, EFTA and the European Community. There should be a concerted official effort overseas, not, as in the past, to offer apologia for Britain's performance and to promise better things, but positively to set out this country's viable standing in trade, and to create confidence in our money.

XV The Cure and Other Solutions

So much for the general line of policy which might be followed. Now for contingency planning.

The possibility has already been envisaged of periodic fluctuations that might throw up deficits of varying degrees, and of an initial boom in imports that would have to be ridden out. Provided confidence is maintained these should, with some official borrowing where necessary, be weathered reasonably smoothly. But it is also necessary to take account of the chances of a sustained imbalance, say over five years. Suppose that, for whatever reason now unknown, the visible balance goes much further into deficit than has been postulated. Suppose the weakened state of investment income delays the growth of the invisible surplus for longer than has been anticipated; or that long-term capital outlays, once free of controls, race up much faster than expected, so causing an interim deficit on current and capital account combined?

It will first of all be necessary to keep a firm hold on the priorities. The country's ultimate advantage lies only in an expanded balance of payments comprising both deficits and surpluses in their proper areas. No benefits will be achieved by switching to other aims, should intervening difficulties be encountered. The basic endeavour should not therefore be abandoned. If problems arise, the Government must have other recourses.

It will be wise to consider at all times whether the best recourse will not still be to do nothing. Provided the sterling balances can be held stable, it is not clear what permanent harm might accrue from a sustained run of, say, five years of deficits. Such annual deficits would be in the hundreds of millions, and even a five-year series would produce a total only of say £1 000 million, which, given the size of overall surplus intended, could be quickly paid back. If of course the sterling balances collapse, then the debt will be thousands of millions within months.

Consideration of the circumstances that would apply suggest few real grounds for presuming that short-term confidence would weaken unless wholly mismanaged. Foreign depositors at present withdraw from sterling because they believe the British economy to be uncompetitive and susceptible to devaluation in the near future. But what would be the position if they were faced with a British Government stating firmly that the economy was sound, and indeed growing healthily; that the visible deficit was normal and undeserving of drama; that the country's commercial exchanges were wholly in surplus; and that the UK was in deficit simply because the nation was spending a great deal of money on international aid and defence. Foreign depositors might well think the British were being over-generous; and that some drastic measure was in the offing. But would they suppose this would automatically take the form of devaluation? They would, presumably, much more assume that Britain would withdraw from this international role, or that other countries would be impelled to volunteer a share in the burden Britain was carrying. None would in short suppose that the British economy was in fundamental imbalance.

The foreign creditors' likely line of reasoning regarding official expenditure, however, requires thought. Were there ever a situation of ineradicable balance of payments deficit, then, as has already been remarked, official expenditures abroad would be the first candidate for removal. In any case, these outgoings would require careful surveillance during the period of balance of payments reform. Until the external private account had grown to comfortable size, it would be foolish to allow Government commitments overseas to grow in arbitrary fashion. But it remains true that if a saving somewhere in the balance of payments became imperative, then the field of official overseas commitments is the most logical place to turn. The underlying object of this expenditure, as was suggested in Chapter IX, is to retain a national voice in international political and strategic events. There is clearly a point at which, in conditions of continuing overall payments deficit, these costs become counter-productive. If a military presence is maintained at key points abroad, but at the cost of the apparent insolvency of the metropolitan territory, then it is doubtful whether the national influence gained by the first is greater than that lost by the second. Certainly where these conditions have applied in recent years, the result seems to have been a net loss of British prestige.

Total withdrawal would be one solution. Another would be to approach other nations, or to be approached by them, on the basis that Britain might certainly provide the services, but that these should be financed in common. The last-named, is, given the desire for national influence, a *pis aller*, and not really likely to attract the British Government's lasting interest. Obviously the political purpose of such expenditures would be lost if they were financed by a consortium of nations. Britain could not then say to the United States that she and the latter alone were maintaining the peace in wide areas of the world and that, as a consequence, world policy-making should also be shared. Is the reluctance of successive British governments to discuss freely the part that official expenditures play in the balance of payments deficit, due to a faint suspicion that such would be the logical outcome?

If a number, for instance, of European nations were contributing to the cost of forces overseas, they would then claim a voice in the deployment and use of these forces and Britain would no longer be free to order these matters in accordance with her own political needs. The foregoing boldly outlines a highly subtle position, and one that is of moment to the nation as a whole. The benefits the Government is seeking for the nation at large are real, in a disunited world. Consequently, it is much more the Government's instinct to dismiss the notion that there is something special about the overseas payments; to roll them up in the whole balance of payments package and to say that Britain must pay her own way. Similarly, it suits other governments' books to leave it that Britain must 'put her house in order' and not to embroider the theory that Britain's balance of payments problem is also their own. In the short term, no government is looking for extra financial commitments. This point will be taken up again.

Finally, it should not be forgotten that a healthier home economy and a properly balanced external payments position will themselves relieve pressure on the British burden of official payments. Thus in 1964 and 1965 the Government decided, in accordance with the Byzantine convolutions of standard balance of payments reasoning that the UK could not afford to develop the home-produced TSR 2 and other military aircraft. Earlier governments, in their wisdom, had made similar, if less sweeping, decisions. Hence the purchase from the Americans of the F111 and other machines, at a foreign exchange cost of £310 million over the period 1964–70.[71] Similarly, past mismanagements of the balance of payments, and the official debts arising out of this, had left the Government with interest charges to pay abroad. The total shown for this item in the balance of payments accounts was £329 million in 1969.[72]

What else could the British Government do that would not interfere with the basic policy of letting the economy expand into normal shape? One self-evident candidate is the use of import quotas. By this term is meant the physical restriction of imported goods; the decree by regulation that only so many tons, or pounds worth of such and such an article may be brought in. The whole arrangement is worked by a system of licences. Obviously this aids the balance of payments, since it cuts down one part of the outflow. Objections to this device are that it reduces the spur of competition on British industry, deprives foreign suppliers of the means to acquire British exports, and starves British industry of the material for production and exports. However, one can fairly easily construct a list of goods that, if restricted, would not unduly offend in this way. A range of luxuries, such as food delicacies—avocado pears, oysters, some wine and the like—tropical hardwoods for furniture-making, jewellery, cosmetics—some manufactured goods, such as a proportion of steel, chemical and car imports, naturally come to mind for study. Many of these are personal luxuries; the individual consumer would be deprived. The Government might feel this would provoke unpopularity. On the other hand, it has been the constant complaint of the individual citizen, when being berated by governments for balance of payments shortcomings, that he is not told exactly how he can help. Here would be his answer. By this method, perhaps £2–300 million a year could be saved.

The advantage of import quotas is that they achieve the same reduction in the import bill as is sought by the huge and elaborate programmes of home market recession, credit restriction and so forth that are part of deflation. They are also mathematically accurate. One knows exactly how much will come off the import bill. They are, above all, legal. It is not commonly appreciated that import surcharges, import deposits, duty increases are instituted in breach of our international pledges. The same international treaties specifically require that a country needing to 'safeguard its external financial position and its balance of payments' must use import quotas and no other expedient.

There are a number of disadvantages. Broadly speaking, the device can be used only for a limited period. Five years might be considered the outside (notwithstanding the import quotas on coal which the UK herself has had in force continuously for twenty years). Five years, in any case, is about the period over which difficulties have been foreseen above. In general, moreover, contractions of trade are uncomfortable things. Import quotas would show Britain in a dependent light—though not so much, some might say, as continuous and weakening deflation. All in all, most people do not like the retrograde aura of import restrictions. Still, the expedient is there, and it would certainly do a useful job in its context. It should not be excluded from the armoury of reserve weapons.

At this point one must broach the three alleviations most in international discussion at the moment: an increase in reserves, the funding of the sterling balances and the floating of exchange rates.

By 'reserves' is meant the stock of gold and foreign currency which each government keeps in order to carry the country through periodic deficits in its overall payments. Thus, if a country has £1 000 million of reserves, as the UK has, for instance, then in theory it could run a £200 million deficit for five years before becoming insolvent. If the world's total stock of reserves were higher, so runs the argument, then we could all run larger deficits for longer and, although nobody would be relieved of the duty to keep in long-term solvency, we would all have more elbow room to work with. In support of the notion that the world needs more reserves—or more 'international liquidity' as it is put—reference is often made to the frequency of deficits and international loan operations, and the ratio of reserves to international trade. Both of these, however, appear to be misnomers.

To take the last point first. It is said that total world reserves,[73] which stand around \$80 000 million, are not an adequate backing for world trade,[74] standing at some \$300 000 million. This proposition seems to be wrong on two scores. Firstly, one would have thought that a ratio of 80 : 300, or 27 per cent, is, on the contrary, quite good. Moreover, the extremely fast rate of world trade growth, noted in the previous chapter, does not suggest any impediment on the part of reserves. Secondly, the figure against which reserves should be contrasted is not really the total of world visible trade, but the aggregate of national deficits at one particular time. This is what reserves are intended to cover. Here the fallacy of considering only merchandise deficits has intervened again. It has been stated that, with Germany running great surpluses of £1 500–2 000 million and the UK running deficits of up to £500 million, the international payments system is subjected to intolerable strain and cannot run without larger reserves. But the real surpluses and deficits to be evened out by the reserves are those arising when all the accounts—visible, invisible, government and long-term capital—have been closed off. Anyone today offering a prize for the best guess as to the average annual result for Germany in the years 1960–69 would probably not lose much money. It is £ – 130 million.[75] Britain, as has been seen, despite her visible deficits and the disastrous policies of the period, has run roughly to balance in the post-war years.

But, even then, the real point lies elsewhere. It is not balance of payments deficits at all that make the true demands on reserves. The true pressure, as has been so clearly seen, is from the movement of short-term funds. These, with their plus and minus effects of thousands of millions over a few weeks, exert the strains which exhaust reserves and threaten insolvency. But what level of reserves will ward off a threat of this magnitude? If an outflow of short-term funds at its habitual rate of, say, £1 000 million a month is to be contained by national reserves, these would have to be

£12 000 million for each major country—perhaps £120 000 million for the world, or $288 000 million—an absurdly huge sum. A yet further point; this short-term capital, the movement of which is the real cause of disarray, itself partly makes up the reserves. Of the total sterling balances of £5 000 million, some £2 000 million are other government's monetary reserves.[76] The world's reserves therefore do not so much iron out international monetary problems as contribute to them; and to increase reserves would be in large degree to increase the problem.

Greater reserves, in general, are obviously worth having; SDR's in particular are most useful. But the cure for international monetary turbulence will lie not in this area. It will be in the consolidation of confidence in national currencies and in the proper management of the international short-term capital market.

Similarly the notion of 'funding the sterling balances' seems to rest on a partial view of the processes at work. Short-term capital funds when in London are called 'sterling balances', because this is simply the proper banking term. The funds come in through the banking system and are measured off against the funds due to British banks from abroad: hence the word 'balances'. They are also known as 'liabilities' as compared with 'claims' because these are also the proper banking terms. The use of this nomenclature in general discussion has given rise to false impressions. The bankers' term 'liabilities' has been taken to mean 'debts', and 'debts' in the sense of something the nation owes because it has bought more than it has sold. Nothing could be farther from the truth. These funds are 'liabilities' in the balance-sheet sense that they are money held by the banks for clients. If the equally appropriate bankers' terms 'deposits' or 'holdings' had been commonly used, the nature of the funds would have been clear. In practice they are just as much imported capital as any other. If the money—as indeed some short-term money is—is brought in and used to buy shares on the Stock Exchange, then it is instantly defined as investment capital, and recorded as 'long-term investment' in the balance of payment accounts. For these reasons, the recurrent talk about 'funding the sterling balances', i.e. converting them into a lump sum debt to be paid off in instalments, is wide of the mark.

It would be wrong to regard sterling balances as 'hot money', still less as unpaid wartime debts or as the liquid equivalents of our current and capital deficits—to name two common descriptions that have also been applied to it. Chapter VII has shown that the speculative element is very small. During the war sterling balances certainly rose, since it was convenient for Britain to repay, for instance, the Egyptian Government for the cost of accommodating British troops, by crediting that Government's account in London; accounts such as this are what the sterling balances contain. But these debts were paid off in the decade after the war. They were, in fact, only a temporary constituent of the balances. There were sterling balances before the war,[77] worth in today's currency as much as £2 000 to £3 000 million, comparing with present-day levels of £5 000 to £5 500 million. Clearly, also, the sterling balances are not the counterpart of annual balance of payments deficits, as the analysis in Chapter VII, and indeed the mathematics of the two demonstrate.

These funds, viewed as an international entity, are the total world's stock of ready cash, or 'bankable' cash, i.e. cash that may be called upon for current purposes at any time, and that is meanwhile held in readily accessible forms.

They are, by the same token, not likely to disappear of their own accord; far from it, they are likely to grow. It is perhaps no coincidence that the holding of balances in sterling, or francs or dollars for that matter, came into general practice in the 1930s, for it was at that time that the world as a whole abandoned the gold standard. The holding of reserves in 'paper', i.e. in national currencies, rather than in gold, and particularly in investable interest-bearing paper, was therefore bound to grow. Short-term holdings must continue to grow. With the increase in trade and international transactions, companies and governments will need to hold ever-increasing reserves. In the period since 1945, the particular kind of company that needs international working balances—the so-called international corporation—has grown apace and will continue to grow. There is a great mass of short-term capital in the world.

This is an expanding banking field. The funds will find a home somewhere; there is no great case to be made against taking them into the UK. True, if mishandled, they can cause great harm, as we have good reason to know. The continued expansion in these monetary flows, incidentally helps to explain why balance of payments crises have got progressively more severe—as economic commentators have frequently remarked, and from this deduced that the UK has got progressively more inefficient. In fact of course the short-term capital flows induced by lost confidence have been greater, and the strain on the parity and consequent degree of foreign borrowing needed, greater also. But if short-term capital comes to London, and stays there, benefits accrue to the UK. They can be used, in the same way as bankers' deposits are used. There is no call for this capital to be unstable, apart from British policy mismanagement. To say, as is said, that the funds are too volatile and therefore unwelcome, is to put oneself in the position of a banker saying that clients cannot be trusted to keep their money with him and that therefore he will not take deposits.

A stable balance of sterling holdings would necessarily grow, since as has been seen, the world supply of short-term capital is expanding. A steady rise in sterling balances would much facilitate the task of opening up the current account into larger dimensions. In the course of this process, large fluctuations in the size of the overall surplus or deficit could occur. Incoming short-term capital—a plus item in the balance of payments, of course—would help to soak up deficits of this sort. More than this, sterling balances that were fully stable would powerfully sustain the long-term capital outflow that is so urgently needed. In other words, as money flowed into the sterling balances, for lodging in bank deposits, Treasury bills and so on, sterling could flow out to finance the building of factories and offices and produce permanent income for the future. The notion of this counter-flow is often dismissed as contrary to the adage that one should not 'borrow short and lend long'. It is difficult to see where this principle arises. Banks in fact take in deposits withdrawable either at sight or at a few weeks' notice, and yet they lend up to five years or more. The principle banks in fact work on, of course, is that although any individual deposit they hold is of very short term, the combined total is at any one time very large and very stable. This is the principle that should apply to the sterling balances.

Floating the exchange rates is a beguiling suggestion that makes a particular appeal to intelligent minds. Not only is it very attractive in theory, but it seems to carry with it a promise of automatically correct operation in practice. Proponents of this device argue that the central problem in international currency matters is that, on the one hand, short-term capital rockets to and fro among currencies expected to be devalued or revalued, and on the other, countries run huge deficits or surpluses because their prices are too high or too low in relation to the world average; the countries in question should devalue, or revalue, but as parities are a prestige symbol they prefer to distort the whole shape of their economies to achieve the same adjustment in prices. Now, say the floaters, if there were no fixed parities, if in other words the exchange rate of currencies were left to find their levels *vis-à-vis* each other according to the demand for each, then all these problems would be removed at one stroke. Firstly, there would be no more surging of short-term money to and fro, since there would be no more devaluations and revaluations. Secondly, the adjustment of national prices to world levels would occur automatically, since a country importing too much would throw up a greater demand for foreign currencies in relation to its own; by the laws of the market place the value of its own currency would fall in relation to that of the others; if the national money was low compared with foreign currencies an importer would have to provide more of his own currency to buy imports, and an exporter would get more of his own currency back for his exports. The discrepancy in prices would have been corrected. Imports would be discouraged and exports fostered, and the country's balance of payments would be righted.

All this is true, and there would be an attractive automaticity in the mechanism as set out. Perhaps this system would work, and provide a stable background for international monetary affairs. But the more the proposal is inspected in detail, the more doubts arise. Firstly, the mechanism relies on the effect on exchange rates, of inward and outward flows of payments on transactions. The implication is that these flows are reasonably big, and it seems certain that the sponsors of the proposal are looking particularly at the big imbalances in visible trade. But, as we have just seen, the actual balances that remain when all national accounts have been closed off are really very small. The actual technical pressure brought to bear, accordingly, on the exchange rates would be very small and the exchange rate variations that resulted would be very small also. We should all end up, therefore, much as before, with our balance of payments patterns of surpluses and deficits much as they are now.

None the less, floating the rates would deal a shrewd enough knock at the volatility of short-term capital flows. There is no doubt of the fact that if the DM could never, from one day to another, be uprated by 9 per cent, or if the pound could never lose 14 per cent of its value by ministerial fiat on one day in the year, the compulsive movements of thousands of millions in the space of weeks would be no more. On the other hand, if the customary conclusions were drawn from the existence of visible deficits and surpluses in various countries, would there not be a slow drain from the 'weak' to the 'strong' countries on the general grounds that the currency rate of the former will fall? The movement of funds in themselves will then accentuate this presumptive fall. The floating school then says, reasonably enough, that the relative fall in the particular country's export prices will pull its trade into surplus. But if the movement of short-term capital is prompted by the existence or otherwise of visible deficits then its effect, applied through the exchange rates, will be towards pushing every country in the world into a visible surplus—a manifestly impossible task. The risks are clearly worse if short-term capital movements flow, a little more sophisticatedly, according to overall imbalances, but where they set in against countries, like the UK, with commercial surpluses but an offsetting Government deficit. The alteration in relative price levels brought about might force visible imports down and visible exports up, and so precipitate that basic distortion of the British economy that the whole of the foregoing suggests should be avoided. It could easily lead to a greater and greater switch of the British economy into high Government expenditure overseas, high exports and low imports, low consumption and low GNP at home. On the other hand, of course, it might facilitate a high growth of invisible earnings and so lead to the outcome envisaged here. All in all, balancing all the preceding points one with the other, there is probably not much reason to suppose that floating rates would do a great deal either of harm, or of good. The prime consideration is that the technical pressures the system is intended to reflect are much smaller than supposed. This reinforces the point that the short-term balances must in the first place be brought into a stable state. Without smooth short-term monetary flows, no international parity system will work; with smooth monetary flows probably any will do so.

However, a somewhat deeper issue needs to be considered. It is not altogether out of regional xenophobia that, for instance, the Community authorities have set their faces sternly against any departure from fixed parities. Of course, they would have endless difficulties managing their intra-Community agricultural prices if the parities were constantly changing. But more is involved than that. The Community aspires to a common currency. The first step to this must unquestionably be a cessation of fluctuations between the existing parities. The currencies must be locked together as one, by means of unchanging exchange rates, after which the mechanics, at least, of substituting a common unit are relatively simple.

Behind this there lies a fundamental point. The 'floaters' assert that abandoning fixed parities really means going back to the natural interrelationship of currencies that existed before governments had made their national parity an emblem of their sovereignty. But before the IMF prescribed fixed rates, there was the international rate scramble of the 1930s. It is certainly not this that the floating school is evoking. Before that, there was gold. This was a stable currency era, without doubt. But was this the free value fluctuation that has been advocated? This was more, if the circumstances are looked at closely, the movement of money in a single form—gold—and the regulation of trade by the simple availability of that money. True, there were variations in national exchange rates, and there was the theory of price rises and declines in exporting and importing countries respectively. But exchange rates varied only between the 'gold points', i.e. between the limits beyond which it was simpler to move gold itself. In other words, a country's trade moved either so far into surplus that it had too much gold, and had therefore to buy other countries' exports and so reduce its surplus; or so far into deficit that other countries had much of its gold and had to buy from it. Similarly, the price effect undoubtedly played a part, but it is to be wondered how central this was. A country, according to the theory, found itself, after over-exporting, in possession of a surfeit of gold. The latter then percolated into the currency, causing inflation, high prices, and a fall in exports.

The reverse happened to a country importing an excess. Undoubtedly these effects did take place, but one can only doubt whether they were very extensive. Obviously the influx or efflux of gold would have been a function not of total trade, but merely of the balance between imports and exports; it was only in order to settle this that gold moved. Now, as the earlier figures have shown, this balance was a very small quantity measured against the main aggregates of the country concerned. In the case of the UK, it was somewhere between 0 and 5 per cent of the GNP, and about an equivalent proportion of the total money supply. This would not have exerted much leverage. There seems little doubt that the regulator of trade was the actual supply of money, in the form of gold, as between countries —which is really the only rational system to operate.

The same is true of the fixed parity system as it exists today. Exchange rates vary marginally between their parity points. The influx of foreign exchange into a surplus country tends to inflate the national currency; but the real sanction of the surplus or deficit trader is the simple exhaustion or surfeit of the means to pay—money—in the form of foreign exchange. This seems, all in all, the best procedure to follow in the future. It is better that trade should be determined by ability to pay, rather than by a refiguration of prices. If we want an eventual world currency, it is certainly the method to preserve.

None of the three expedients examined above offers the hope of much assistance if the UK should find herself in sustained balance of payments trouble. We are left, then, with the general prescription to grit one's teeth and see it through until the eventual surplus is attained, but in no case to revert to old habits and to dismast the economy in the interests of a few hundred million in the external account. In short, the country must either break its way through to higher output and higher surpluses, or something other than the economy must be sacrificed. In face of such a principle, there is really no choice. If the alternative is between prolonged economic shrinkage, and the political advantages of official spending abroad, then on any evaluation the latter must go. With a respite to re-deploy economic forces at home, the UK could return to the international arena and resume its duties; but the reverse could not take place. The case of Germany in the 1960s is a clear example of this. But with good management and good fortune, it should never come to this.

At this juncture, as at so many others, the implications of joining the Common Market have a bearing. The British public, including particularly its business and financial sectors, have shown only lukewarm enthusiasm for this venture since it was revived towards the end of 1969. Small wonder. The roseate image of a new dispensation in Europe, of a new political union, intelligently co-operating as a continental body, to which we were so eager to become attached in 1961, quickly faded. The Six showed themselves in short order to be broadly incapable of common effort, still less of political unity. For the best part of a decade they were led by the nose by an aged autocrat in Paris, and a team of hugely articulate casuists from the Quai d'Orsay; no one in the Community had apparently either the will or the ability to curb the transparently murderous onslaughts that were being made on their organisation. They advanced nowhere in their common policies except in the one—agriculture—that outrageously favoured France. And their progress towards the simple goal of free trade was in the event slower than that of EFTA. Finally, *comble de tout*, they let it be known that they were fearful of Britain's real ability to co-operate in a political Community.

Be that as it may, the ideal remains good, and one to be achieved, even if it means joining the Community and bringing it about through our own major efforts. Now, it has been said, rightly, that the essential purpose of the Community is political in that it provides, or is certainly intended to provide, a means whereby the countries of Europe can achieve an equal say in a world of continental powers about the fate of the civilisation of which they are so much a part. But this is precisely the motive for which Britain is now disbursing such large and problematical sums on aid and military defence overseas. The emergence of an effective Community—including Britain—would inevitably require the UK to consider whether her individual efforts had become supererogatory. Moreover, an effective Community would be one which will presumably be ready, in the shorter rather than the longer term, to assume its due share of world police and resuscitation activities. The burden of official expenditure, and with it the core of our balance of payments problem, might well be lifted as an early consequence of adhesion to the Community. It might well be said that the UK on adherence will merely exchange one form of balance of payments deficit for another. One is bound to recognise that admission to the Community, and to a desirable balance of payments situation, will not be free. There will be the well-publicised short-term costs of membership themselves, which are expected to be in the neighbourhood of £500 million a year. Nevertheless, the position in the medium-term future, if not earlier, is by no means so pessimistic.

A cursory analysis will suffice to show that these costs are concentrated in the Community's agricultural policy and its effects. They consist, in fact, of the contributions that will have to be paid across the exchanges by the UK for the support of the agricultural policy. The contributions are wanted because of the extraordinarily high prices for agricultural produce within the Common Market which the members have to support. The balance of payments cost of these contributions is compounded by the higher prices Britain will have to pay, for the same reason, for such agricultural products which she buys from other Common Market countries. These high prices derive from the Community countries' dedication to the unconditional welfare of their farmers and to the notion of agricultural self-sufficiency for the Six as a whole. It is self-evident that these aims are unreal. Self-sufficiency for the minute European countries in a world encompassing the vast wheatlands and pastures of America, Russia, Canada, the Argentine and Australasia, is an economic nonsense, as was clearly recognised long ago in Britain's history. The accompanying immobilisation of much needed human resources in unproductive labour on farmlands is equally a diseconomy that cannot persist. If the Community is to exploit its own potential to the full, then it will have to abandon protective farm policies that relate more to past centuries than to this. The Government of the Six have heard this often enough from their own Commission; they have reached the stage of giving lip service themselves to the principle. When they move to the stage of action the problem of high agricultural prices, and with it the high cost of membership for this country, will recede.

Thus, it may well be that the Community will furnish a viable alternative to the international expenditures which the British Government now finds it necessary to incur in the national interest. In balance of payments matters, as in so much else, all roads seem to lead eventually to the Community.

XVI Much Ado

One of the purposes of the present book is to assist in banishing for ever the balance of payments from the arena of serious economic concern. If the foregoing has attempted anything, it has tried to prove that the British balance of payments is not a reasonable cause for national anxiety. It has sought to show this by reference to the real structure of the balance of payments, the real position of the UK in the world at large, and the real dangers outside the balance of payments which press on sterling. But the balance of payments is an inconsiderable subject also in terms of pure size.

The whole turnover of the UK's external transactions, public and private, current and long-term, is some £23 000 million. This includes all imports and all exports of goods and services: all Government expenditure and receipts: all ouflows and inflows of capital including Government loans. The overall deficit we are worried about averaged just short of £400 million in the period 1964–68—and these were bad years, as we know too well. The percentage of our nation's external turnover that gave us recurrent economic vapours is therefore 1·7 per cent—or about one-sixtieth. To put this in another way: in each year about £11 300 million worth of trade and investment flowed into this country, and about £11 700 million flowed out, and it is on the tiny residual between these that anxiety centres.

Turning to the core of the anxiety, the position on merchandise trade, the average volume of total trade in the five years was £10 500 million annually. The average deficit, even in those five tense years, was £350 million, or 3·3 per cent. In other words, again, each year we exported about £5 075 million and imported about £5 425 million of goods and it is about the difference between these that we are concerned.

Lastly, we should look at these quantities in terms of our overall national activity, in terms of GNP. The average GNP in the period 1964–68 was £33 000 million.[78] In contrast to this, the figure we are worrying about is, as noted, £350 million. It can immediately be seen that in relation to GNP the trade deficit is not just a small sum; it is so minute as to be almost imperceptible. It is almost exactly a one-hundredth part of the GNP.

This book has given a number of economic reasons why we should not consider our balance of payments situation a serious one. We now have, cast over the scene, a whole new doubt based simply on the pure size of the matter.

It really is straining credulity to claim that this minute sum represents a significant failing on the part of the economy. Can we really say in all seriousness that a fractional difference between imports and exports accounting for about one-hundredth of the annual turnover of the country is a symptom of desperate imbalance in the economy, which must be corrected at all costs? Yet this is precisely the conclusion drawn by post-war governments. Even more extraordinary, it is the pretext upon which enormous and prolonged strictures are placed upon the normal working of the economy, and massive efforts are made to divert it on to another course. There is only one rational conclusion that can in fact be drawn from a figure of this minuscule nature: that it is of no material significance for the economic performance of the country.

It is bad enough to see an economy of the size of Britain's being subjected to contortions for this purpose. It is far worse to see an economy on the scale of that of the United States, whom we seem to have infected with the same passion for minutiae, being made to stagger under similar inflictions for an even smaller crumb of statistics. The GNP of the United States of America[79] now amounts to a figure resembling the distances quoted to faraway planets. In 1970 it is believed to have just topped the billion dollar mark, that is to say, a million million $. The American balance of payments deficit in 1969 was about seven thousand million dollars.[80] Accordingly this deficit is seven-thousandths of the US gross national product. In order to adjust this minuscule margin the whole of that mighty economic machine was, literally, brought to a standstill. A squeeze on the monetary supply and other measures against 'overheating' were instituted in 1969. Under the official definition, a recession is considered to be in progress in America when the GNP per cent fails to grow for two quarters in succession. In early 1970 a recession was declared.

There is another implication in the midget dimensions of our balance of payments figures. This is that they are so small as to be, in fact, within the margin of statistical error. When numerical data is being collected, there is an inevitable twilight zone of possible error in the figure assembled. Ambiguities of definition, misunderstandings and sheer mistakes mean that the totals shown cannot be perfectly accurate, but will vary round an approximate figure. The Central Statistical Office, in issuing the official balance of payments statement each year, sets out what these margins of error are. For the total of visible and invisible exports and imports combined (Government included), they are up to 10 per cent either way: thus in the devaluation year 1967 the position as recorded was the following:

Imports	*Exports*	*Balance*
8 564	8 242	−322

But, given the margins of error,[81] this could equally well have been:

Imports	*Exports*	*Balance*
9 420	7 418	−2 002

or, equally well, at the other extreme:

Imports	*Exports*	*Balance*
7 706	9 066	+1 360

In short, in statistical terms the deficit of 1967 may never have existed.

When the theme under treatment is for practical purposes exhausted, there arises simply out of a view of the numbers involved a further remarkable demonstration of the mythology to which this subject has been prey.

Needless to say, the forces which have been earlier identified as actually imperilling the external account, that is, the flows of short-term capital, are very real quantities in relation to the overall business of the economy. Money streams moving at a rate of £1 000 million a month generate an annual volume equal to 33 per cent of the GNP.

The tiny proportions of the present balance of payments figures also throw a fresh perspective on the possible trade and investment magnitudes suggested in Chapter XIV. Surpluses and deficits many times bigger than the microscopic quantities now achieved should not be especially difficult to attain: and, indeed, in the light of the statistical measures just seen, there is nothing spectacular in recommending that they should be brought into being.

All of the above illustrates in a new fashion the point made in Chapter XV, to the effect that all external payments tend to move to balance.

What is so seldom recognised about the balance of payments is that this is one of the fields of economic affairs where all concerned are dealing, not with the actual activities themselves, but with the residual between them. Thus the UK authorities and commentators have been concerned, not with the absolute size of this country's exports and imports, but with the margin between them. In most other activities, gross aggregates, only, come under scrutiny: how many schools and hospitals built, how many nuclear submarines, how big a national income, how large the total of private consumption, etc. Were this essential fact better perceived, then the external accounts balances would be more easily recognised as self-cancelling residuals. We are dealing with a subject the purest expression of which is the figure 0.

What we should really be worrying about is the size of the real aggregates themselves. In Chapter XIV it was urged that the individual balances within the whole should be allowed to enlarge, so as to give breathing space for economic expansion in the system; but the overall result would still tend to zero. A poor country will automatically balance its overseas payments just as a rich country will: there is no magic in that. But the poor country will balance its payments at a much lower level of all-round prosperity and effectiveness than a rich country. It will sell abounding quantities of cheap goods produced with much toil and effort to buy the expertly manufactured products of the richer nations; at a lower level still, it will not produce enough to maintain an appreciable level of exports at all, and so will be reduced to a poor level of imports. It is not the fact of the balance, but the quality and volume of the inflow and outflow, that should capture the attention of policy makers. It is no use Britain's balancing her trade at around 15 per cent of her GNP, when she could do it much more rewardingly around 25 per cent. It is no use Germany's exporting a major part of her wealth in direct form, when she might export capital and import a surplus of goods. A national economy is like a lung. The UK breathes in largely goods and investment income, and breathes out services and investment capital. Undue concern about the balance of external payments is like worrying about the difference between the amount of air a lung breathes in and the amount it breathes out. The difference is of course negligible; it may vary slightly from moment to moment, but the balance enforced by nature is nil. To worry whether this balance will get out of control is one thing; infinitely worse would be to constrict the working of the lung to ensure that the transient imbalances were as small as possible. This is, however, the precise purpose of recent British balance of payments policy.

Nevertheless this is not even what successive British Governments avow they are doing. The final paradox of the situation is that what the Government are consciously trying to do is to control to within a few pounds the actual size of this microscopic residual, imperceptible as it is to the statistical eye. It is endeavouring to bring down a £300 million overall deficit, to £200 million or £100 million, or to change it to a surplus of £100 million or £200 million. It is swinging a £38 000 million economy about in order to achieve these indistinguishable differences. This unrealised aim is called 'fine tuning'. Moreover, it employs teams of economists and committees of Civil Servants to predict what these infinitesimal quantities will be, not a month or so hence, but a year, or two years or five years ahead.

This leads to a further broad conclusion, foreshadowed in the preceding chapters. This is that in all this national perturbation over the balance of payments, too much detailed involvement in business affairs has been undertaken by the Government and too much political responsibility has inevitably been shifted on to the economists.

Economists are the practitioners of a new branch of knowledge—one based on the discovery that the business life of a nation answers to natural laws—and they are willing to test out their armoury of analysis in whatever new field may be offered. But they are frequently called upon to produce superhuman results. This occurs when, as cited above, they are asked to measure the statistically incommensurate, years ahead of the event, or when, as earlier mentioned, they are called on to show whether, and to what degree, British export prices are higher or lower than the variegated export prices of the remaining countries of the world. They are asked to state the effect on British exports, to within tens of £million, of a strike in America, a student revolt in France, or a change of parity in Peru. There is nothing inherently wrong in these inquiries. Provided it is known that the answer is impossible, it is right for economists to try. They must expand the frontiers of their art: by continually pushing forward into obscure areas they will eventually find that the answers are attainable, and they will throw up much knowledge on the way. But economists are also asked to judge. They are asked to say why British exporters fall short of the sales deemed requisite; whether it is because prices are too high, marketing abilities inadequate, packaging unattractive, and so on. Economists are encouraged to work out 'price elasticities' and say how low the average prices of motor cars, petro-chemical plants and handkerchiefs must be in order to capture the share of world trade considered correct for those articles. They are asked to report on whether overseas investment is profitable to manufacturers. They state whether manufacturing industry is employing too much labour, and whether services are employing too little. They say whether the economy as a whole is efficient, and what measures are required to make consumers spend less, to make manufacturers invest more in their plants, pay more or fewer dividends to their shareholders, allot higher or lower sums of cash to research.

This is to mistake both the nature of the economist's calling, and the subject to which he is applying his attention. The economist is essentially an observer, and the economy is still largely unexplored. Moreover, it is clear that the economy is not merely a process that can be calibrated mathematically and regulated by precise methodologies. Company boards of directors, as was remarked in Chapter X, make investment decisions, not on a pure calculation of cash flow and interest rates, but on their sense of well-being or otherwise in the general business climate. The most cursory acquaintance with any of the great markets of the country—the Stock Exchange, Lloyds, the foreign exchange market—will show that decisions proceed not from mathematical concepts, but from a consensus of feeling about the rightness or otherwise of things. When studying the ebb and flow of these activities, measures such as price and income elasticities are useful in isolating in numerical terms some of the facets of the whole process; but this does not give a picture of the whole, any more than calculation of the effect of capillary action gives a complete understanding of plant growth. Economic activity is a product exclusively of human behaviour; it belongs almost certainly in the realm of social sciences; its basis is more likely psychology than mathematics. John Stuart Mill insisted that he was expounding 'political economy', not economics. Certainly, the economist is studying a living organism, which is constantly growing and changing, and whose laws are complex.

As for economists, so for governments. The Government, as a corporate entity, can no more run a motor car factory or an investment trust than it can put on five acts of *Hamlet* or play the banjo. Yet since the Second World War there has been an unending stream from governments, multiplied tenfold in the last six years, of strictures, complaints and judgments on industry's efficiency, its methods and techniques, its 'profit-oriented thinking', its 'technological horizon' and its 'market initiative'. Government has striven, by cajolery, flattery and threats, to induce industry to comply with its own views on industrial activities of which it has no experience and little understanding. Institutions, commissions and public bodies have proliferated on every aspect of industrial and commercial life. Training Boards, the Prices and Incomes Board, the Industrial Reorganisation Commission, the mooted Commission on Manpower and Industry, and many others. Numberless committees have been formed, at which industrialists and businessmen who have spent a lifetime making real sales and real profits, have been lectured on their opportunities by teams of officials who have done neither. Not content, it has invaded large slices of private enterprise, captured its assets, and proceeded to make the product itself—not surprisingly, at an invariable loss.

This is no part of the function of government. The Government is not a technician, cannot be the actual operator, in any part of the business community. What it must do, is govern; it must hold the ring, check abuses, prevent fractricide, succour the weak, remove obstacles, encourage the strong, open doors, widen horizons and lead the nation. Some intrusion into industrial affairs is in the modern State inevitable. With the constant enlargement of the role of business and industry in the community, the call for regulation, if nothing else, grows bigger every year. At innumerable points the Government will, as a major property owner, as responsible for a number of public services, as an employer in its own right, be drawn into the commercial arena. But it should draw the line as to where its mandate ends. It cannot do industry's job and it cannot teach industry how to do it. If there were not the great national affray about the country's trade, this would not even need saying.

And so to the last point. The balance of payments is the English sickness. This is not because the British have a balance of payments that is any different from any other. It is because only the British make it a point of national conscience. True, other countries have their spells of national anguish. These have, however, been rare and recent. One suspects that the industrialised world has learnt to worry about balance of payments from the British.

There is a marked particularity about the UK's attitude to her trading and economic fortunes. The United States has run a consistent balance of payments deficit since 1950. So little was made of this that it was not until the 1960s that most other countries thought that the deficit existed, let alone that it was serious. Even now, though the Americans worry about their deficit, they do not imagine that it is to be a sign of the original sin of American nationhood. In France, the external problem is felt to be a pity and to be the harbinger of hard times, but it is not thought to reflect the lost valour of Frenchmen. And the Japanese, romping in and out of deficit as they do, are they exultant when in surplus and deeply shocked when in deficit? Perish the thought. Why have the British reacted so differently? Why have they taken it so *personally*?

The answer throws an intriguing sidelight on British history. The UK's self-revulsion over the balance of payments is only part of a larger, and more long-lived process. For many years, since the 1939 war, and probably the war before that, Britain has felt herself to be on a gentle slide. She would not call it actual decadence, but she feared it could be something not far removed. The reason, of course, was that she was slowly moving from a world in which she dominated all her coevals, through physical strength and an extensive empire, to one in which the standard of size is the continental nation, needing no empire to sustain its strength. In a world of these national dimensions, Britain can have no prominence. The world of today is for nations of the scale of Soviet Russia and the United States of America and the world of tomorrow is for China, India, Australasia. England saw this coming long ago. She knew herself to be physically overtaken by the United States in the 1890s. She foresaw the growth of Russia from the moment that the Tsarist regime was toppled. India was a predestined world power in the 1930s. Any ordinary British serviceman, coming back in 1945 from a Europe where a war begun between Germans, Frenchmen, Poles and Englishmen had virtually been concluded by Americans and Russians, had no doubt as to where the future leadership of the world lay. The year 1956 and Suez saw the final end of independent British power. This was hard for the British. After all, they alone of the now medium-rank European states had enjoyed world dominance. The French had receded steadily from the tidal mark of Napoleon, and after Sedan had never really rated. The Germans had never managed it at all. Despite their apparent *amour propre*, the British took it very hard. It is indeed painful to see pre-eminence slipping away. The experience bred about a curiously inverted frame of mind. The British presumed, since the world was getting bigger around them, that they were getting smaller in themselves. Like the passenger in a stationary train seeing an adjacent train pulling out, they thought they were moving backwards. Confusedly, they saw in all the signs of greater power around them, evidence of failing ability and shrinking strength in themselves. Nothing, of course, could be farther from the truth. Objectively seen, Britain's problem was that, through no fault of her own, the world had grown into dimensions beyond her own; she remained no less effective by her own standards, and her task was to overcome, where possible, the disadvantage under which she now lay. But Britain persisted in the belief that she was in absolute decline, that she was less productive, less imaginative, less industrious than before.

Into this atmosphere erupted, for reasons of subtly similar causation, the postwar balance of payments problem. This, as though pre-ordained, became the magnet for all these disconsolate feelings. The trade balance was a first-class gauge of the country's recovery. If we attained a surplus, we were on the mend. If we persisted in deficit, and our share of world trade went on declining, we were still heading for decay.

To this, from the economist there is only one valid comment. Loss of confidence, as a generalised indulgence, may be one thing. Loss of confidence in balance of payments matters carries with it, for strictly technical reasons, a particularly severe penalty.

Appendix I—Notes on Sources

General

Reference throughout the book to British balance of payments statistics in the postwar period are based on:

For 1946–66: Central Statistical Office, '*The UK Balance of Payments*', 1969.

For 1967–69: Central Statistical Office, '*Economic Trends*', March, 1970.

All references to the pre-war British balance of payments statistics in the book are drawn from Tables I, II, III, V and VI in the Appendix (sources of these are shown at the foot of the tables).

References by Chapter:

Chapter II

1 Population Growth—Abstract of British Historical Statistics.

2 Historical Comparisons for British Output and Exports—PEP, *Growth in the British Economy*, London, 1960.

3 *et seq.* Statistics of Trade—much of the detail drawn from Professor G. N. Clark, *Guide to English Commercial Statistics in the 18th Century*; Sir John Clapham, *Concise Economic History of Britain*; Werner Schlote, *British Overseas Trade from 1700 to the 1930s*, in particular.

4 The Rev. Woodforde and Smuggling—G. M. Trevelyan *English Social History*.

5 The Younger Pitt—Sir John Clapham *Concise Economic History of England.*

Chapter III

6 Services as percentages of GNP—European Economic Community *Basic Statistics*, Ninth edition.

7 Share of in services; *Annual Abstract of Statistics*, 1969, Table 132.

8 Return on overseas investment, *Board of Trade Annual Enquiries.*

9 Totals of investment—Central Statistical Office *National Income and Expenditure*, 1969

Chapter IV

10 Government of India payments: *Board of Trade Journal*: articles appearing in February of each year during the 1930's.

11 Official balances of twelve countries—UK, USA, Germany, Canada, Australia; national balance of payments accounts: others, IMF *Balance of Payments Yearbook*.

12 Maintenance of overseas armed forces. Reprinted from *The Banker*, June 1968, with permission of the Editor.

13 United States balance of payments 1960/66—O.E.C.D. Survey of the United States, 1967. 1967/69—International Monetary Fund *International Financial Statistics*, June 1970.

14 German receipts from foreign military agencies: *Deutsche Bundesbank Zahlungsbilanzstatistik*, March 1970. Japanese receipts, op. cit.

Chapter V

15 Details of the United States economy—*Britannica Book of the Year*, various issues 1965 to 1969.

16 Iron ore consumption in the UK—British Iron and Steel Federation *Statistical Yearbook*, 1967.

17 Breakdown of UK imports 1968—Board of Trade *Report on Overseas Trade*, May 1970.

18 British maritime expansion—much of the detail et seq. drawn from Sir John Clapham and Trevelyan, op. cit.

19 History of Financial Institutions—Sir John Clapham, op. cit. Henley Administration College *History of the City*.

20 Growth of the British population—Imlah, op. cit., page 182 (footnote).

21 Prices—ibid.

22 Mid-nineteenth-century debate on the trade, et. seq. Much of the detail drawn from Imlah, op. cit.

23 Import content of output and imports. CSO Input Output tables for the UK, pp. 9–10, HMSO, 1970.

Chapter VI

24 Lord Cecil, Restoration Council of Trade—Sir John Clapham, ibid.

25 Mr Reginald Maudling—*The Director*, November 1967.

26 J. S. Jeans, Secretary of the Iron and Steel Institute, Carr and Taplin *History of the British Steel Industry*.

27 Bourne—*Journal of the Royal Statistical Society, 1882.*

28 Giffen, ibid.

29 Sir John Clapham quotation—*Economic History of England*, 2nd vol.

Chapter VII

30 External debts. Chancellor's budget speech, April 1970.

31 Proportion of World Trade Settled in Sterling: *Britain's Invisible Earnings*, p. 255.

32 Hans Bär (partner in Julius Bär and Co., Zurich), 'The Swiss Perspective' address to Economic Research Council, 16 November, 1966.

33 Short-term UK movements in 1964—*Economic Trends*, March 1965.

34 Short-term capital flows in Germany—Bundesbank Reports.

35 Short-term capital flows in France—May–June 1968 newspaper reports; May–November OECD Economic Survey of France, April 1969, p. 23.

Chapter X

36 West European Visible and Invisible balances—Source, International Monetary Fund, *International Financial Statistics*, June 1970.

37 Balance of Payments of Germany 1968—International Monetary Fund, *International Financial Statistics*, June 1970.

38 Germany's standard of living—European Economic Community *Basic Statistics*, 4th and 9th Editions.

39 Germany's long-term capital movements—Bundesbank reports.

40 UK coal, iron and steel production 1910—Abstract of British Historical Statistics, 1968—*Annual Abstract of Statistics*, 1968.

41 Growth of the economy and of individual industries 1910–66—London and Cambridge Economic Service, *Key Statistics*, 1967 edition.

42 UK technological innovations—Confederation of British Industry, *Fanfare for Britain.*

43 UK and European research—OECD Report on Technological Gaps, table published in *OECD Observer*.

44 Fast- and slow-moving export markets—*Annual Abstract of Statistics.*

45 Historical direction of trade—*Abstract of Historical Statistics.*

46 Product pattern of UK exports—Abstract of *Historical Statistics—Annual Abstract of Statistics*, 1969.

47 International comparison of fast-moving exports—EEC Statistics.

48 1954 Quantity and Volume of Steel products—*UK Trade and Navigation Accounts*, December 1954.

Chapter XI

49 International comparison of retail prices—*European Community Basic Statistics:* London and Cambridge Economic Service, *Key Statistics.*

50 Government expenditure—Central Statistical Office, *National Income and Expenditure 1969*. Tables 49 (for public section expenditure) 1 (for consumers expenditure) and 52 (for private sector gross domestic fixed capital formation).
51 Government borrowings and investment, ibid., Table 44.
52 Government overspending—ibid., Table 39.
53 Public and private sector spending—Central Statistical Office, ibid. (see reference 50 above).
54 Private consumption as a percentage of GNP, ibid., Tablc 14.
55 Private consumption in the Community—European Economic Community, *General Statistical Bulletin*, 1969, No. 10, Table 1.
56 Average annual gross income of wage and salary earners—Parliamentary reply by Mr Harold Walker, Parliamentary Under-Secretary of State for Employment and Productivity (based on a 'recent Community publication'), April 1970.
57 Average hourly wages—European Economic Community *Basic Statistics* 1967: *Department of Employment and Productivity Gazette*, May 1970.

Chapter XII

58 Private investment in manufacturing—*Economic Trends*, various issues in 1962, 1969 and 1970.
59 Motor car production in Japan—Society of Motor Manufacturers and Traders.
60 Exports as percentage of GNP in major countries—OECD National Statistics published in *OECD Observer*, February 1967 and 1970.
61 Industrial production in European countries—European Economic Community *General Statistical Bulletin*, 1969, No. 10, Table 3.
62 Output per manhour in manufacturing—*National Institute Review*, No. 50, November 1969, Tables 6 and 19.
63 Shares of world manufactured trade—*National Institute Review*, No. 50, November 1969, Table 20.

Chapter XIII

64 Monthly visible deficits—*Board of Trade Journal*, 22 October, 1969, and 21 January, 1970.

Chapter XIV

65 Trade as a percentage of GNP—OECD National Statistics published in *OECD Observer*, February 1970.
66 UK Historical trade in relation to GNP—GNP prior to 1900, *Abstract*

of Historical Statistics; post-1900 and pre-1939, London and Cambridge Economics Service, *Key Statistics*. Imports and Exports, Appendix Tables. Pre-1939 GNP figures are the mean of expenditure and income basis. Pre-1939 import figures are reduced by 10 per cent to eliminate c.i.f. element.

67 World Trade—1937/38: League of Nations, *Network of International Trade*, 1942. Present-day, GATT *International Trade*, 1969

68 Percentage change in trade over previous year 1958–67: *Annual Abstract of Statistics*, 1969; 1968, 1969—*Board of Trade Journal*, 12 August, 1970.

69 UK Overseas Assets 1939, Command 6707: 1968, 'Pink Book', 1969.

70 Public Expenditure—Central Statistical Office, *National Income and Expenditure*, 1969.

Chapter XV

71 Foreign exchange cost of F111 and other US military aircraft—'Pink Book', 1969, and *Economic Trends*, March 1970.

72 Government interest charges, 1968—*Economic Trends*, March 1970.

73 Total world reserves—International Monetary Fund: *International Financial Statistics*, June 1970.

74 Total world trade; GATT, *International Trade*, 1969.

75 Average annual basic deficit for Germany 1960/69—Bundesbank Reports.

76 Sterling balances—Central Statistical Office, *United Kingdom Balance of Payments*, 1969.

77 Pre-war sterling balances—London and Cambridge Economic Service, *Key Statistics*.

Chapter XVI

78 GNP 1964/1968—Central Statistical Office *National Income and Expenditure* 1969.

79 United States GNP—US Department of Commerce *Survey of Current Business*, May 1970.

80 US Balance of Payments deficit 1969—US Department of Commerce *Survey of Current Business*, May 1970.

81 Margins of error in the UK Balance of Payments Statistics—Central Statistical Office, *United Kingdom Balance of Payments*, 1969, page 86.

Appendix II—Statistical Tables and Chart

Index

Table

Appendix II—Statistical Tables and Chart

Table I—Visible trade of the United Kingdom, 1796–1969 £m

	Imports	*Exports*	*Balance*
1796	39·6	38·6	−1·0
1797	34·4	36·8	+2·4
1798	49·6	43·5	−6·1
1799	50·9	46·2	−4·7
1800	62·3	52·4	−9·9
1801	68·7	53·5	−15·2
1802	54·7	58·8	+4·1
1803	53·9	46·0	−7·9
1804	57·3	49·2	−8·1
1805	61·0	48·1	−12·9
1806	53·3	50·1	−3·2
1807	53·8	45·5	−8·3
1808	51·5	43·8	−7·7
1809	73·7	61·7	−12·0
1810	88·5	60·9	−27·6
1811	50·7	39·6	−11·1
1812	56·0	50·8	−5·2
1813	—	—	—
1814	80·8	70·3	−10·5
1815	71·3	68·4	−2·9
1816	50·2	54·3	+4·1
1817	61·0	51·9	−9·1
1818	80·7	58·8	−21·9
1819	56·0	45·4	−10·6
1820	54·2	46·8	−7·4
1821	45·6	46·2	+0·6
1822	44·6	44·8	+0·2
1823	52·0	42·6	−9·4
1824	51·2	45·9	−5·3
1825	73·6	47·1	−26·5
1826	50·4	38·8	−11·6
1827	58·8	44·0	−14·8
1828	57·3	43·3	−14·0
1829	54·1	42·4	−11·7
1830	55·9	43·9	−12·0
1831	62·0	43·9	−18·1
1832	52·5	43·8	−8·7
1833	58·9	46·6	−12·3

	Imports	*Exports*	*Balance*
1834	64·7	49·6	−15·1
1835	68·0	56·6	−11·4
1836	84·4	62·6	−21·8
1837	70·1	51·1	−19·0
1838	80·1	59·3	−20·8
1839	90·8	63·4	−27·4
1840	91·2	61·4	−29·8
1841	83·9	61·5	−22·4
1842	76·4	55·8	−20·6
1843	71·0	60·1	−10·9
1844	78·9	66·6	−12·3
1845	88·4	69·4	−19·0
1846	87·3	67·0	−20·3
1847	112·1	70·5	−41·6
1848	88·2	61·2	−27·0
1849	101·4	75·7	−25·7
1850	103·0	83·4	−19·6
1851	109·5	86·9	−22·6
1852	110·0	91·1	−18·9
1853	148·5	115·7	−32·8
1854	152·4	115·8	−36·6
1855	143·5	116·7	−26·8
1856	172·5	139·2	−33·3
1857	187·8	146·2	−41·6
1858	164·6	139·8	−24·8
1859	179·2	155·7	−23·5
1860	210·5	164·5	−46·0
1861	217·5	159·6	−57·9
1862	225·7	166·2	−59·5
1863	248·9	196·9	−52·0
1864	275·0	212·6	−62·4
1865	271·1	218·8	−52·3
1866	295·3	238·9	−56·4
1867	275·2	225·8	−49·4
1868	294·7	227·8	−66·9
1869	295·5	237·1	−58·4
1870	303·3	244·1	−59·2
1871	331·0	283·6	−47·4
1872	354·7	314·6	−40·1
1873	371·3	311·0	−60·3
1874	370·1	297·7	−72·4
1875	373·9	281·6	−92·3
1876	375·2	256·7	−118·5
1877	394·4	252·4	−142·0
1878	368·8	245·4	−123·4
1879	363·0	248·8	−114·2
1880	411·2	286·5	−124·7

	Imports	*Exports*	*Balance*
1881	397·0	297·1	–99·9
1882	413·0	306·7	–106·3
1883	426·9	305·4	–121·5
1884	390·0	295·9	–94·1
1885	371·0	271·5	–99·5
1886	349·9	268·9	–81·0
1887	362·2	281·2	–81·0
1888	387·6	298·5	–89·1
1889	427·6	315·6	–112·0
1890	420·7	328·2	–92·5
1891	435·4	308·1	–127·3
1892	423·8	291·6	–132·2
1893	404·7	277·2	–127·5
1894	408·3	273·8	–134·5
1895	416·7	285·8	–130·9
1896	441·8	296·3	–145·5
1897	451·0	294·2	–156·8
1898	470·5	294·1	–176·4
1899	485·0	329·5	–155·5
1900	523·1	354·4	–168·7
1901	522·0	347·8	–174·2
1902	528·4	349·2	–179·2
1903	542·6	360·4	–182·2
1904	551·0	371·0	–180·0
1905	565·0	407·6	–157·4
1906	607·9	460·7	–147·2
1907	645·8	517·9	–127·9
1908	593·0	456·7	–136·3
1909	624·7	469·5	–155·2
1910	678·3	534·2	–144·1
1911	680·2	556·9	–123·3
1912	744·6	598·9	–145·7
1913	768·7	634·8	–133·9
1914	696·6	526·2	–170·4
1915	851·9	484·0	–367·9
1916	948·5	603·9	–344·6
1917	1 064·2	596·8	–467·4
1918	1 316·2	532·3	–783·9
1919	1 626·2	963·3	–662·9
1920	1 932·6	1 557·3	–375·3
1921	1 085·5	810·3	–275·2
1922	1 003·1	823·2	–179·9
1923	1 096·2	885·8	–210·4
1924	1 277·4	941·0	–336·4
1925	1 320·7	927·4	–393·3
1926	1 241·4	778·5	–462·9
1927	1 218·3	832·1	–386·2
1928	1 195·6	843·9	–351·7
1929	1 220·8	839·0	–381·8
1930	1 044·0	657·6	–386·4

	Imports	*Exports*	*Balance*
1931	861·3	454·5	−406·8
1932	701·7	416·0	−285·7
1933	675·0	417·0	−258·0
1934	731·4	447·2	−284·2
1935	756·0	481·1	−274·9
1936	847·8	501·4	−346·4
1937	1 027·8	596·5	−431·3
1938	919·5	532·3	−387·2
1939	885·5	485·5	−400·0
1940	1 152·1	437·2	−714·9
1941	1 145·1	378·1	−767·0
1942	1 206·2	401·7	−804·5
1943	1 886·1	350·9	−1 535·2
1944	2 362·2	346·5	−2 015·7
1945	1 517·9	485·6	−1 032·3
1946	1 063	960	−103
1947	1 541	1 180	−361
1948	1 790	1 639	−151
1949	2 000	1 863	−137
1950	2 312	2 261	−51
1951	3 424	2 735	−689
1952	3 048	2 769	−279
1953	2 927	2 683	−244
1954	2 989	2 785	−204
1955	3 386	3 073	−313
1956	3 324	3 377	+53
1957	3 538	3 509	−29
1958	3 377	3 406	+29
1959	3 639	3 522	−117
1960	4 138	3 732	−406
1961	4 043	3 891	−152
1962	4 095	3 993	−102
1963	4 362	4 282	−80
1964	5 003	4 486	−517
1965	5 042	4 817	−225
1966	5 211	5 168	−43
1967	5 576	5 122	−454
1968	6 807	6 273	−534
1969	7 153	7 056	−97

Sources: 1796–1945: Abstract of British Historical Statistics Tables: *Overseas Trade*, 2 and 3
1946–66: Central Statistical Office, *United Kingdom Balance of Payments*, 1969.
1967–69: Central Statistical Office, *Economic Trends*, March, 1970.

Notes

1. For the period 1796–1945, imports are shown c.i.f., exports f.o.b. For 1946–69, both are shown f.o.b. (For a uniform f.o.b. series 1825–1969, see Tables III and V.)
2. The column 'exports' includes exports and re-exports.
3. Imports shown for 1964–69 do not include purchases of US military aircraft and missiles.
4. Exports shown for 1964–69 include correction for statistical under-recording.

Table II—Visible trade of the United Kingdom, Official and Real values, 1796–1853 £m

	Official			Real		
	Imports	Exports	Balance	Imports	Exports	Balance
1796	23·2	30·5	+7·3*	39·6	38·6	−1·0*
1797	21·0	28·9	+7·9*	34·4	36·8	+2·4*
1798	27·9	33·6	+5·7*	49·6	43·5	−6·1*
1799	26·8	36·0	+9·2*	50·9	46·2	−4·7*
1800	30·6	43·2	+12·6*	62·3	52·4	−9·9*
1801	31·8	35·3	+3·5	68·7	53·5	−15·2
1802	29·8	38·4	+8·6	54·7	58·8	+4·1
1803	26·6	28·6	+2·0	53·9	46·0	−7·9
1804	27·8	31·7	+3·9	57·3	49·2	−8·1
1805	28·6	31·1	+2·5	61·0	48·1	−12·9
1806	26·9	33·7	+6·8	53·3	50·1	−3·2
1807	26·7	31·1	+4·4	53·8	45·5	−8·3
1808	26·8	30·4	+3·6	51·5	43·8	−7·7
1809	31·8	46·3	+14·5	73·7	61·7	−12·0
1810	39·8	43·6	+4·3	88·5	60·9	−27·6
1811	26·5	28·9	+2·4	50·7	39·6	−11·1
1812	26·2	39·2	+13·0	56·0	50·8	−5·2
1813	..	..	..	..	..	..
1814	33·8	53·6	+19·8	80·8	70·3	−10·5
1815	33·0	58·6	+25·6	71·3	68·4	−2·9
1816	27·4	49·2	+21·8	50·2	54·3	+4·1
1817	30·8	50·4	+19·6	61·0	51·9	−9·1
1818	36·9	53·6	+16·7	80·7	58·8	−21·9
1819	30·8	43·4	+12·6	56·0	45·4	−10·6
1820	32·4	49·0	+13·6	54·2	46·8	−7·4
1821	30·8	51·4	+20·6	45·6	46·2	+0·6
1822	30·5	53·4	+22·9	44·6	44·8	+0·2
1823	35·8	52·4	+16·6	52·0	42·6	−9·4
1824	37·5	58·9	+21·4	51·2	45·9	−5·3
1825	44·2	56·4	+12·2	73·6	47·1	−26·5
1826	37·8	51·1	+13·3	50·4	38·8	−11·6
1827	44·9	62·0	+17·1	58·8	44·0	−14·8
1828	45·2	62·7	+17·5	57·3	43·3	−14·0
1829	44·0	66·8	+22·8	54·1	42·4	−11·7
1830	46·3	69·7	+23·4	55·9	43·9	−12·0
1831	49·7	71·4	+21·7	62·0	43·9	−18·1
1832	44·6	76·0	+31·4	52·5	43·8	− 8·7
1833	45·9	79·8	+34·9	58·9	46·6	−12·3
1834	49·4	85·4	+36·0	64·7	49·6	−15·1
1835	49·0	91·2	+42·2	68·0	56·6	−11·4
1836	57·3	97·6	+40·3	84·4	62·6	−21·8
1837	54·8	85·7	+30·9	70·1	51·1	−19·0
1838	61·3	108·2	+46·9	80·1	59·3	−20·8
1839	62·0	110·2	+48·2	90·8	63·4	−27·4
1840	67·5	116·5	+49·0	91·2	61·4	−29·8

* Excluding Ireland.

		Official			Real	
	Imports	Exports	Balance	Imports	Exports	Balance
1841	64·4	116·9	+52·5	83·9	61·5	−22·4
1842	65·3	113·9	+48·6	76·4	55·8	−20·6
1843	70·2	131·9	+61·7	71·0	60·1	−10·9
1844	75·4	146·0	+70·6	78·9	66·6	−12·3
1845	85·3	150·9	+65·6	88·4	69·4	−19·0
1846	75·9	148·6	+72·7	87·3	67·0	−20·3
1847	90·9	146·1	+55·2	112·1	70·5	−41·6
1848	93·5	151·0	+57·5	88·2	61·2	−27·0
1849	105·9	190·1	+84·2	101·4	75·7	−25·7
1850	100·5	197·3	+96·8	103·0	83·4	−19·6
1851	110·5	214·4	+103·9	109·5	86·9	−22·6
1852	109·3	219·5	+110·2	110·0	91·1	−18·9
1853	123·1	242·0	+118·9	148·5	115·7	−32·8

Source: Abstract of British Historical Statistics, Tables: *Overseas Trade*, 1 and 2

Table III—The visible and invisible accounts of the United Kingdom, 1826–1969

Years	*Visible (Deficit)*	*Invisible (Surplus)*	*Balance (£m)*
1826–1830	−5·0	+10·0	+5·0
1831–1835	−4·5	+10·3	+5·8
1836–1840	−13·2	+14·9	+1·7
1841–1845	−6·6	+14·9	+8·3
1846–1850	−14·0	+17·7	−3·7
1851–1855	−10·2	+23·3	+13·1
1856–1860	−10·0	+36·7	+26·7
1861–1865	−24·6	+48·8	+24·2
1866–1870	−20·0	+67·6	+47·6
1871–1875	−19·3	+94·9	+75·6
1876–1880	−78·9	+102·6	+23·7
1881–1885	−56·4	+112·9	+56·5
1886–1890	−44·3	+129·7	+85·4
1891–1895	−84·4	+139·9	+55·5
1896–1900	−118·4	+147·0	+28·6
1901–1905	−115·0	+156·2	+41·2
1906–1910	−79·1	+226·6	+147·5
1911–1913	−61·3	+273·1	+211·8
1920–1925	−116	+314	+148
1926–1930	−276	+327	+51
1931–1935	−229	+204	−25
1936–1938	−294	+259	−35
1946–1951	−249	+307	+58
1952–1955	−260	+426	+166
1956–1960	−96	+522	+426
1961–1965	−215	+705	+490
1966–1969	−282	+998	+716

N.B. For Sources and Notes see Appendix Table V.

Table IV—World invisible trade, 1967 **$m**

	Exports	*Imports*	*Balance*
World	67 346	68 677	—
United States	15 353	9 819	+5 534
United Kingdom	8 585	6 804	+1 781
France	6 255	5 583	+672
Germany	4 699	7 060	−2 361
Italy	4 298	3 102	+1 196
Netherlands	2 671	2 107	+564
Japan	2 625	4 271	−1 646
Canada	2 363	3 574	−1 211
Norway	1 788	1 056	+732
Switzerland	1 692	1 057	+635
Spain	1 601	719	+882
Belgium-Luxemburg	1 600	1 845	−245
Sweden	1 065	1 414	−349
Mexico	1 005	1 091	−86
Denmark	885	726	+159
Austria	853	556	+297
Australia	669	1 473	−804
Yugoslavia	563	426	+137
South Africa	558	1 055	−497
Portugal	538	318	+220
Ireland	443	295	+148
Singapore	425	189	+236
Israel	390	469	−79
Greece	372	235	+137
Finland	339	455	−116
Philippines	293	373	−80
India	245	738	−493
United Arab Republic	245	224	+21
Argentine	238	517	−279
Brazil	235	732	−497
Turkey	198	222	−24

Source: Committee on Invisible Exports.

	1826–1830	*1831–1835*	*1836–1840*	*1841–1845*	*1846–1850*	*1851–1855*	*1856–1860*	*1861–1865*	*1866–1870*	*1871–1875*	*1876–1880*	*1881–1885*	*1886–1890*	*1891–1895*
Visibles														
Imports	−47·5	−52·6	−72·5	−69·3	−85·6	−115·5	−159·1	−215·4	−254·7	−316·8	−336·8	−351·6	−342·8	−371·9
Exports	42·5	48·1	59·3	62·7	71·6	105·3	149·1	190·8	234·7	297·5	257·9	295·2	298·5	287·5
Net	−5·0	−4·5	−13·2	−6·6	−14·0	−10·2	−10·0	−24·6	−20·0	−19·3	−78·9	−56·4	−44·3	−84·4
Invisibles (*Net*)														
Services	5·4	4·9	6·9	7·4	8·2	11·6	20·2	27·0	36·8	44·9	46·3	48·1	45·5	45·9
Investment returns	4·6	5·4	8·0	7·5	9·5	11·7	16·5	21·8	30·8	50·0	56·3	64·8	84·2	94·0
Total	+10·0	+10·3	+14·9	+14·9	+17·7	+23·3	+36·7	+48·8	+67·6	+94·9	+102·6	+112·9	+129·7	+139·9
Current Balance	—	—	—	—	—	—	—	—	—	—	—	—	—	—
Government	+5·0	+5·8	+1·7	+8·3	−3·7	+13·1	+26·7	+24·2	+47·6	+75·6	+23·7	+56·5	+85·4	+55·5
Overall Balance	+5·0	+5·8	+1·7	+8·3	−3·7	+13·1	+26·7	+24·2	+47·6	+75·6	+23·7	+56·5	+85·4	+55·5

	1896–1900	*1901–1905*	*1906–1910*	*1911–1913*	*1920–1925*	*1926–1930*	*1931–1935*	*1936–1938*	*1946–1951*	*1952–1955*	*1956–1960*	*1961–1965*	*1966–1969*
Visibles													
Imports	−422·1	−482·2	−566·9	−655·2	−1 163	−1 075	−689	−857	−2 022	−3 088	−3 603	−4 509	−6 187
Exports	303·7	367·2	487·8	593·9	997	797	460	563	1 773	2 828	3 509	4 294	5 905
Net	−118·4	−115·0	−79·1	−61·3	−116	−276	−229	−294	−249	−260	−96	−215	−282
Invisibles (*Net*)													
Services	46·8	43·2	75·2	85·1	—	—	—	—	69	200	182	196	378
Investment returns	100·2	113·0	151·4	188·0	—	—	—	—	238	226	340	509	620
Total	+147·0	+156·2	+226·6	+273·1	+314	+327	+204	+259	+307	+426	+522	+705	+998
Current Balance	—	—	—	—	−13	+13	−7	−20	−166	−99	−293	−532	−766
Government	+28·6	+41·2	+147·5	+211·8	+148	+51	−25	−35	+58	+166	+426	+490	+716
Overall Balance	+28·6	+41·2	+147·5	+211·8	+135	+64	−32	−55	−108	+67	+133	−42	−50

Sources: 1826–1913: This table is an abbreviated version of the one furnished by the present author to the Committee on Invisible Exports and published in their Report 'Britain's Invisible Earnings', pp. 20–23. The latter table was itself an adaptation to an f.o.b. trade basis of the series shown in Albert H. Imlah's 'Economic Elements in the Pax Britannica', 1958, pp. 70–75 (a full explanation of the method of adaptation was shown in 'Britain's Invisible Earnings'.)
1913–38: London and Cambridge Economic Service, *Key Statistics.*
1946–66: Central Statistical Office, *United Kingdom Balance of payments 1969*; 1967–69: Central Statistical Office, *Economic Trends*, March, 1970.

Notes:
1. Notes 2, 3, 4 of Appendix Table I apply. (Payments for US military aircaft and missiles are included under 'Government'.)
2 'Services' and 'Government' include transfer payments.
3. For 1946–57 official debt interest payments were deducted by the Central Statistics Office from returns on private investment before showing the latter; these cannot now be separated. The effect is to reduce simultaneously the apparent official outgoings and apparent investment income, probably by £100–£150m in 1957.
4. The above table is for current transactions only (i.e. sales and purchases of goods and services and the like) and excludes capital inflows and outflows. Between 1826 and 1913 it is calculated that there were capital exports roughly equivalent to the surpluses on current account. Between the wars, there were capital exports which in some cases aggravated the current deficit. Since 1952 exact figures have been collected and these are shown in Table VI.

Table VI—The balance of payments of the United Kingdom, 1952–1969

£m

	1952	1953	1954	1955	1956	1957	1958	1959	1960
Visibles									
Imports	−3 048	−2 927	−2 989	−3 386	−3 324	−3 538	−3 377	−3 639	−4 138
Exports	+2 769	+2 683	+2 785	+3 073	+3 377	+3 509	+3 406	+3 522	+3 732
Balance	−279	−244	−204	−313	+53	−29	+29	−117	−406
Invisibles									
Payments	−1 041	−1 076	−1 162	−1 347	−1 487	−1 509	−1 336	−1 404	−1 546
Receipts	+1 544	+1 531	+1 614	+1 643	+1 817	+1 915	+2 011	+2 019	+2 117
Balance	+503	+455	+452	+296	+330	+406	+675	+615	+571
Current Balance	+224	+211	+248	−17	+383	+377	+704	+498	+165
Long-term Capital Exports (Net)	−114	−145	−163	−60	−119	−172	−146	−131	−89
Current and Long-term Capital Balance	+110	+66	+85	−77	+264	+205	+558	+367	+76
Government									
Current	−61	−66	−131	−138	−175	−146	−360	−355	−430
Long-term Capital	−20	−49	−28	−62	−68	+66	−50	−124	−103
Total	−81	−115	−159	−200	−243	−80	−410	−479	−533
Government and Private Balance	+29	−49	−74	−277	+21	+125	+148	−112	−457

	1961	1962	1963	1964	1965	1966	1967	1968	1969
Visibles									
Imports	−4 043	−4 095	−4 362	−5 003	−5 042	−5 211	−5 576	−6 807	−7 153
Exports	+3 891	+3 993	+4 282	+4 486	+4 817	+5 168	+5 122	+6 273	+7 056
Balance	−152	−102	−80	−517	−225	−43	−454	−534	−97
Invisibles									
Payments	−1 541	−1 576	−1 697	−1 880	−2 016	−2 051	−2 160	−2 530	−2 657
Receipts	+2 185	+2 297	+2 405	+2 566	+2 783	+2 832	+3 028	+3 561	+3 967
Balance	+644	+721	+708	+686	+767	+781	+868	+1 031	+1 310
Current Balance	+492	+619	+628	+169	+542	+738	+414	+497	+1 210
Long-term Capital Exports (Net)	+113	+6	−44	−247	−117	−32	−82	−110	+116
Current and Long-term Capital Balance	+605	+625	+584	−78	+425	+706	+332	+387	+1 326
Government									
Current	−496	−507	−514	−550	−592	−674	−736	−806	−847
Long-term capital	−45	−104	−105	−116	−85	−80	−57	+21	−95
Total	−541	−611	−619	−666	−677	−754	−793	−785	−942
Government and Private Balance	+64	+14	−35	−744	−252	−48	−461	−398	+384

Sources: 1952–1966: Central Statistical Office, *The United Kingdom Balance of Payments, 1969.*
1967–1969: Central Statistical Office, *Economic Trends*, March, 1970.

Notes:
1. Notes 2, 3 and 4 of Appendix Table I apply. (Purchases of US military aircraft and missiles are shown under 'Government'.)
2. Imports and exports are f.o.b.
3. The 'Invisibles' section shows total earnings and total payments of the whole invisible sector, i.e. of services (including transfers) and investment income combined.

Table VII—The current balances of Western European countries, 1960–1968 $m

	1960		*1961*		*1962*		*1963*		*1964*		*1965*		*1966*		*1967*		*1968*	
	Vis.	*Inv.*	*Vis.*	*Inv.*	*Vis*	*Inv.*	*Vis.*	*Inv.*	*Vis.*	*Inv.*	*Vis.*	*Inv.*	*Vis.*	*Inv.*	*Vis.*	*Inv.*	*Vis.*	*Inv.*
Belgium Luxemburg	+14	+85	−40	+74	—	+58	−80	−12	+22	−36	+86	+64	−114	+36	+122	+130	−40	+124
France	+92	+581	+417	+495	+501	+323	+177	+349	−89	+109	+388	+93	−104	+37	+381	+376	−157	−81
Germany	+1 327	+699	+1 622	+210	+746	+19	+1 413	+193	+1 351	+24	+24	−269	+1 875	−192	+4 166	−127	+4 490	+144
Italy	−634	+750	−577	+718	−910	+826	−1 901	+839	−645	+972	+646	+1 237	+334	+1 445	−21	+1 292	+1 051	+1 302
Netherlands	−116	+459	−347	+547	−279	+456	−443	+518	−747	+588	−515	+576	−634	+497	−558	+564	−335	+469
Austria	−210	+120	−190	+154	−196	+179	−297	+294	−394	+354	−472	+374	−596	+344	−474	+303	−455	+318
Denmark	−211	+149	−241	+131	−363	+122	−111	+141	−379	+185	−368	+193	−403	+206	−458	+185	−436	+199
Finland	−77	+30	−102	+32	−129	+36	−69	+45	−220	+50	−232	+43	−237	+42	−180	+39	+25	+40
Norway	−520	+390	−630	+426	−635	+442	−692	+501	−625	+543	−699	+590	−771	+617	−962	+754	−713	+873
Portugal	−173	+105	−267	+78	−161	+75	−188	+94	−214	+152	−297	+151	−341	+220	−332	+236	−382	+162
Sweden	−332	+255	−178	+231	−190	+216	−190	+199	−148	+289	−365	+165	−283	+105	−144	+77	−171	+24
Switzerland	−317	+411	−617	+406	−753	+415	−777	+417	−901	+770	−650	+837	−569	+955	−525	+1 015	−384	+1 187
Greece	−310	+151	−350	+151	−448	+175	−452	+197	−574	+179	−702	+211	−727	+251	−673	+247	−766	+290
Iceland	−16	+6	—	+5	+2	+6	−7	+2	−9	+1	+4	+2	−7	—	−53	+1	−50	+3
Ireland	−229	+144	−281	+143	−313	+144	−311	+148	−359	+178	−424	+224	−363	+217	−292	+243	−363	+210
Spain	+41	+254	−293	+351	−655	+470	−1 026	+573	−1 077	+782	−1 759	+913	−1 992	+1 009	−1 781	+874	−1 574	+725

Sources: 1960–62: International Monetary Fund, *International Financial Statistics*, June, 1967 (France, 1960–1966).
1963–68: International Monetary Fund, *International Financial Statistics*, June, 1970 (France, 1967–68).

Notes: Government current transactions included. In the case of Germany, in particular, the invisibles shown include incomes from foreign troops valuing some $1 100 per annum. Transfers are excluded.
Visible balances for Germany, Finland and Greece are based on exports f.o.b. and imports c.i.f. For all other countries exports and imports are f.o.b.

Table VIII—Visible trade of France, 1911–1966 (*1911–1958: F 00 m*
1959– : NF m)

Year	*Imports*	*Exports*
1911	81	61
1912	82	77
1913	84	69
1914	65	48
1915	110	39
1916	207	62
1917	271	60
1918	223	48
1919	358	118
1920	499	269
1921	288	198
1922	243	214
1923	329	309
1924	402	424
1925	445	466
1926	596	593
1927	552	552
1928	537	521
1929	582	501
1930	525	429
1931	422	305
1932	298	197
1933	284	185
1934	231	178
1935	210	155
1936	255	155
1937	424	240
1938	461	306
1939	438	316
1940	457	175
1941	249	158
1942	260	297
1943	140	354
1944	98	255
1945	571	114
1946	2 447	1 014
1947	3 972	2 233
1948	6 726	6 340
1949	9 263	7 839
1950	10 732	10 777
1951	16 153	14 843
1952	15 912	14 161
1953	14 578	14 064
1954	15 221	15 095

Year	*Imports*	*Exports*
1955	16 743	17 357
1956	19 781	16 255
1957	22 674	18 892
1958	23 572	21 528
1959	25 149	27 721
1960	31 016	33 900
1961	32 992	35 667
1962	37 134	36 356
1963	43 100	39 916
1964	49 719	44 408
1965	51 063	49 629
1966	58 672	53 837

Table IX—Visible trade of France, 1827–1910
General trade *Fm*
Official values

Year	*Imports*	*Exports*
1827	566·0	602·0
1828	608·0	610·0
1829	616·0	608·0
1830	638·0	573·0
1831	513·0	618·0
1832	653·0	626·0
1833	693·0	766·0
1834	720·0	715·0
1835	761·0	834·0
1836	960·0	961·0
1837	808·0	758·0
1838	937·1	955·9
1839	947·0	1 003·3
1840	1 052·3	1 010·9
1841	1 121·4	1 065·4
1842	1 142·0	940·3
1843	1 186·9	992·0
1844	1 192·9	1 146·8
1845	1 240·1	1 187·4
1846	1 256·3	1 180·3

	Imports		*Exports*	
	Official values	*Current values*	*Official values*	*Current values*
1847	1 343	1 290·3	1 270	1 049·3
1848	862	708·3	1 153	936·4
1849	1 142	1 021·3	1 423	1 269·5
1850	1 174	1 119·8	1 531	1 435·3
1851	1 158	1 093·8	1 629	1 520·3
1852	1 438	1 392·0	1 682	1 680·2
1853	1 632	1 695·7	1 861	2 083·4
1854	1 709	1 805·4	1 788	1 932·4
1855	1 952	2 159·7	2 027	2 167·2
1856	2 267	2 740·2	2 320	2 659·2
Average 1847–56	1 503		1 672	

Current values

Year	*Imports*	*Exports*
1857	2 689	2 639
1858	2 164	2 561
1859	2 355	3 057
1860	2 657	3 148
1861	3 085	2 660
1862	2 899	3 050
1863	3 237	3 526
1864	3 408	3 921
1865	3 528	4 087
1866	3 845	4 281
Average 1857–66	2 987	3 293
1867	4 031	3 934
1868	4 258	3 721
1869	4 009	3 994
1870	3 498	3 456
1871	3 953	3 278
1872	4 502	4 757
1873	4 576	4 822
1874	4 423	4 702
1875	4 462	4 807
1876	4 909	4 548
Average 1867–76	4 262	4 202
1877	4 570	4 371
1878	5 089	4 111
1879	5 579	4 270
1880	6 113	4 612
1881	5 996	4 724
1882	5 962	4 764
1883	5 887	4 562
1884	5 239	4 218
1885	4 930	3 956
1886	5 117	4 246
Average 1877–86	5 448	4 383

Current values *Year*	*Imports*	*Exports*
1887	4 943	4 238
1888	5 187	4 298
1889	5 320	4 804
1890	5 452	4 840
1891	5 938	4 731
1892	5 136	4 551
1893	4 982	4 326
1894	4 795	4 125
1895	4 920	4 589
1896	4 929	4 594
Average	5 157	4 510
1897	4 717·0	4 358·6
Average 1893–97	4 549·4	4078·7
1898	5 582·6	4 673·5
1899	5 848·0	5 523·5
1900	5 988·6	5 521·6
1901	5 606·2	5 219·7
1902	5 698·6	5 597·0
Average 1898–1902	5 744·8	5 309·1
1903	6 079·5	5 577·5
1904	5 721·5	5 744·5
1905	6 061·5	6 302·3
Average 1901–5	5 837·5	5 688·2
1906	7 090·4	6 828·2
1907	7 874·6	7 256·1
1908	7 180·4	6 620·3
1909	7 856·5	7 482·3
1910	9 102·6	8 104·9
Average 1906–10	7 820·6	7 258·4

Source: Direction Générale des Douanes, Paris: Tableau décennal du commerce.
Note: The French, like the British, used official values until 1847.

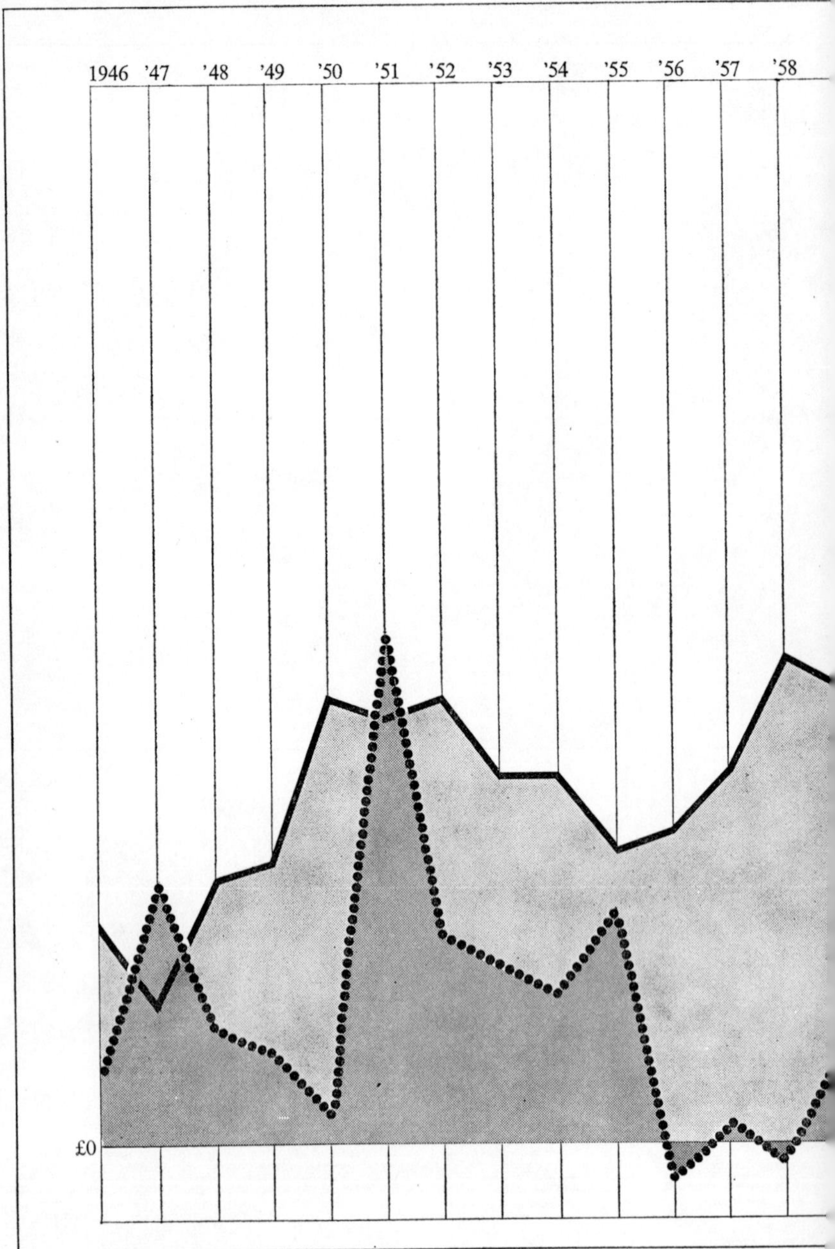

Figure 7. Invisible Surplus and Visible Deficit

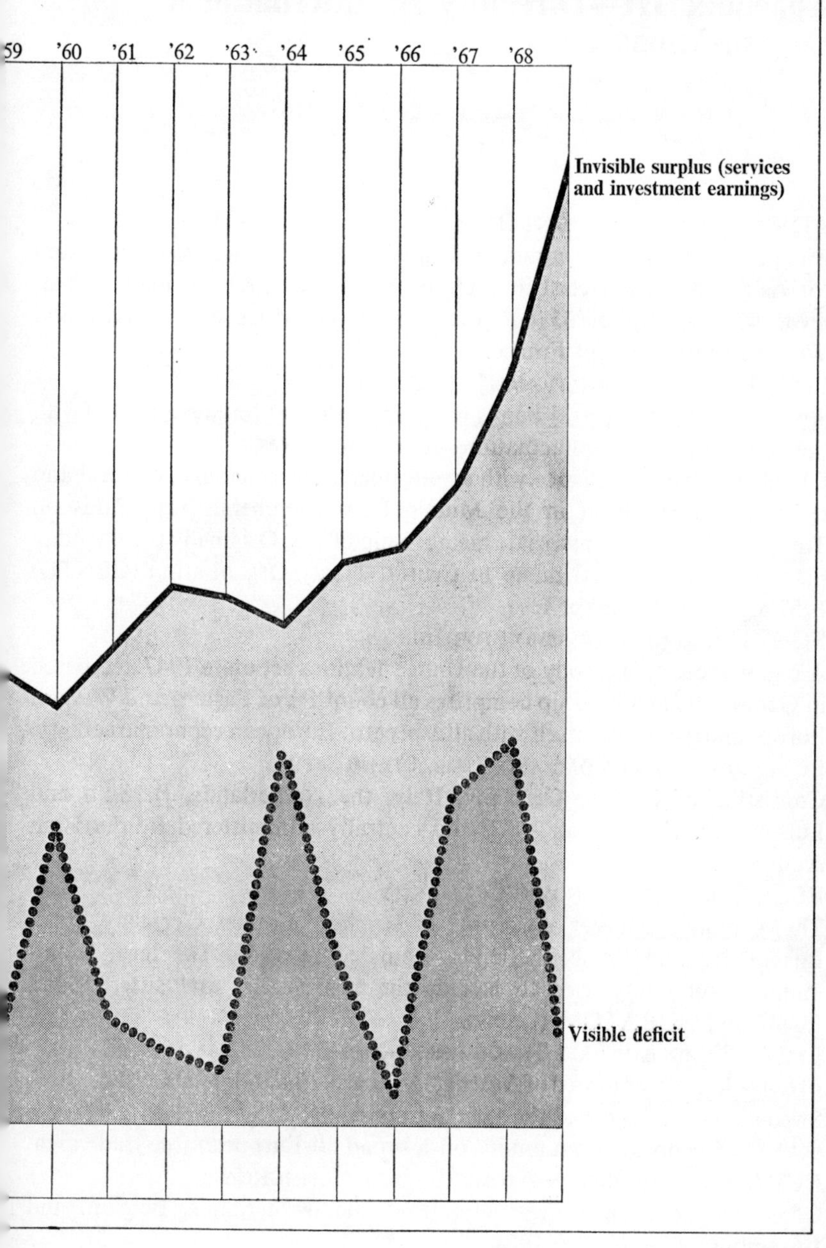
59
'60
'61
'62
'63
'64
'65
'66
'67
'68
Invisible surplus (services and investment earnings)
Visible deficit

Appendix III—Directory of International Organisations

ADB ASIAN DEVELOPMENT BANK
Financial institution set up under United Nations Economic Commission for Asia and the Far East in 1966 to provide development loans in that area. Membership of 33 comprising most countries of Far East and Western Europe except France.

BIS BANK OF INTERNATIONAL SETTLEMENTS
An association of Central Banks based in Basle and founded in 1930 with the aim of moderating fluctuations in exchange rates.

CENTO Defence alliance with arrangements for economic, cultural and technical co-operation in the Middle East. Members: Iran, Pakistan, Turkey and UK, with associate membership of US. Originally the Baghdad Pact of 1955, changed name to Central Treaty Organisation (CENTO) 1957 after withdrawal of Iraq.

ECE ECONOMIC COMMISSION FOR EUROPE
A regional economic body of the United Nations set up in 1947 and based in Geneva. Its membership comprises all countries of Eastern and Western Europe and it concerns itself with all aspects of European economic activity.

ECSC EUROPEAN COAL AND STEEL COMMUNITY
Consisting of France, Germany, Italy, the Netherlands, Belgium and Luxemburg. Founded in 1952, and centrally administered by the High Authority.

EEC EUROPEAN ECONOMIC COMMUNITY
The 'Common Market' consisting of Belgium, France, Germany, Italy, Luxemburg and the Netherlands. Founded in 1958. The term 'Community' commonly used to include the two smaller and sister bodies ECSC and EURATOM (below).

EFTA EUROPEAN FREE TRADE ASSOCIATION
Free trade area composed of Austria, Denmark, Finland, Norway, Portugal, Sweden, Switzerland and the UK. Set up in 1960 after the failure to agree with the European Community on a broad all-European free trade area.

EURATOM EUROPEAN ATOMIC ENERGY COMMUNITY
Consisting of France, Germany, Italy, the Netherlands, Belgium and Luxemburg. Founded in 1958.

GATT GENERAL AGREEMENT ON TARIFFS AND TRADE
An international trade organisation under the aegis of the United Nations designated by the name of the first Convention signed. Its aims are to improve trading relations between nations and generally to remove obstacles, such as tariffs, in the way of this. It was founded in 1947 and has 75 members drawn from all parts of the world, including some communist countries.

GROUP OF TEN Ten major countries who under the 'General Arrangements to Borrow' of the IMF in 1962 agreed to lend $6 000 million at any time to cope with an emergency in the international monetary system: Belgium, Canada, France, Germany, Italy, Japan, Netherlands, Sweden, UK and US.

IDA INTERNATIONAL DEVELOPMENT ASSOCIATION
Affiliate of the World Bank created in 1960 for special loan operations in developing countries.

IBRD INTERNATIONAL BANK FOR RECONSTRUCTION AND DEVELOPMENT ('The World Bank').
Founded in 1945 for the provision of investment finance, particularly to developing countries.

ILO INTERNATIONAL LABOUR ORGANISATION
Founded originally by the League of Nations in 1919 as the International Labour Office. It became part of the United Nations complex.

IMF INTERNATIONAL MONETARY FUND
Founded in 1945 as world body with general powers of supervision of parity rates and having finances for the support of national reserves.

NATO NORTH ATLANTIC TREATY ORGANISATION
Defence organisation founded in 1949 for the defence of Western Europe and the Atlantic Basin consisting of Belgium, Canada, Denmark, France, Germany, Greece, Iceland, Italy, Luxemburg, the Netherlands, Norway, Portugal, Turkey, the UK and the USA.

OECD ORGANISATION FOR ECONOMIC CO-OPERATION AND DEVELOPMENT
Comprising Austria, Belgium, Canada, Denmark, France, Germany, Greece, Iceland, Ireland, Italy, Japan, Luxemburg, the Netherlands, Norway, Portugal, Spain, Sweden, Switzerland, Turkey, the UK and the USA. Created in 1961 out of the original OEEC (Organisation for European Economic Cooperation) founded to implement Marshall Aid in 1949.

SEATO SOUTH-EAST ASIA TREATY ORGANISATION
Alliance formed in 1955 and comprising Australia, France, New Zealand, Pakistan, the Philippines, Thailand, the UK and the USA for the collective defence of South-East Asia.

Bibliography

The bibliography which follows is broadly a compilation of Works consulted when writing this book. It is, however, intended as a guide to those interested in further reading on the subject.

Bank of England Quarterly Bulletin, 'Inventory of UK External Assets and Liabilities' (September issue each year); also reproduced in the 'Pink Book'.

BOWLEY, A. L., *Some Economic Consequences of the Great War*, Thornton Butterworth Ltd., London, *1930*.

– *A Short Account of England's Foreign Trade in the 19th Century*, Swan, Sonnenschein & Co., revised edition, *1905*.

BRITTAN, SAMUEL, *Steering the Economy*, Secker & Warburg, London, *1969*.

BROADWAY, F., *State Intervention in British Industry*, Kaye & Ward, London, *1969*.

CAMERON, RONDO E., *France & the Economic Development of Europe, 1800–1914*, Princeton University Press, *1961*.

CLAPHAM, SIR JOHN, *A Concise History of Britain*, Cambridge University Press, *1957*.

CLARK, G. N., *Guide to English Commercial Statistics, 1696–1782*, Roy. Hist., London, *1938*.

COMMITTEE ON INVISIBLE EXPORTS, *World Invisible Exports, 1970*.

– *Britain's Invisible Earnings*, Thomas Skinner & Co., London, *1967*.

CONAN, A. R., *Rationale of the Sterling Area*, Macmillan, *1961*.

– *The Problem of Sterling*, Macmillan, *1961*.

– 'Britain as creditor', *National Westminster Bank Review*, August, *1970*.

– 'Sterling: The Problem of Policy', *Westminster Bank Review*, November, *1967*.

– 'Sterling: The Problem of Diagnosis', *Westminster Bank Review*, August, *1967*.

– 'Britain as Creditor', *National Westminster Bank Review*, August, *1970*.

– 'Does Britain Pay its Way?', *National Westminster Bank Review*, February, *1969*.

CONFEDERATION OF BRITISH INDUSTRY, *Overseas Investment—Why and How*, October *1967*.

CROSLAND, C. A. R., *Britain's Economic Problems*, Cape, *1953*.

DEANE, PHYLLIS, and COLE, W. A., *British Economic Growth, 1688–1959*, Cambridge University Press, *1962*.

DEVONS, ELY, World Trade in Invisibles. *Lloyds Bank Review*, March, *1961*.

DUNNING, J. H., *American Investment in the UK.*

ECONOMIC COMMISSION FOR EUROPE, *Economic Survey of Europe, 1948*.

ECONOMIC RESEARCH COUNCIL, 'A Programme for National Recovery', Research Papers 1, 2, & 3, *1968–69*.

EINZIG, PAUL, *Leads and Lags*, Macmillan, 1968.

ELTIS, W. A., 'Is Stop–Go Necessary?' *National Westminster Bank Review*, March, *1969*.

HALEVY, ELIE, *A History of the English People in the 19th Century*, Ernest Benn, *1961*.

HARROD, SIR ROY, *The Role of Sterling*,

HATTON, G., *Le Commerce Extérieur de la France*, Berger-Levrault, *1968*.

HOBSON, C. K., *The Export of Capital*, Constable, London, *1914*.

IMLAH, A. H., *Economic Elements in the Pax Britannica*, Harvard University Press, *1958*.

INTERNATIONAL ECONOMIC POLICY ASSOCIATION, *The United States Balance of Payments*, Washington, *1966*.

LEAGUE OF NATIONS, *The Network of World Trade*, Princeton University Press, *1942*.

LONDON AND CAMBRIDGE ECONOMIC SERVICE, *The British Economy Key Statistics, 1900–1966*, Times Newspapers Ltd., *1967*.

MAIZELS, A., 'The Overseas Trade Statistics of the United Kingdom', *Journal of the Royal Statistical Society, 1949*.

MCMAHON, CHRISTOPHER, *Sterling in the Sixties*, Oxford University Press, *1964*.

MITCHELL, B. R., and DEANE, PHYLLIS, *Abstract of British Historical Statistics*, Cambridge University Press, *1962*.

MOREAU, CESAR, *State of the Trade of Great Britain with all Parts of the World*, London, *1822*.

MUN, THOMAS, *England's Treasure by Foreign Trade*, Hatchard, *1664*.

OEEC, *A Decade of Co-operation*, Paris, *1958*.

PARNELL, SIR HENRY, *Financial Reform*, Murray, London, *1831*.

PEP, *Growth in the British Economy, 1960*.

PORTER, G. R., *The Progress of the Nation*, London, 3rd Edition, *1847*.

RAMSAY, G. D., *English Overseas Trade during the Centuries of Emergence*, Macmillan, London, *1957*.

REDDAWAY, W. B., *Effects of UK Direct Investment Overseas: Interim Report and Final Report*, Cambridge University Press, *1967* & *1968*.

ROBERTSON, D. J., and HUNTER, L. C., *The British Balance of Payments*, Oliver & Boyd, *1966*.

ROSTOW, W. W., *The Stages of Economic Growth*, Cambridge University Press, *1968*.

SCHLOTE, WERNER, *Entwicklung und Strukturwandlungen des Englischen. Aussenhandels von 1700 bis zur Gegenwart*, Jena, *1938*. Translated into English by Drs Henderson and Chaloner of the Department of Economic History of the University of Manchester and published under the title *British Overseas Trade from 1700 to the 1930s*, Blackwell, Oxford, *1952*.

SCHUMPETER, E. B., *English Overseas Trade Statistics, 1697–1808*, Oxford University Press, *1960*.

SECRETARY OF STATE FOR ECONOMIC AFFAIRS, *The National Plan*, HMSO, *1965*.

SHONFIELD, ANDREW, *British Economic Policy Since the War*, Penguin Books Ltd, London, *1958*.

TAUSSIG, F. W., *International Trade*, Macmillan, New York, *1927*.

TORRENS, ROBERT, *Essay on the External Corn Trade*, Hatchard, *1815*.

TREVELYAN, G. M., *English Social History*, Longmans, Green & Co., London, *1942*.

TURNER, H. A., *Is Britain Really Strike-Prone?*, Cambridge University Press, *1969*.

WELLS, SIDNEY, *Trade Policies for Britain*, Oxford University Press *1966*.

Statistics and Reports

Official Bodies

BANK OF ENGLAND:

Quarterly Bulletin: statistics on financial and balance of payments matters, together with useful articles.

BANK OF INTERNATIONAL SETTLEMENTS

Annual Report; broad commentary on balance of payments position of major countries.

BANQUE DE FRANCE

Balance des Payements—annual.

BOARD OF TRADE

Board of Trade Journal—weekly; comprehensive reporting of most matters of economic interest, inter alia overseas investment surveys, monthly reports on foreign trade, including indices of volume and unit value of imports and exports.

Report on Overseas Trade—monthly; analysis of imports and exports by direction and product.

UK Trade and *Navigation Accounts*—monthly; detailed account, by product, destination and origin, of UK imports and exports.

CENTRAL STATISTICAL OFFICE:

United Kingdom Balance of Payments—annual (the 'Pink Book').

Economic Trends—monthly; contains quarterly balance of payments accounts.

National Income and Expenditure—annual (the 'Blue Book'); contains main GNP figures and components.

Annual Abstract of Statistics; broad review of the nation's statistics, covering large range of subjects.

DEUTSCHE BUNDESBANK

Monthly report; Statistical Supplement, *Series 3*, on balance of payments.

EEC

Basic Statistics—annual; compact survey of main data about Community countries with comparisons with other major countries.

General Statistical Bulletin—monthly; summary of main economic data about Community countries.
Industrial Statistics; monthly; summary of data on production by individual industries.
Foreign Trade Statistics—monthly; analysis of trade of Community countries and other major countries.

GATT
International Trade; annual report on trade developments of all countries.

INTERNATIONAL MONETARY FUND
International Financial Statistics—monthly; internal economic and balance of payments data of all IMF members.
Balance of Payments Yearbook—annual with frequent updatings; detailed balance of payments accounts of all IMF members.

OECD
Annual Economic Surveys; detailed surveys of development and prospects of each OECD country.
Main Economic Indicators—monthly; summary of principal economic data of each country.

UNITED STATES DEPARTMENT OF COMMERCE
Survey of Current Business—monthly.

Semi-Official and Private Bodies

NATIONAL ECONOMIC DEVELOPMENT COUNCIL
Periodic reports on individual industries.

NATIONAL INSTITUTE FOR ECONOMIC AND SOCIAL RESEARCH
National Institute Economic Review—quarterly; survey of UK economic position, with copious statistics on UK and international developments.

INSEE
INSTITUTE NATIONAL DE STATISTIQUE ET D'ETUDES ECONOMIQUES
Etudes et prévisions—monthly.

Index